Books by Peter Maas

NONFICTION

Killer Spy
In a Child's Name: The Legacy of
a Mother's Murder
Manhunt
Marie: A True Story
King of the Gypsies
Serpico
The Valachi Papers
The Rescuer

FICTION

China White
Father and Son
Made in America

UNDERBOSS

SAMMY THE BULL GRAVANO'S
STORY OF LIFE IN THE MAFIA

Peter Maas

HarperPaperbacks
A Division of HarperCollinsPublishers

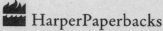
HarperPaperbacks
A Division of HarperCollins*Publishers*
10 East 53rd Street, New York, N.Y. 10022-5299

ISBN 0-06-109664-4

Cover design by Rick Pracher
Cover photograph © 1997 by John Earle

A hardcover edition of this book was published
in 1997 by HarperCollins*Publishers.*

First HarperPaperbacks printing: December 1997

Printed in the United States of America

Visit HarperPaperbacks on the World Wide Web at
http://www.harpercollins.com

20 19 18 17 16 15 14

For my loved ones—my wife, Suzanne, and my sons, John-Michael and Terrence

And in loving memory of Audrey

UNDERBOSS

**SAMMY THE BULL GRAVANO'S
STORY OF LIFE IN THE MAFIA**

Preface

In what law enforcement officials described as the American Mafia's highest-ranking desertion, John Gotti's right-hand man in the Gambino organized-crime family has defected and is expected to be a Government witness against Mr. Gotti on charges that he is the nation's top Mafia leader, law enforcement officials said yesterday.

The Gotti confidante, Salvatore Gravano, who was indicted last year as a co-defendant with Mr. Gotti on murder and racketeering charges, has entered the Federal Witness Protection Program and was secretly transferred last week from a Federal jail in Manhattan where he had been held without bail with Mr. Gotti, officials said.

The authorities asserted that because of the two men's close ties, Mr. Gravano's testimony could provide a crushing blow to Mr. Gotti, who has been acquitted on lesser charges at three trials in the last five years and has become the No. 1 target of Federal investigators.

—*The New York Times,* November 12, 1991

1

They're bad people,
but they're our bad people.

"YEAH, YOU COULD SAY I CAME FROM A PRETTY tough neighborhood," Salvatore (Sammy the Bull) Gravano said.

The neighborhood was Bensonhurst, roughly two miles square, in southwestern Brooklyn bordering Gravesend Bay and the Atlantic Ocean.

Unlike the first Italian communities in New York, such as Manhattan's Little Italy, which was being swallowed up by an aggressively expanding Chinatown, or East Harlem, clinging to a narrow strip along the East River against the inroads of a booming Hispanic population, Bensonhurst remained vibrantly and definitively Italian-American. Even today it is where recent arrivals from southern Italy and Sicily settle. In Roman Catholic churches, some masses are sung in Italian.

As with other ethnic migrations in the city, the

subway paved the way when in the early 1900s the first rapid transit lines linking Brooklyn to Manhattan went into service, one of them going directly from the dark and crowded tenements of Little Italy to the open spaces of Bensonhurst.

It has a small-town feel. Many of the cross streets lack traffic lights. Cruising taxis, common in most of the city, are rare. Houses are mostly two-family dwellings of aluminum siding, stucco or brick with wrought-iron gates painted white and porches with their ubiquitous steel awnings. Tiny front lawns feature potted flowers and statues of the Virgin Mary and in backyards, more often than not, are vegetable gardens. Bensonhurst's main street, 18th Avenue, also officially designated Cristoforo Colombo Boulevard, is lined with Italian delicatessens, bakeries, fresh mozzarella shops, food markets overflowing with packaged products imported from Italy, pizza parlors boasting traditional wood-burning ovens, and espresso bars.

In Bensonhurst, everyone knows everyone else on every block. Its mainly blue-collar residents are insular, closemouthed, and suspicious of outsiders. Strangers are remarked on at once. As a result, the rate of common street crimes—rapes, robberies, felony assaults—is low compared to other parts of the city, according to police statistics. Murder is a third less than the citywide average.

But Bensonhurst was tough in a very special sense. A great number of these murders were mob related. It was a prime spawning ground for Cosa Nostra—"Our Thing"—which filled its ranks from local youth street gangs that hung out at candy stores and luncheonettes throughout the area. One of the original members of Cosa Nostra's national commission, Joseph Profaci, the so-called Olive Oil King because of his monopoly on the importation of olive oil from Italy, lived in Bensonhurst. So did his successor as a family boss, Joseph Colombo. One of the grandest underworld funerals ever seen in New York, complete with thirty-eight carloads of flowers, took place in Bensonhurst following the Prohibition-era slaying of a celebrated mobster named Frankie Yale, who had a falling out with Al Capone.

As in a Sicilian village, Cosa Nostra's shadow loomed large over Bensonhurst and was spoken of only in whispers. "They just shoot themselves," a resident confided after two corpses were found in a car, gazing vacantly into space, each with a bullet hole behind the ear. "The thing is, you mind your own business. You don't hear nothing. You don't see nothing." Another said, "You got to admit the Mafia, whatever, keeps the neighborhood safe. You don't see all them other people coming in to mug and burglarize here. So their presence is kind of good is my opinion."

•   •   •

Salvatore Gravano was born in Bensonhurst on March 12, 1945. He had two older sisters. Another sister and a brother had died before his arrival. His mother, Caterina, was born in Sicily and brought to America as a baby. His father, Giorlando, also from Sicily, was on the crew of a freighter when he jumped ship in Canada and slipped into the United States as an illegal alien.

For Sammy and for friends and neighbors, his parents were always Kay and Gerry. English was the language of the house, except during visits from his grandmothers, who spoke a Sicilian dialect. Sammy was especially close to his maternal grandmother and picked up enough to be able to converse with her, but forgot it all after she died.

He was called Sammy instead of Salvatore or Sal for as long as he can remember. Someone had said that he looked just like Uncle Sammy, a brother of his mother's, and the name stuck. The uncle was Big Sammy and he was Little Sammy. He grew up on 78th Street in the heart of Bensonhurst near 18th Avenue. His father owned the house, the middle one of three identical brick row houses, each with a garage. Steps led up to the front porch. The basement apartment was rented out, as well as an apartment on the second floor. The Gravanos lived in the middle apartment. In a small plot behind the house, Sammy's father cultivated tomatoes and beans and tended to his prized fig tree.

Kay was an exceptionally skilled seamstress who worked for a Jewish dress manufacturer in Manhattan's garment center. Gerry was a house painter until he was felled by lead poisoning and could no longer continue his trade. The dress manufacturer then financed the Gravanos in a satellite factory of their own in Bensonhurst. Kay supervised the filling of the orders he sent her and rode the subway to the garment center to sew the sample dress for a forthcoming line, while Sammy's father took care of the business end. Things went so well that Gerry was able to afford the purchase of a summer cottage for $8,000 near Lake Ronkonkoma in the middle of Long Island.

On Sunday mornings, Sammy usually accompanied his father to mass at the Church of Our Lady of Guadalupe. Down the block, they would pass a corner saloon. There would always be a cluster of men in front of it, still others at the bar inside. They were all smartly dressed in suits, or in sharply creased slacks and Italian knit shirts. Sammy could see the glitter from the diamond rings many of them wore. There often was a crap game in progress right on the sidewalk with wads of bills being passed back and forth. Sometimes a police car parked there, and two or three of the men would saunter over and banter with the cops. Sammy could hear the laughter. He noticed that while his father always stayed on the opposite side of the street, some of the men would wave to him and call out, "How you doin', Gerry?" and his father would nod back in acknowledgment. Finally, when Sammy was about eight, he asked, "Who are those men, Dad? You know them?"

"Yes, I know some of them. They are not hard-working, nice people. They're bad people, but they're our bad people."

This only excited Sammy's curiosity and he kept pressing his father for more details. "What I got from him little by little," Sammy says, "was that these men were people I should stay away from and not ever talk about. But they had ties to the community. He told me that there was a lot of prejudice against the Italian people when they first came over here, especially from the Irish cops and politicians, and Italians went to these men to resolve their problems when the police, whatever, wouldn't do nothing. So the community would back them up if there was a beating or a shooting that the cops were trying to find out about. I guess my father was trying to school me that they were bad guys, but we should never go against them, never call the police about anything we saw them doing. We don't know anything. We don't ask questions. We don't get involved. We walk on the other side of the street."

At age nine, Sammy had a traumatic experience that changed the whole course of his life. He was held back in the fourth grade. When his parents went to P.S. 186 to find out what was wrong, they were told that Sammy, unfortunately, was "a slow learner." As they persisted in their inquiry, the analysis grew harsher. Sammy was exhibiting all the signs of being mentally retarded.

Sammy, in fact, was the victim of a severe case of dyslexia. For Sammy, a *d* became a *b*. A letter like *r* reversed itself. Words got jumbled—*god* transposed into *dog*. The number 3 became 8. But in the elementary schools of Bensonhurst in the 1950s, nobody seemed to know about dyslexia. There were no remedial options available.

In repeating the fourth grade, humiliation piled on humiliation. He was relegated to the back of the class. A student seated up front would be asked to spell *invitation*. Another would be asked to spell *independence*. Then the teacher would call out to Sammy and ask him to spell *cat*. Knowing titters would ripple through the class. "You just felt like you were a moron," he says. "When I felt like that, I started to reject school as something that wasn't for me. And authority, too. Being rejected by teachers like you were a retard. The hell with that. So I fought back. I rejected them."

At first, to cope, he tried being the class clown. When that didn't work, he took another tack. Although as an adult he is only five feet five, he didn't stop growing until his teens. At nine years old, he was about the same size as the other boys and physically strong. If someone ridiculed him, he beat him up after school. That instantly ended the slights. "That's when I found out that violence paid," he says. "They stopped laughing."

The only people who didn't care about his reading and spelling abilities were the men at the corner saloon. They were the ones who named him Sammy the Bull. "It was my tenth birthday, I think," said Sammy, "and my father and mother gave me a brand-new bike. We didn't have a lot of money to throw around, so when they gave you something, you had to take care of it. I was real happy, but then the bike was robbed. It was my fault. I left it unwatched, unprotected. Maybe a week later a couple of my friends, little kids like me, told me that they saw the bike near a fruit stand on the corner across from the bar where those wiseguys hung out. I ran down there and sure enough two kids bigger and older than me from 79th Street had it.

"I went and grabbed the handlebars and I said, 'Hey, this is my bike.' But they wouldn't give it back. So I started fighting both of them. It was hard going. I mean, I was getting a little beat up, but I was fighting my ass off. I wasn't giving up that bike. I was doing pretty good, but I wasn't winning, either. It was like when somebody would look at you and say, 'Wow, you must have been in some fight,' and you'd say, 'Yeah, well, you ought to see the other guy.'

"Now some of the wiseguys outside the bar were watching all of this, and a couple of them came over and broke us up. I was so mad I was crying, and one of the guys rubs my head and says, 'Sammy, what are you crying for? You're destroying these kids.' And the other guy says, 'What's this all about, anyway?'

"And I said, 'This is my bike and they took it and I'm taking it back.' These two wiseguys that came over started to laugh. It was amusing to them, I guess. Then they told the two kids to beat it, it was my bike and I was keeping it. If their fathers had any problems with this, they should come see them. Then one of the guys says to me, 'Come on, Sammy, stop crying.' And he calls out to some of the other wiseguys who were watching, 'Did you see this Sammy? He's like a little bull.'

"Word got around, and pretty soon all the kids were calling me Sammy the Bull and that was that. Even later on, when I started getting into trouble, the cops would come by looking for me and they would say they were looking for 'the Bull, Sammy the Bull.' So you see, it wasn't how good I was sexually that I got the name."

Sammy and his sisters often helped out at the dress factory Kay and Gerry Gravano had on 15th

Avenue in Bensonhurst. The regular workforce averaged fifteen cutters, sewers, pressers, and finishers. Payday in cash was on Friday. And the employees were all nonunion.

Sammy was thirteen and in the office helping his father prepare the weekly envelopes when the two men walked in. "I mean, these guys were huge," he says. "I think they were Irish. I'm not sure. They had reddish complexions. They come in and tell my father they're from the union. What union I don't know. All I know is these goons are really big and rough with their language, and my father is pretty small, and they're telling him that all his workers are nonunion and if he wants to keep operating, he's going to have to start making payoffs. One of them says, 'You don't, the end result is you can get hurt. You won't be walking so good.'

"I don't say nothing. I don't do nothing. But I am on fire. Listening to them talk to my father this way has sparked a rage in me. There is no fucking way that I'm letting these bums hurt my father. And my father is just sitting there, calm as a cucumber. 'Yeah, yeah, OK, you come back, I talk to you,' he says with a little Italian accent. He isn't fazed at all. I tell you, I'm plenty fazed, but he isn't.

"So one of them says they'll be back on Monday, and this better be settled. After they leave, my father must have sensed my emotion, but I don't think he understood the depth of my rage or the violence I was capable of. Instead, he tried to calm me down. I said, 'Dad, what's the story? Who were they?' And he said, 'Ah, nobodies. Big mouths. Don't worry about it. It's nothing. I'll talk to Zuvito about it.'

"Zuvito? I think. Old man Zuvito? What good's he? He's a frail little old guy, half the size of my dad. A strong wind would knock him right off his feet. I don't know Cosa Nostra. I don't know Zuvito's power. I'm a kid. I'm with a gang. My thing is to fight with my fists. I figure these goons would cripple my father and I'm definitely not letting them hurt him."

By then, Sammy had hooked up with the Rampers, the dominant youth gang in his part of Bensonhurst. "There were Ramper seniors and Ramper juniors. I was a Ramper midget. I tell some of the Rampers what happened. I was thinking that maybe two or three of my pals would come in with me and bang it out with those bastards when they came back. I'm thinking in terms of a fistfight. Instead, one of them tells me, 'Sammy, these guys hit your father, blow the fucking bums away.' So, without really thinking about it, I got a gun from one of them. I'm totally geared, nervous as a bastard, but I was ready to whack the two of them out if they got into my father.

"I got the gun stuck in my belt. I have a jacket on to cover it when they come in. I can't believe it. They are totally different. 'Hey, Gerry,' one of them says, 'why didn't you tell us Zuvito is your *compare*? We're sorry. We apologize. You ever have any union trouble, call us up, we'll resolve the problem. Don't forget, Gerry. Please tell Zuvito we were here, that we apologized.' And they grabbed my father's hand and shook it and kissed him on the cheek.

"I'm watching this in total amazement. After they walk out, I said, 'Dad, what was that? What happened?' And he said, 'It's nothing. I told you. They talk too much, those people. There was no problem. Like they said, Zuvito is my *compare* from Italy. Zuvito spoke with them. Remember I told you about our bad guys. Well, Zuvito is one of our bad guys.'

"I said, 'And if they didn't listen, he'd shoot them, no?'

"'I don't know what he would do, but he didn't have to do any more than talk. No shooting, no nothing.'

"'If those guys would have done anything, I was ready,' I said and I opened up my jacket and showed him the gun. His eyes just glared at me, like ice. My dad never laid a hand on me, but that was a time he came pretty close. 'What are you doing?' he said. He took the gun. 'I told you. This is not our life. We don't live by these things. That's not what we do. We're legitimate, honest people. We work hard and if we have a problem, we go to

Zuvito, people like him. They understand hardworking people. We're not bothering nobody. They'll help us.'

"That really opened my appetite to know more about Zuvito, what the hell he was, what made him so feared. Boy, I thought, wasn't it something to be that physically unimposing and still have that kind of power and strength? I really didn't understand it then.

"Eventually, I found out that he was a made guy in Cosa Nostra who was very respected. I met him a few times. Once, when I got into trouble, he caught me on the corner and gave me a kick in the ass. I couldn't believe what a kick he gave me. 'Go home, you son of a bitch!' he said. 'Your father's such a beautiful man. Go to school. Study. Make something of yourself!' "

But that was not to be, at least as far as Sammy's formal education was concerned. Still with no inkling as to the root cause of his learning disability, and with no professional help, Sammy began on his own to improvise. If a teacher wrote what looked to him like an 8 on the blackboard, he automatically assumed—correctly—that it was a 3. He tried to concentrate on his reading, realizing that if he went over a sentence five or six times, he could finally make some sense of it. But it was slow going, and at Shallow Junior High he was held back another year.

"That's when I decided school wasn't for me.

You had to go to school, but I was cutting classes most of the time and being with the Rampers. We were pretty tough and when I was there I was getting into fights all the time. Then one day one of my friends told me that a teacher had touched the ass or something of this girl I was going out with, and me like a hambone went in and I just punched the shit out of him. I got suspended for a while for that, but the straw that broke the camel's back was when I was playing hookey and got a little drunk with some other kids. They caught us and they brought us back to the school. We went up to the principal's office and he started yelling and blasting me out, and then he finally said to another teacher in the office, 'It's their upbringing. Their mothers and fathers are irresponsible.' In other words, he was blaming everything on my mother and father. About halfway through listening to this, I hit him a shot in the mouth and I guess I broke his jaw.

"I was thrown out of school. I went in front of the Board of Education, and they reinstated me in school, but not at Shallow. I was officially switched to McKinley Junior High School. McKinley's on Fort Hamilton Parkway. I had to take buses there. It was out of the neighborhood and there weren't any Rampers around. There are different gangs, different guys. Like there were Irish gangs, and I got to make my bones all over again in that neighborhood, which I did. I was in a lot of fights!

"But the one thing I remember from McKinley was a teacher, a math teacher, who also was my home-study teacher. I still remember his name. Mr. Mandracchia. He looked like a football player, strong-looking, about five eleven. He wore glasses. Really wanted to take you out of this problem situation you were in and move you into the mainstream. And it wasn't just with me. He gave everybody a chance to shine. Whether it was in class, in gym, whatever, he figured out what you could do well and he gave you the chance to do it.

"I got to like him, trust him, and for a while everything seemed to improve: my attendance, my marks. When you had a problem, he wouldn't just look at you like you were an idiot. He'd say, 'OK, everyone has a problem with that.' I never heard of the word *dyslexia* then and I don't think he did either, but he would sit with you and work out different ways of how to solve the problem, which maybe wasn't the system's way, but it made it easier for me. One time, he told me, 'Sammy, I've gotten to know you. You're far from being stupid. You just don't want to try anymore. Try for me. If something's a problem, if you feel frustrated in class, let me know. I'll give you a pass. You want to go into the yard? You want to play handball or something? You want to walk out of class? Don't do it on your own. Don't defy me. Just tell me. I'll let you do it.'

"It became easy to live with the guy. After a while, you don't even want to walk out on him. Because here's a guy who's put such an effort, an honest effort, into you, and you wanted to make him look good. If it wasn't for him, I would never have got out of that school, but I graduated and went to New Utrecht High School.

"In two or three months, it was the same thing all over again. I couldn't keep up. For all the teachers, I was a dummy. That was it. So OK, I'm stupid. The other thing I thought is that when I was in the neighborhood hanging out with the Rampers, it was those other kids who went to school and really tried who were nerds. They were nothing. They were taking the easy track. We were the guys who did it the hard way, helping our families by robbing and getting money, which a lot of them didn't have too much of. I felt that *we* were doing the right thing.

"You have to understand that the people I was looking up to by now, almost like they were my big brothers, were people in the mob. These guys knew me and I knew them. Even as a kid, before the bike thing, they knew me because they knew my father. After the bike, I was 'Sammy' to them. Plus, I had two older sisters and they were attractive. It's not like I was trying to impress these guys or anything like that, but when I fought and I got a pat on the head from them, it was a compliment. You did right defending yourself, taking back what was yours, like with the bike and the wiseguys on the corner. You didn't let nobody bully you. They helped teach me all that.

"But this thing that the mob does to you when you're young is that they compliment you if you rob, if you kill. The ultimate compliment is when you kill. So I was getting these compliments from them, and because I looked up to them, it felt good. At school, except for Mr. Mandracchia, I never got compliments. It would take me a long time to realize who was taking the easy way out, who the nerds really were.

"Anyway, with all the fights and my attitude, I was thrown out of New Utrecht and thrown back into the Board of Education, which sent me to a '600' school for incorrigibles. I think everyone in the one I went to was nuts. The second day, there was a kid in front of me reading the Bible, mumbling to himself, and the teacher asked me something that I gave a smartass answer to that got the other kids laughing, and this other kid all at once started quoting from the Bible and calling me the devil. So I banged him out right then and there and I'm back before the board with my parents, and they were told I was out of the school system, period. Either they would sign me out on my sixteenth birthday, which was coming up, or the board would take other steps against me. I stopped going to school, and when I was sixteen, my family did sign me out.

"My mom and dad were disappointed. Sad, I guess. But they never ranted and raved that I was no good. They knew that I was having education problems. They were used to hearing that from the schools and about the truancy and all the trouble I was getting into. That was the reality. There wasn't anybody they could turn to for help. Believe me, there weren't a lot of psychiatrists in Bensonhurst, even if they would have thought that way.

"They knew I had this reputation on the street that I was a tough, tough kid. They heard it from people they knew, but they never saw it themselves. They loved me and looked at the good in me. I mean, I never did drugs or acted up at home. I respected my parents. As the only son in the family, I did what was expected of me, like when my mother told me to take out the garbage, wash down the walk, shovel the snow, lug home groceries. Maybe I'd piss and moan a little, but I did it. I got along great with everybody who lived on our block. I liked them and I think they liked me. The old lady who lived a couple of houses down and had a sick husband would say, 'Sammy, could you get this prescription filled at the pharmacy?' Sure, why not? No big deal.

"My father didn't give up on me. He was still trying to get me to do the right thing. 'You can learn a trade,' he said. 'Use your hands, your back. A little honest sweat never hurt nobody.' He tried to bring me into the dress factory, which I did do from time to time. Some of his friends would say they could get me a job in construction, a machine shop, car repair. But it was too late. I was into another life now, running with the Rampers."

"When we were young and in the Rampers, we took an oath. We were gonna be together forever. Fuck the world. Fuck everybody, even the mob. Later on, that changed, but that was our attitude then.

"We became so tough, with such a dangerous reputation, that the other Italian gangs, the Irish gangs, the black gangs, the Puerto Rican gangs, from different neighborhoods, from Coney Island, downtown Brooklyn, guys from Avenue U, used to come to us in the summer and say, 'Listen, we don't want no trouble with you.' In the sixties, there was nothing but gangs all over the place, and none of them would fuck with us.

"There was a mob war going on in the Profaci family. The Gallo brothers from President Street, downtown Brooklyn, were in that family—Larry Gallo and his brother Joey and their crew—and they didn't think they were getting a big enough piece of the action. One time we—me and Jimmy Emma, Gerry Pappa, Joe V., Tommy Snake, Lenny the Mole, a bunch of us—were in this bar we hung around at 79th Street and Utrecht Avenue.

And there were some Gallos there. Actually it turned out they weren't the Gallos themselves, but people with them. Anyway, they were a lot older than us and there was some kind of beef with Jimmy Emma. So now they're gonna fuck us around, but not with their hands. They got guns. So we left and loaded up and went back into the bar.

"It was a long bar. They were at one end and we were at the other end. It seemed like one of them went for a gun. We went for guns. There was a ton of shots thrown back and forth. It was like a cowboy movie. Totally unbelievable. Glass breaking, women screaming, things falling on the floor. One of the Gallo guys got hit, like eleven times. He staggers out of the bar and falls in the street. And lived, believe it or not. Another guy in the bar, an innocent bystander, got hit in the foot. He went on his own to a doctor and never said nothing. The Gallo guy at the hospital don't say nothing, either.

"But now the Gallos let it be known they are coming after us. Everybody in the neighborhood is talking about it and the neighborhood wise-guys on the corner get involved. There are huge sit-downs. The Profaci family is involved. The Gambino family gets into it. People from the neighborhood tell the Gambinos we're tough kids, but good kids. So they step in for us. They say, 'Hey, you ain't doing shit to these kids. They're good neighborhood kids. They didn't come into your neighborhood and fuck with you. They're in their own neighborhood. You ain't doing nothing.' We only hear about all this. We're ready for anything, but then we're told it's over, it's been straightened out. But we stayed heeled. You never could be sure."

The Rampers had a network in operation—for guns, for fences to handle stolen goods, for bail bondsmen, for lawyers—long before Sammy joined up. "We did mostly burglaries and stealing cars," he said. "We did cars for their parts or to be shipped out of the country. We never burglarized homes. That was against what we wanted to do. It was all commercial places. We'd break in at night, robbing clothing stores, hardware stores, stuff like that. We'd hold up jewelry stores, you know, with ski masks on. They all had insurance.

"My old enemy was the teachers in school. My new enemy was the law, cops. I started boxing a lot in local gyms where guys were training to go into the Golden Gloves tournaments. It made me feel like I was somebody. You didn't have to read to learn how to box. I was quick and I had some pretty good moves. I learned how to feint and jab and use my body the right way in a punch. They wanted me to join the Police Athletic League, so I could work my way up in the Golden Gloves. They said I had real potential. Forget it. I wasn't fighting for no cops.

"Cops would always be hassling you. It got me my first arrest. We were in front of a luncheonette and this cop car pulls up. The cop driving was Italian. I can't remember his name exactly. Let's say Benocchi. He was a real pain in the ass. He yells at us to get off the street. Everybody scatters. I go down the block and stand in the doorway of a little bar. So I was off the street. This Benocchi had followed me and he says, 'I told you to get off the street.' I said, 'You got eyes? I'm off the street.'

"With that, he's out of the car and starts towards me. 'Think you're smart, you punk bastard?' he says. I assume he's ready to hit me with his nightstick, whatever, like they normally did. As soon as he got within range, I set myself and I nailed him with a shot to the jaw. He goes down. I kicked him in the face. Now the other cop in the car is on his way. His gun is out. I'm pinched for assault on an officer.

"Through some of the Rampers, I get this lawyer. He's supposed to know his way around the state courts. And he does! And I get a good lesson about real life and how important it is to be connected. A couple of times my case is postponed. I was out on bail. Then, the third time, it's on. When I meet this lawyer outside court, he says, 'Stay downstairs till I come for you.' In court, my name is called. 'Gravano. Not here. Gravano. Not here.' The judge issues a bench warrant for me, and the cop, Benocchi, leaves.

"Next, the lawyer gets me and brings me up into court. First he talks to the prosecutor. He's been getting delays to get this particular prosecutor. Then he says to the judge, 'Your Honor, my client just arrived. He was delayed because of a car accident. I know you have a full calendar and there are extenuating circumstances to this case. Your Honor, what I would like is to plead my client guilty to a misdemeanor.' The judge goes for that. He doesn't have to reschedule the cop and start this over again. He grants the motion. All I get is a five-hundred-dollar fine. Benocchi don't know it, but he's been set up.

"Right after court, me and my friends go back to the luncheonette where this started. It is right by the precinct house. We're eating hamburgers, and sure enough, Benocchi walks in. He sees me, and real cocky, he says, 'You didn't show up in court. There's a bench warrant out for you. I'm taking you in.'

"'Not me,' I said. 'They got a bench warrant out for your mother, is what. The case is over. I went to court. I copped to a misdemeanor. I got a fine and I got to go back in a couple of days and pay it.'

"My guys are laughing. He's all red in the face. 'I don't believe it,' he says. 'I'm checking this out.' He's so confused he sits down on a stool. I say to the guy behind the counter, 'Hey, Bo, what's Benocchi eating? Hamburger? Put it on my tab. I'm celebrating today.'

"He says, 'You can't pick up my tab.'

"'Yeah, well, that must be a first for you,' I said, and we walked out, giggling."

Sammy's next encounter with the police, however, was not so amusing.

"There were four of us Rampers," he said. "We're looking to score in this lumberyard. We break in. There must have been an alarm we didn't know about because all of a sudden the cops arrive. The other kids get away. I'm the only one who gets collared. They bring me into the precinct and it's the old story. Who were my accomplices?

"'What accomplices?' I say.

"In those days, there wasn't no Miranda warning. The cops did what they want. They asked me a couple of more times and I'm not giving them anything. So they handcuff me to a pipe and started working on me. I mean, they beat me to a pulp. It was bad. There was blood all over the place. My nose was busted. I couldn't see out of my eyes. I could hardly hear. Finally, they gave up and threw me into a holding cell.

"When my mom and dad came, she fainted dead away when she saw me. In court, my lawyer got it knocked down from a burglary felony to a misdemeanor. The case wasn't all that strong. I got caught in the lumberyard, all right, but I hadn't actually taken anything out, and they didn't have the other kids. I was eighteen then, and the war in Vietnam was heating up. What my lawyer told the judge was that if there wasn't any jail time, I would join the army. That way, everyone was a winner. The judge agreed, and all I got was another fine.

"Afterwards, I told the lawyer, 'I ain't joining no army,' and he says, 'You don't have to. I just said that to get you off.'

"I ended up in the army, anyway. I got drafted."

2

I wouldn't have minded
going to Vietnam. You got medals
for killing people there.

SAMMY SHRUGGED OFF THE DRAFT NOTICE TO appear for a physical. All his pals told him that you took the physical and came home. It would be months before there was a call to report for duty, if it came at all, and in any event, plenty of time to find the right doctor or lawyer to keep him out of military service. But it was 1964 and America's involvement in Vietnam was rapidly escalating.

Sammy never got home.

"After the physical, they told us we were going that day. They took us down to a room where you had to take the oath. I refused. I figured my name must have been flagged from when my lawyer told the judge I was going to enlist in the army. I told them I wasn't joining no army. This wasn't my fight. I wasn't the only one. They took us to another room where some FBI people told us it was the army or jail. So I called up my mother and told her I was drafted.

"She said, 'Get home.'

"I said, 'I can't.' I had to put the sergeant on the phone to explain what was happening. I really didn't have such a big problem with it, because I figured I'd be sent to Fort Dix over in Jersey for basic training and I'd be home on the weekends, whatever. I was in a long line of guys and an army guy was calling out, 'Fort Dix, Fort Dix, Fort Dix.' But about six guys in front me, he starts saying, 'Fort Jackson, South Carolina, Fort Jackson, South Carolina.' When I get up there, he tells me, 'You're going to Fort Jackson.'

"I told him, 'I think you made a mistake. I'm from Brooklyn. I'm supposed to go to Fort Dix.'

"He said, 'Fort Jackson.'

"So that was basically it. I was on my way to South Carolina that night. On a bus. Actually, I ended up kind of liking the military. It wasn't all that bad. Most of it was physical. I was nineteen and in real good shape. The sit-ups and push-ups, the running, the obstacle courses, all that stuff, didn't bother me at all. I was right at the top of my company and that made me feel good about myself.

"Every week they had boxing between the companies. I had been working out on the bags in the gym and my sergeant came to me and said one of the guys on the company team was sick and would I fill in? So I did, and I won. Now he wants me to be on the team. I said I wasn't interested. There'd be some benefits, he said. When the company was sleeping out in the field, I could be in my bunk. If I had guard duty, it'd be in a nice warm barracks while everybody else was outside freezing their asses off. I could get three-day passes into the city, which was Columbia.

"So I was on the team and I won a few times. But I quit. I found out the sergeants were betting on the bouts. Small amounts, but they were betting nonetheless. I just didn't want to be used. It wasn't so much that they were betting. It was that they weren't up front about it. Thinking about this now, I realize that has always been and will be an obsession with me. So long as people are straight up with me, everything is OK. But when they try to do things behind my back, when they betray me *first,* I can't stand that. I hate it. Down the road, it was the same sort of thing between me and John Gotti.

"The discipline didn't bother me, either. The rules and regulations, when I thought about it, made a lot of sense. I only got into trouble once. I was on KP, kitchen duty, with this black guy who I was friendly with and we were on the serving line when I had my first real experience with rebels and rednecks and racism and all that bullshit. Now I use words all the time like *nigger, spick, Polack, Jewboy, Mick,* even *greaseball,* which is people from Italy. That's just the way you talk on the street. I don't think I'm racist. But these rednecks, they are real hard core.

"Anyway, I'm on the line and this rebel, whatever, gives the black guy a hard time about how he's dishing out the food. Then he gets to me and says, 'Whip it on me, boy.' I'm using a big long metal spoon and I'm putting stuff in the little compartments on his tray until it starts dripping over and I stopped. I looked at him and he dumped the tray upside down on the counter. 'When I tell you to whip it on me,' he says, 'I tell you when to stop. You niggers, you fucking New Yorkers, better learn to listen to us.'

"I think he might have gotten to the word *us* before I whacked him right in the head with the spoon. I didn't realize that the guy next to him was his buddy, and he clocked me with his metal tray. With that, the black guy jumped over the counter and we went at them. A war broke out. Guys battling all over the place. It was crazy. Afterward, me and the black sat there on the floor, laughing.

"It didn't get to the higher-ups. It was settled right in the kitchen area. Everyone got chewed out, with warnings that if anything like this happened again, it would be the stockade. One of the deciding people was a sergeant, who was black. His tone was harsh, but then he winked and grinned at me. I guess he felt I was defending a brother. Not that I wouldn't have, but actually the black guy jumped in to help me. He just said, 'Gravano, we can't put you on the line anymore. From here on in, you're out back peeling potatoes.' I told him, 'Fine, I could care less.'"

Following basic training, Sammy finally got back to Bensonhurst. Most of the time he hung out with his girlfriend, a girl from the neighborhood named Lorraine. They'd been going together since junior high. She promised to wait for him until he was discharged.

"Then I got shipped to Fort something-or-other in Indiana and started making some extra money in the army. Me and a guy from Boston and a couple of New York guys started a crap game on payday, which went on for a couple of days until everybody went broke. We were cutting the game, taking a percentage, taking, you know, a cut. When the MPs showed up, I grabbed one of the head guys, one of the head sergeants, and said, 'What are you doing?' He said, 'You can't gamble on the base. It's illegal.' I said, 'Are you nuts? You're getting a piece.'

"'What are you talking about?' he said.

"I said, 'You're in this. You're in, for Chrissake.' It took him maybe a minute to get my drift, but all of a sudden, he's nodding his head and smiling and he tells the other MPs, 'Hey! Come on, let's get out of here.' From there on in, I had him on the payroll. I had a booming game. I think I had everybody on the payroll but the general. We had protection. In other words, these guys playing in our game knew they couldn't get into trouble gambling with us. No MPs were going to raid us. You're not going to the stockade and you're not going to lose your stripe, if you have a stripe."

The crap game led to another profitable line of business—loan-sharking. "We backed our game a hundred percent with cash money. When guys went broke, we shylocked them. We paid off their debts and they owed us. Sometimes we had to chase them at payday, but mostly they came back. If you played in another game, and guys busted out, how could you know you'd be paid? With us, nobody had to worry. We were full service."

Sammy brought the crap game and the loan-sharking with him to his next post—Fort Meade, Maryland. "I was assigned to the headquarters company, Second Brigade, Fifth Infantry Division. There was a major in charge of the office. I was part of his staff. We were in communications. He had a black guy for his driver and a buck sergeant who handled the paperwork. Me, I was his bodyguard. When we went into the field in a Jeep, I sat behind him. My thing was to secure his position if we were in combat. But we weren't, so it was nothing really. The major was a real good guy. He told me that I was a damn fine soldier and I should think about the army as a career. As a matter of fact, he had me to his home for dinner several times. He had a daughter around my age, a real good-looking girl. He wanted me to take her out. 'You kids want to go to the movies?' he'd say. Believe me, I was very careful around her.

"All in all, I did very, very good in the army. It was a hell of a lot better than jail. I got promoted to corporal. By the end of my two years, they wanted me to reenlist. They offered me sergeant's stripes and any place I wanted to go in the country if I signed up for four more years. Orders had come down for the company to go to Vietnam. But I had only four months left, and you needed something like ten months before they shipped you out. There were about a hundred guys and maybe twenty of us were scratched for different reasons. I wouldn't have minded going to Vietnam. You got medals for killing people there. Anyway, I got an honorable discharge."

Back in Bensonhurst, Sammy returned to robbing with the Rampers, hanging out at their favorite corner luncheonette at 79th Street and Utrecht Avenue. His mother and father had retired. They had enlarged and winterized the vacation cottage on Long Island and were now living there permanently, but they still owned the house on 78th Street and Sammy moved into the downstairs apartment for a while. Then his father sold the house. He urged Sammy to join him and Kay in Ronkonkoma. "There's a lot of construction work out here," Gerry told him. "You could make a nice living."

"Instead, I had made a nice little score," Sammy said, "and I rented an apartment in Bensonhurst near the water. It had a doorman. Like she promised, Lorraine had waited for me. But now she wanted to get married. I should get a steady job and settle down. But I was high-rolling again. I wasn't interested in a legitimate job."

Still, he was torn. He loved her, and despite his reputation as a tough street kid, he had excellent relations with her family. "Her father was a baker, Nick the Baker. A real sweetheart of a guy. I'd go by her house and watch TV with him. I'd go to the bakery. Not to work. Just to go there. They had a family operation. Her grandmother was the actual owner. I'd go in the back room. They had a big table where they'd all eat. I got along great with them. But me and Lorraine were living in two different worlds. She wanted me to get a job, have kids. But I was too far gone. There was never an argument or a beef. It's just that she was going for a legitimate life and I was a thousand miles in the other direction."

Breaking up with Lorraine became much easier when he met another neighborhood girl, Louise Grimaldi. "She was the most beautiful girl I'd ever seen in my life. Absolutely, totally gorgeous. She had big blue eyes, blond hair, beautiful skin. A completely innocent kid, too. Eighteen years old, just out of high school. We were going to get married. No question about that. It was just a matter of when."

Her family was diverse, to put it mildly. Her mother had died just after Sammy met Louise, but he hit it off at once with her streetwise father, Little Louie, even though he was close to the Gallos. One of her brothers excelled in computers. Another would earn a Ph.D. in the same field and teach college-level computer science. Her third, youngest brother, Johnny, was another story. He stayed on the Bensonhurst streets as a tough kid.

Most of the Rampers who were Sammy's age still clung to the one-for-all, all-for-one notion that they could make it on their own. They would take care of themselves. They didn't have to be mobbed up beyond their own circle. Only a few of them had ended up being drafted into military service. Claiming to be the sole support of their families was a favorite dodge.

During Sammy's absence, one of the Rampers, Louie Milito, had developed a thriving operation in which stolen vehicles were shipped out of the country for sale overseas. "I was close to Louie. I needed a car. He offered to get me one at cost— the cost being what it took to rob the car, changing the engine number and the plates, getting the registration and so forth. Louie calls me and says the car is all ready in a yard he uses. So I go down with a kid named Tommy Spero who had hooked up with the Rampers. I pick up the car and I'm headed for a car wash when all of a sudden there are fucking police cars chasing me, lights flashing, sirens full blast, and they pull me over. The cops were coming at us with guns out. I said, 'What's the matter? What happened?' This cop says, 'You're in a stolen car.'

"I said, 'No, I'm not. Here's the registration. Here's my license. Here's everything.' I was real cocky.

"He tells me, 'Look, the plates don't match. These are stolen plates.' So now I know what happened. The guy in the yard didn't change the plates. Next thing the cops are under the car with mirrors and they spot where the numbers have been changed. I can't believe it. I've been breaking in, doing stickups all over the place, and this is my first pinch since I'm out of the army. I told the cops that Tommy Spero was just riding with me, keeping me company, he don't know nothing, and they just took his name and let him go.

"Louie Milito is fucking fuming. He was even thinking of whacking the guy about the plates, but I told him, 'Louie, I mean, come on, the guy forgot. Maybe it's, you know, partly my fault. Maybe I was anxious to get the car out of the yard and I could be just as much to blame.'

"The guy, naturally, is scared to death. He pays for my lawyer and he tells the cops that yeah, I had come in to buy the car legitimately. He's in the used-car business. He didn't know it was stolen. He said that if he had ever thought it was stolen, he wasn't stupid enough to leave the wrong plates on it.

"So even though I knew it was a swagged car, my lawyer's argument is that I'm an innocent victim. He talks to the prosecutor, and they knocked it down to a misdemeanor. I don't mind taking a plea, because misdemeanors really don't count. It's felonies that screw up your life. I think the lawyer got twenty-five hundred, three thousand. My fine was five hundred. The yard guy paid that, too."

"In those days, we were young and stupid enough, I guess, to think we were invulnerable. Nothing could touch us. That changed. One night I was with one of the Rampers, Joe V. We were going on a robbery and we had to rob a car first. I had a .45 with me and a ski mask. I was getting known well enough that I was using masks. We saw this car and hot-wired it. I was driving. We were about four or five blocks from where we took it. We stopped at a light and another car comes right up to us. There's a guy driving and another guy half-hanging out the window with, like, a rifle and he's yelling, 'Pull over, you cocksucker, or I'll fucking kill you!'

"Right away, I say, 'Whoa, take it easy. Relax. What's the problem?' and he's screaming, 'You stole my fucking car!'

"'All right, all right, now take it easy,' I said again. 'Don't do anything crazy.' As I'm putting up a hand saying this, I reached down for the .45. I see this bum turn toward the driver for a second, telling him something. I bring up the .45 and pull the trigger. I pulled it three times. Click, click, click. Nothing. Believe me, beads of sweat start coming down my forehead. He hears the clicks and he swings his rifle back toward us.

"Joe's sitting next to me and he's screaming, 'Hit it. Hit it.' And I'm hitting it. I've got this thing floored. They're right behind us. We hear shots.

"Then I hear Joe groan, 'Ooh.' He's clutching his stomach. A bullet has gone through the rear of the car, through the backseat, then the front seat, hits him in his back, comes out of his stomach, hits his knee, and winds up hitting the dashboard. I'm turning and wheeling, driving like a bastard, and all of a sudden, bang! Another one blasts through the window and hits me in the back of my head. It blows out a whole section of my head on the right side. Joe is bent over, holding himself. There's blood all over his lap. There's blood all over me. I make a turn. I'm starting to get dizzy. I'm doing maybe seventy miles an hour and I hit like six or seven parked cars. I'm ramming into them, bouncing off them. The car I'm driving spins around and now this car is headed right for us. Forget it. It's over. But now I hear the police sirens. And this other guy jams on his brakes. I see him backing up. Whoever they are, they don't want nothing to do with the cops.

"'Joe,' I say, 'let's get the fuck out of here.' We get out of the car and hobble halfway up the block. Joe collapses on a lawn. I grab him and drag him into an alleyway. We're laying under like a little shed, or some fucking thing. We hear the cops down the street.

"'Joe,' I say. 'We're OK.'

"'Sammy,' he says. 'I'm dying.'

"'Joe, you ain't dead yet,' I say. 'So come on.'

"I help him down the alleyway. We're on another street near a main avenue. I flag down a cab. We're trying to act normal with blood all over us. When we're in the cab, the cabbie sees the blood. Remember, it was dark outside. And he says, 'Hold it.'

"'Hold it, my fucking ass,' I say. I don't have my gun. I left it in the car. I make my finger like a knuckle and press it into his neck. 'Start driving, or I'll blow your fucking brains out.'

"I make him take us back to our neighborhood, where my car is. That cabbie doesn't bother waiting to get paid. I get Joe into the car and I drive to the house of another Ramper, Gerry Pappa. Only now he's hooked in with a made guy in the Genovese family. His name is Dutchie. Pap helps get a bandage on Joe to stop the bleeding. I tell Pap, 'We need a doctor, or something, right away. We can't go to a hospital. We'll be pinched. Maybe Dutchie could help.'

"'All right, Sammy,' Pap says. 'I'll drive.' Finally, he locates Dutchie. Me and Joe are laying in the backseat. By this time we're just about out of it. I remember opening my eyes and seeing Dutchie staring at us and I hear him say, 'Pap, they're dead. What the fuck can I do? Look at them.'

"Pap gets back in the car and says, 'What I'm gonna do, I'm drivin' you to Coney Island Hospital and you jump out and try and walk in.' Joe was moaning real bad now. But I said, 'Fuck the hospital. I ain't going.'

"He says, 'Joe'll die.'

"'Well, take Joe there then.' And that's what happened. We pull up to the emergency entrance and open the door and push Joe out. He just flops there. That was all we could do."

Pappa told Sammy that he could end up bleeding to death himself. But Sammy said, "You know, I think I'll be all right. I feel dizzy and weak, but I'm still conscious. The bleeding is stopping."

That same night Pappa drove Sammy some distance to a doctor in upstate New York who could be relied on for his discretion. According to the doctor, the bullet, instead of plunging into his brain, had taken off a small piece of his skull behind and slightly above his ear.

In the hospital, Joe V. also miraculously survived. "They took out his spleen and I don't know what else," Sammy said. He knew the police had been alerted by the hospital about Joe's gunshot wound and he stayed out of sight until his own wound healed. "There are all sorts of rumors in the neighborhood about me and Joe, and what did or didn't happen. I hear the cops are looking for me, so I go in. They tell me that they know I shot Joe. 'What the fuck are you talking about, I shot him?' I said. 'He's my friend.'

"One of the cops said, 'That's what he told us. You two were in a shoot-out.' Now I know they're trying to bullshit me. So I said, 'If that's what he told you, then you're crazy and he's fucking crazy. Maybe you should sign him into a mental institution.' I'm jerking them off now and they know it. I said, 'I didn't shoot nobody and nobody shot me.'

"Later, I found out that Joe had said that he was walking down the street and this bullet hit him in the back, just like that. He didn't know who did it or why. He didn't know how he got to the hospital, who brought him. He was out of it. After the cops heard these rumors circulating in the neighborhood, they somehow got it mixed up that we had shot it out, or else the rumors did, and they were making inquiries.

"I visited Joe in the hospital and he said, 'I'll never forget it. You saved my life.'

"I said, 'Fuck saving your life. When you get

out of here, we got to find that fucking bum. He tried to kill us for a fucking car?' We looked all over where we stole the car, but we never found him."

While Sammy was recuperating, he happened to bump into a friend from his old neighborhood, Gerry LaTorroca, who had been drafted around the same time he was. "Sammy," he said, "I got a situation where you could make some good money."

"Doing what?"

"There's this beauty school in downtown Brooklyn where they teach all about skin care, things like that, how to cut hair."

"Are you nuts, or what? I'm not a beautician."

"No, no. You'd just put in for the haircutting classes. You're ex-G.I., right? The government pays for the whole thing. And you get unemployment tax-free because you're learning a trade. I know the guy who runs the place. He's just interested in the government's money. You walk in, walk out, do whatever you want. And listen to this. There's about six hundred girls in there, fulltime and part-time. And only five guys, including me. Two of them are stone faggots. You can consider them women. Of the other three of us, one is part-time. He only goes at night."

"I don't know," Sammy said. "I'll think about it."

Then he met a neighborhood girl named Lorraine who turned out to be attending the school. "It's a different Lorraine, not the one I used to go out with but one I was always looking to nail. She said, 'I hear you might be enrolling.' I said, 'I'm thinking about it. Why?' She starts to laugh. 'This school is loony,' she says. 'The girls are all crazy.' I said, 'Really? What's going on?' and she said, 'All they think about is sex. You should hear them talk. Believe me, you're going to need a cast-iron cock. After a couple of days, you won't be able to walk.'

"Well, that sounded good to me, so I go down with Gerry and meet the guy. He's an older guy. I tell him, 'If I do this, all I'm interested in is the unemployment money. I'll be in and out. I'll check in, but when I'm bored, I'm taking off.' He said, 'No problem. I do that with Gerry. But there are certain times you have to listen to me.'

"In those days, I always carried a gun. I opened up my jacket and he sees the .38 laying there. 'I don't listen to nobody,' I said, and he says, 'Right, all right, you do what you want.'

"'Good,' I said. 'We have an understanding.' Then he wants me to fill out the forms for the government and the unemployment. I told him I was bad at that. I'll give him the information and he should do the paperwork. He sneaks another peek at the .38 and says, 'Fine, no problem.'

"That was some school. They had classes for

doing nails. I'm not there for that. I was the one they practiced on. I'm getting a manicure every other day. And the facials. Again, I don't take that. I'm the one getting the massages and stuff. Right off the bat, this girl is giving me a facial and the next thing she's going down on me. I'm getting blown. I'm getting laid every three minutes. In closets, on massage tables, every time I turn around, practically.

"What I'm supposed to be learning is haircutting. And I am the worst, the absolute and total world's worst. One day I'm doing a haircut on some lady. She had straight hair, nothing fancy, so it's fairly easy. Just even everything out, shoulder length. She's sitting in the chair chatting away and I'm talking to her. All of a sudden, she ain't saying nothing. I feel like I'm talking to the wall. I look down at her and there's a wire hanging on her chest. I'm thinking, what the fuck is that? I said, 'Sweetheart, I'm talking to you. Are you deaf?' She turns around and says, 'What?' That's when I saw it. She has a hearing aid and I cut the wire going to it. Un-fucking believable!

"In haircutting, you had to learn how to color hair, too. But I pushed it off. The girls at the school would do it for me. One day, this older woman comes in. She wasn't really that old, maybe in her fifties, but that was old to me then. She's got gray hair and she wants a blue rinse. Everyone's tied up, and they tell me, 'Sammy, you can do it. It's nothing.' I just have to put this blue stuff in her hair, like shampoo, that brightens it up, takes the yellow, whatever, out, gives it a sheen. Let it sit for a while and wash it out.

"So I said OK. I put this blue stuff in her hair. And it's blue, I mean, really blue. Next I take her over to the sink to wash it out and nothing happens. It's still fucking blue. It turns out you're supposed to mix this blue stuff first and water it down. But how was I supposed to know? I never done it before. I put it in her hair the way it was in the bottle.

"'Excuse me for a minute,' I say, and she says, 'Is something wrong?' I said, 'No, I'll be back in a second.' I grab the boss and tell him that there's this woman in the back. 'You can't miss her, her hair's fucking sky blue and the blue won't come out. I'm going to lunch. Take care of her.' 'What do you mean?' he says. 'She's your customer.' He tries to give me another shampoo. 'Use this. This is sure to work.' 'I ain't taking nothing,' I said. 'I ain't going near this woman again. When she looks in a mirror, she'll go nuts.'

"When I got back, the whole school was hysterical. Of course, the guy couldn't get the blue out either. And the woman did go bananas. He had to promise her I don't know how many free haircuts and everything else.

"Another thing I learned at that school is how women—I mean, the customers—talk in beauty parlors. They're loose as a goose. They talk about every fucking thing. It's incredible. You can't believe how dirty they talk. One day, I'm working on a woman and she starts telling me, 'I was with my husband last night and I put ice cubes in my mouth and gave him the best blow job ever.' And she's telling about a lot of other things she has in mind. She ain't bad-looking and she's turning me on. I can't concentrate no more. I say, 'You can't tell me these things. What do you think, that I'm a fucking fag?' And I throw down the comb and walk out.

"I had another problem. My girlfriend Louise finds out about what's going on at the school, that I'm supposed to be screwing everything in sight, and she joins up to keep an eye on me. These other girls know she's my girlfriend, but they don't give a fuck. They're real cagey and sneaky. Louise never actually catches me, but she hears rumors. I luck out, though. She blames them.

"When it's time to graduate, to get my license, I figure I don't stand a chance with the state board tests. And by now I'm thinking I want the license. I'm looking ahead. Somewheres down the line, I might open a string of beauty salons and I'll need it. Some of the girls tell me what to do. I used my sister Frannie as a model. I had her hair cut professionally. And I saved what was cut. I take it in a bag down to where the board tests are. So it's haircut time, and OK, boom, boom, I take the hair out of

the bag, wet it and sprinkle it around her chair. I'm
pretending to cut, then I'm done. The woman
inspector comes over. She looks at Frannie. She
looks at the hair on the floor. I think she checks it
out with a comb. I'm on the money. I passed! She
nods and says, 'You're good, pretty good, at cutting
hair.'

"I said, 'I know. Thank you very much.'"

For the Rampers around Sammy's age, a new reality set in as they grew older. They could rob commercial establishments and steal cars all they
wanted to, but there was a ceiling on how far they
could expand their activity. To take the next step up,
to open a business, say a bar, a disco, an after-hours
club, which were especially popular in Bensonhurst,
or to run a gambling operation, to loan-shark, to
pull off a major hijacking, they had to be connected,
mobbed up.

Some Rampers drifted into legitimate blue-
collar work. The rest, if they could, became associated with one of the five Cosa Nostra families in
New York. In Bensonhurst, the Profaci family had
been dominant. When Profaci died, and Joe
Colombo was anointed his successor as boss, it
became the Colombo family. The Gambino family
also had a major presence locally. The Genovese,
Bonanno and Lucchese families were in the picture as well. A few Rampers ended up in the

DeCalvacante family across the Hudson River in New Jersey.

And for Sammy, the message was especially clear when Jimmy Emma was murdered. "Of all the Rampers," he said, "Jimmy was the wildest. One time, we're standing on our corner and we're all heavy, and a police car pulls up. A cop rolls down the window and says, 'Hey, Jimmy, we got a report somebody saw you with a gun. We're going to have to search you.' We're all nervous. Every one of us has a gun on him. Jimmy walks forward three or four feet towards the car and opens his jacket. He's got two guns in his belt. 'Draw!' he shouts, and the cop who's driving hits the gas. You could hear the tires squealing. We all ran up to him and said, 'Jimmy, what the fuck, are you crazy? There's going to be eight million cops back here.' 'Fuck 'em,' he says. 'We'll hide the guns.' Which was what we did. When they came back, we had no guns. But they pulled in Jimmy. I don't know what happened, but he was out in an hour. No arrest, nothing. Lack of evidence, I heard.

"Now the Rampers are tough. We're always banging heads. And there was a club that was run by a captain in the Colombo family. His name was Dominick Scialo. They called him Mimi, a real mean rough-and-tumble guy. So we're in his club a lot and it seems there's always trouble with Jimmy in the middle of it. Fights and so forth. Finally, there's one fight too many. I don't remember what it was about, but Mimi has had enough. When Mimi has a problem with somebody, his solution is to kill. He goes to his boss and asks permission to whack us out. And he got permission. He sends a team of shooters down to the corner where we hung out, at 79th and Utrecht. It was late afternoon and only Jimmy and Gerry Pappa were there, washing their cars. These shooters ran up and they blew Jimmy away.

"They start shooting at Pap. Just then a car passes by and Pap dives into an open window. It was some neighborhood kid who didn't know from nothing. The kid was so scared when they started shooting at his car that he took off. Pap got lucky and got away.

"I was home at the time. It wasn't late enough yet. I got to the corner about an hour after they took Jimmy's body away. Then I hear the story. One of the guys says, 'Pap's at the precinct, I think.' We all get together at this bar called Doc's and decide what to do. We're going to strike back. Fuck the Colombos. It sounds nuts, but we're full of piss and vinegar, and stupid. Now the cops have us down at the precinct questioning us. A million and one questions. I think it was Joe Vitale who called me over and said, 'Sammy, look at this.' On the desk there was a protection order filled out for Gerry Pappa and he'd signed it. He'd signed himself in. A rat move. We were going to stick together and fight back. What's this? Fuck signing anything. Our relationship and friendship and everything died out from that point on.

"There were a lot of sit-downs amongst the families about us. Basically, what we heard was, the decision was that Jimmy was enough. This Dutchie spoke up for Pap and they gave him a pass.

"Pappa eventually became a made member in the Genovese family himself. And then got killed. He was shot to death in a restaurant. On 69th Street and 14th Avenue. A guy blew his head off with a shotgun. Point-blank."

Shortly afterward, Tommy Spero, who had been with Sammy in the stolen-car arrest, came to him. He said, "My uncle would love to meet with you."

"About what?"

"He just wants to talk to you and stuff."

"Now I know who Tommy's uncle is. His name is Tommy, too, except everybody calls him Shorty. He's a big shot, whatever, with the Colombo family. So I say, 'Sure, why not?'"

You can't live your whole life on your own. Sooner or later, you're going to get in real trouble or get killed.

IN 1931, WARRING FACTIONS OF THE ITALIAN underworld, primarily Sicilian and Neapolitan, came together to form Cosa Nostra. This union enabled it to completely dominate organized crime, both ethnic and homegrown American, throughout the country during the next decade. By the end of World War II, Cosa Nostra consisted of twenty-four crime families from coast to coast, each with an identical organizational structure. It flourished in cosmopolitan New York City as well as cow-town Kansas City. Two resort cities were ordained to be open to the activities of any family—Las Vegas and Miami. Policy was determined, and interfamily disputes settled, by a national commission composed of eleven of the most powerful bosses.

Then, in 1957, when Sammy was twelve years old, Cosa Nostra was wracked by a series of internal convulsions. After Lucky Luciano, one of its original architects, had been deported to Italy, Vito Genovese sought control of his family by attempting to assassinate the acting family boss, Frank Costello.

Costello decided to step down, and the Luciano family became the Genovese family. Still, Genovese feared retaliation from another trigger-happy family boss and Costello ally, Albert Anastasia, the most notorious killer in Cosa Nostra's history. So he conspired with a wily Anastasia underling, Carlo Gambino, to do away with "the Mad Hatter," as Anastasia was called. On October 25, 1957, Anastasia was relaxing under a pile of hot towels in a Manhattan barbershop when two gunmen walked in and gunned him down. The Anastasia family was now the Gambino family.

Even more unsettling was the discovery that while Anastasia was still alive, memberships in his family were being secretly sold for $50,000 each.

To deal with all of this, a national conclave of Cosa Nostra's leadership was scheduled for November 14, 1957, in the small upstate New York village of Apalachin, where a captain in the Buffalo family lived. The idea was that a meeting in such an out-of-the-way rural setting would go unnoticed. Just the opposite happened. An alert New York State trooper spotted an unusual number of black limousines full of silk-suited strangers converging on the residence. Roadblocks were set up, and soon the nation's top mobsters were scampering through the woods trying to avoid detection. Many of them were arrested and convicted on charges of obstructing justice by refusing to explain their presence in Apalachin. These convictions were reversed on the ground that merely meeting as they had was not by itself a crime. However, they effectively ended any more national Cosa Nostra commission get-togethers. If families around the country had to communicate with one another, emissaries were dispatched. Only in New York City, where five families uniquely rubbed shoulders, did the commission system continue to function.

Both Vito Genovese and Carlo Gambino were officially recognized as family bosses. And to regain some measure of stability, because of the sale of memberships, the membership books of the New York families were closed.

Eleven years later, in 1968, when Sammy the Bull had his meeting with Shorty Spero, the books remained closed, which was why Spero was an associate rather than a made member of the Colombo family. It was really a technicality. "Everyone in the neighborhood knew that Shorty pulled a lot of weight in the family," Sammy said. "Shorty was a veteran. It was all around on the streets about the books being closed, but when they opened up, Shorty would be made right away.

"Shorty was an ex-pug, but he'd gotten to be a polished guy, nice clothes, nice jewelry, nothing overdone, who knew how to talk without beating around the bush. When we met, he got right to the point. His message wasn't anything I hadn't heard before. Eventually, I'd have to hook up with the right people. But the way he put it was different. 'I've had my eye on you,' he says. 'Why not come with me? You're a tough guy, but you can't keep doing things your own way. You can't live your whole life on your own. Sooner or later, you're going to get in real trouble or get killed. I'll give you a different relationship, where you can be somebody. I'll never stab you in the back. I'll never bullshit you. I'll never ask you to do anything I wouldn't do myself.' Those were the words, that was the pledge, I wanted to hear. Like I've said, I'm obsessed with people being up front with me."

Once Sammy had agreed to "go on record" with Shorty—to be associated officially with the Colombo family—he was taken to meet Shorty's captain, Carmine Persico, Jr. Persico was called "Carmine" or "Junior" to his face and behind his back a name he detested—"the Snake"—because of the suddenness with which he would strike when provoked. "It was an honor for me to meet him," Sammy said. "He was a living legend, not just in Bensonhurst, but all over. He shook my hand and said, 'I'm real happy about this. I heard a lot of good things about you.' I still have high regard for him. When I look back, he was one of the few mob guys who never went around scheming, who was always on the up-and-up."

Word of Sammy's recruitment was passed on to the family boss, Joe Colombo, and to the other New York families, as required by Cosa Nostra rules. Shorty told Sammy that the boss himself had signaled his special pleasure at the news.

Sammy had already had an encounter with Colombo. "I beat up both his sons one time. In a movie house. We had this argument and I got in a fight with Joseph Junior, who was younger than me, and I broke his ass. He went and got his big brother, Anthony, who comes and it's the same result. I'll never forget it. Joe Colombo sent for me, he called me down. He looks at me and says, 'You beat up both my sons? You must be pretty tough. Did you know they were my sons?' I said, 'No, not at the time. They were just two young guys at the movie house.' He says, 'Anthony, you almost knocked him out. You could have kicked his face in. How come you didn't do that?' I said, 'Why would I want to do that? It was just a fight. It was nothing personal.' He says, 'Now you know they're my sons, right?' and I said, 'Absolutely.' He says, 'You must be good with your hands because I know my sons are pretty tough. And that's good how you conducted yourself. When you got a guy down, know when to let him up. Good-bye.'

"So I liked this Joe Colombo. That was another reason I was glad to be with the family. I never got a bad decision from him. I'd be with Shorty, and Shorty would be talking to him, maybe giving him a message from Junior. I would stay across the street or out of the way, and a couple of times he would say, 'Sammy, how come you didn't come over and say hello?' I said, 'I didn't know if it was my place.' 'It's always your place to say hello,' he told me. That's the kind of guy he was."

The benefits of being connected became quickly apparent.

"So now I'm in Shorty's crew and my 'new friends' are this Frankie, Ralphie Ronga, Joe Colucci, Lenny the Mole, who also was from the Rampers—Lenny would only come out during the day when he had to—and Tommy Spero, Shorty's nephew.

"And right around then, me and Tommy and Lenny stick up this clothing store at closing time. I go in first, I don't have a mask, I don't want to alert the guy. I put a gun in his face and Tommy and Lenny come in. We took all the cash and carried a lot of clothes out the back way, where we had the van parked. But the guy picks me out of a mug book. It looks bad. It's a heavy felony. Grand larceny, forcible theft with a deadly weapon. But it turns out the guy, the owner of the store, is a friend of a made guy in Sam the Plumber's family— the DeCalvacante family—over in Jersey. Shorty, whoever, gets in touch with him and he talks to the owner. It was all set up the next time I was in court. The owner walks in and goes in front of the judge and says, 'Your Honor, I picked the defendant out from his picture, but now that I see him in person, that's not him.' And the case is thrown out. I didn't have to make restitution or anything. The guy was covered by insurance. So he's got it going both ways. He gets his losses back and he's done us a favor, too. For sure, he doesn't have to worry about no more robberies.

"The same kind of thing happened in a bank robbery. This looked like big money and Shorty was all for it. He got a piece of everything we scored. The bank was on a corner, and Tommy Spero had a guy on the inside. The bank had a side door on the street and then there was a little foyer and another door to the bank itself. This was the route the armored car people used to pick up money from the bank. Tommy said that at this particular branch, they only used one guard to bring out the money bags. Tommy's inside guy would leave the side door on the street open, so I could slip into the foyer and get the guard when he comes out of the bank. It sounded good.

"Tommy is at the corner by the bank to get the signal from his guy. Frankie is at another corner to cover us. Lenny's driving the getaway car. The guy in the bank must have given Tommy the nod, because Tommy nods to me. Sure enough, the side street door is open and I go in. Perfect.

Nobody walking outside can see me. I get my gun out and set myself. The inside door to the bank opens up and lo and behold, there ain't one guard, there are four of them! I'm in shock. Three of the guards are holding money bags and the fourth has got his hand on his gun. I pointed my gun at him and yelled, 'Hit the floor!' And they do. I guess they're in shock, too. I got my gun in one hand and I grab two of the bags with the other, and now I don't know what the hell to do. I back out through the street door. It's a solid door, no windows. I slam it shut, just as the guards are coming at me, pulling out their guns. I yell to my guys that there are a gang of guards in there. I get my foot against the door to jam it. I don't know what the fuck else to do. I feel the guards pushing against the door and I'm telling my guys to run.

"I see them running. They're yelling to me, 'Come on, Sammy, come on.' I'm afraid to let the door go. I'm panicking. How far could I get? Ten feet? These guards will blow me away. By now I've dropped the two bags. One of them opened up and some of the money comes out. Bills are actually flying all over the street. By now a crowd has formed, people are looking, yelling, screaming. People are chasing the bills. Fuck it! I take a shot and let go of the door. Instead of running to the car where Lenny is, I run straight into the crowd, figuring the guards won't shoot with so

many people around. I run through the crowd. As
I'm running up the block, there's a guy standing
there, and he's yelling at me, 'Sammy, come here,
come here.' Zoom! he takes me into his house. I
never knew who the fuck he was, but he knows
me. This is at 86th Street and 21st Avenue. It's not
far from my old neighborhood. He must know me
from there. He tells me he's going to look outside
and I'm wondering if he went to tip the cops.
Finally, he comes back and says they were searching all over, but they're gone. He asks me if I want
to leave my gun with him. I say thanks, but no
thanks, I'm keeping it and walk out. 'Good luck,'
he said.

"I make it to Tommy Spero's father's house.
The other guys are there. Shorty comes down and
finds out what happened. We all stay low at the
house in the basement playing cards. Sure
enough, we find out one of the guards made me.
And the cops are looking to arrest me. They have
an identification from the mug book and all that
shit again. But guess what? The guard knows
Carmine Persico's cousin and is a little crooked
himself. The guard reaches out and says for ten
thousand he ain't going to see nothing. He won't
testify.

"Great! The case will be over.

"I go down with Shorty to see Carmine.
Carmine says, 'We'll do it.' I said, 'Carmine, I don't
have five cents.'

"He says, 'I'll pay the ten thousand. We'll squash this. But you're going to give me three points on the money.'

"From being happy, now I'm totally disappointed. Three points is three hundred a week until the principal is paid off. You don't knock it down. 'Carmine,' I say, 'I'm telling you, I'm broke. That's why I was robbing the bank.'

"He gives me a look. 'Yeah,' he says, 'but you don't get nothing for nothing in this life. Let me tell you how it works. I *get* money. I don't give you money, you give me money. That's number one. Number two, you have the opportunity to beat this case because of my strength and power. And number three, you're paying for the case with my money. You want to go through the door, I'm the guy who opens it. You don't seem to appreciate that.'

"I sat and thought about it for a minute. I said to myself that he was right, basically. Streetwise, he was a hundred percent right. In other words, I'm beating the case, I was looking at seven and a half to fifteen years, minimum. I'm borrowing the money to do it. So I got to pay the vig. That's the life. I realized that he was training and schooling me in the right direction. The money don't come down free of charge. You don't get nothing for nothing. First off, I'm scrambling to come up with the three hundred a week so I don't look bad with Carmine. And then I go after the ten. I know how to do it. With a gun. Robbing and stealing left and right, jewelry stores. It took me about three weeks. I just couldn't live with paying out that three hundred."

Gradually, Sammy's new status enabled him to begin moving out of his old routine of stickups and break-ins. "I'm starting to become more of a true gangster and racketeer, getting into business. Even if they're not stone legitimate businesses, they're real on a business level.

"One of the first was this after-hours club on 62nd Street and 17th Avenue. This guy Billy Stag told me about it. Billy wasn't mobbed up, but he knew the ins and outs of running a club like that. He said old man John Rizzo, who was a made guy in the Gambino family, and Matty Gambino, who wasn't made but pulled weight because he was related to Carlo Gambino, a nephew or something, were opening this club. 'Sammy,' Billy said, 'they want me to manage it, but I'll need somebody on my side. They'll drive me crazy, especially Matty, who thinks he's a big fucking gangster. Why don't you get a piece of it?'

"I've accumulated some money and I go down to see John and ask could I have a piece of the joint. Now I know an old-time wiseguy like him ain't interested in being there every night. He just wants to collect his end. And when I go down,

Louie Milito, who's close to him, happens to be there, and Louie says, 'Sammy will be great for the fucking club because Matty Gambino is a fucking waste.' And the old man says, 'I love the idea. You're in.'

"The joint was half done at that point. I done construction work on and off and I dived in to help finish it up. When you went in, there was a big front room. To the right and along the back was an L-shaped bar. There were café tables and chairs and a little dance floor and nice soft lighting. Behind the front room, there was another room with a big green-felt table where we ran a poker game that we cut and there's a small kitchen for sandwiches and stuff. Right from the start, the place was extremely successful.

"I put it on record with Shorty and the Colombo family that I got a piece of this club. I'm there like every minute, working like a dog with Billy, stopping fights, seeing everything is OK. I'm taking shifts in the card game. I'm watching the door. If there's a fight, I'm in between guys. Hey, I'm five feet five. Some of these fucking guys fighting are six one, six two, and they don't give a fuck. It's an after-hours club. They're drunk. We'd start around ten or eleven at night. People would come in and leave and then others would come in, and we'd be filled to seven, eight in the morning. Sometimes a poker game would go on for two or three days straight without stopping.

"The only problem was Matty Gambino. He'd strut in with his overcoat draped over his shoulders. He'd come in like a fucking Don Juan— he was a good-looking kid—have a couple of drinks, pick up a girl or two and leave. Louie Milito would be around a lot. He's got nothing to do with the joint, he's just helping out, bringing in people to drink, play cards, whatever. 'Sammy,' he'd say, 'how things going?' and I'd tell him, 'It's going good.' He'd say, 'How come you and Billy got it all on your backs. Why don't Matty work?'

"'Louie,' I said, 'you trying to break my balls? He's only his nephew, but he thinks he's Carlo Gambino himself. He comes in and he's gone.'

"The truth is that I wish he would never come into the club at all. One night me and Billy had finished doing the books, breaking down all the ends everybody got, and sure enough this Matty Gambino comes in with a couple of guys and some broads. He walks over and he said, 'You know, Sammy, the bills don't seem right with the amount of liquor we're selling.' He keeps on about this and that. 'It don't seem right,' he says. 'What do you think is wrong?'

"'Wrong!' I said. 'Do you think me and Billy are robbing you? If I were you, I wouldn't even answer that.' He kind of draws back, stunned. 'I tell you what,' I said, 'why don't you take that fucking greaseball coat off, roll up your fucking sleeves, come in here and roll on the floor every time there's a fucking fight and work the fucking joint. As a matter of fact, you handle the cash. *You* divvy it up.'

"'Sammy,' he says, 'don't you think you're out of order?'

"'Fuck you, out of order! You come in here, you want to abuse people, you're a fucking punk! You come in here with your friends and don't do no fucking work. Then you make a fucking accusation that something ain't right? Let's stop this conversation because it's going to get worse and worse and I'll knock your fucking head in, you understand, you fucking greaseball! Just make another accusation about something that ain't right here with me or Billy.'

"The next thing I know there's a massive meeting. Shorty's there. John Rizzo says, 'Sammy, he went to his uncle, he went to Carlo. I'm sent down to talk to you about it. How could you do that? How could you say those things?'

"'How could I do it? He's lucky I didn't put my motherfucking foot up his ass. Who the fuck does this bum think he is? John, I give you the respect, I give Carlo the respect. But this fucking bum ain't going to come in on Carlo's name and reputation, or your name and reputation, and make accusations against me and Billy.'

"I turned to Shorty. 'Shorty,' I said, 'I'll declare it right now. I'll take my end back. I'm out of this club if that's what everybody wants.'

"Old man Rizzo starts laughing. 'Take it easy,' he says. 'Don't get so fucking hot. You're hundred per- cent right. Fuck this bum. He'll come in like a mouse from here on in. I know what happened, I heard it from Billy, but I had to come down about it and hear the story from you. Let me go back to Carlo and tell him how his nephew was acting. There's nothing to worry about. Don't pull out. Shorty, tell him to calm down.'

"So I learned a big lesson. Number one, you got to stand up for yourself. Number two, I didn't stand a chance if I wasn't hooked up with the Colombo family. Shorty's getting a piece of my end. That's how it works. After the expenses of the club, and paying off the cops, I'm taking out for myself about two thousand a week cash—which is not bad in those days—and five hundred of it goes up the ladder that I give to Shorty. I wait to see what Carlo Gambino is going to say about all this—Shorty has already told me where Joe Colombo stands—and the answer is that when this Matty comes in again, he's gonna be like a fucking mouse. As a matter of fact, every time he came in with his girls, it was, 'Say hello to Sammy.' The whole picture changed.

"I started on my own another little club on the side in Bensonhurst, which was making some money. It was just a club to gamble, poker. And Shorty got a piece of that. I started shylocking, too, in a small way. Shylocking was considered your personal business, so what you got, you kept.

"At first it was bullshit loans. Not like later on when I became and had the reputation of a shylock's shylock. I used to lend ninety-six for a hundred-twenty for twelve weeks. It was hard work. It was easy to give the money out, but when you're dealing at that level, you're lending to the bottom of the barrel. A lot of these guys would wind up taking off and you'd have to chase them down. But even so, during those years, there's only two people I had to hit to collect. Physically hit, I mean. Only two people. I think that says something about the reputation I had.

"There was this one guy. He didn't pay me for months and months. I kept having to chase him. I was yelling at him and he told me to lower my voice. I said, 'Lower my voice? You take my money, you give me a tough time and then you tell me to lower my voice?' *Boom!*

"And there was this other guy who owed me money. My friends were teasing me in a bar one night about it. He had made an appointment and didn't show. He made another appointment and still didn't show. They're breaking my chops that he wasn't never going to pay. He don't care. As they were joking and laughing and teasing, he comes into the bar with some heavyweights in the Colombo family. I grabbed him and took him outside. First off, I tell him he's going to pay up. 'Second thing, when you make an appointment with me, you better show. Or send somebody down to tell me you ain't going to show. Don't fucking make me just stand on a street corner waiting for you.'

"He got a little nervy. 'Sammy,' he says, 'I'm tied up. I'm not paying the loan. I'm with Joe Colombo and the Italian-American Civil Rights League.' I said, 'You're with what? The Italian-American League? And you ain't paying? Who the fuck do you think I'm with, the Jewish Defense League?'

"I gave him a tremendous beating right there. And then this other guy, who's going to be made—remember, all them years the books were closed and nobody got made—comes out of the bar and says, 'What are you doing, Sammy? He's with Joe Colombo and the league.' I said, 'He owes me money and that's the bullshit answer he gives me, that he ain't paying up. Fuck him and fuck that!'

"'How much does he owe?' the guy asks. I tell him it's a couple of hundred and he takes out the money and paid me. The next day Shorty got in touch with me that Joe Colombo wanted to see me again. The boss himself. I go down to the real estate office on 86th Street, where he stayed. He came out and said, 'Sammy, you know that kid, the one you beat up the other night? He's working with the league.'

"I said, 'Joe, before you say anything or get mad, let me tell you what happened.' I explain the whole circumstance about him borrowing the money, not paying, and then telling me to my face that he's not paying, not showing, that he's with the league. Joe Colombo starts laughing and says, 'Are you paid?' I said, 'Yes.' He says, 'OK, this is the end of it.' I said, 'Of course, Joe. That kid just got me to a point where I lost it.' 'Well, make sure it never happens again,' and I said, 'All right.'

"Joe Colombo was a street guy. I heard from Shorty that after I left, Joe said that if I hadn't given the kid the beating I did, 'he'—meaning me—'wouldn't be one of us. A guy gives a fucking answer like that, he's supposed to get a beating.' As far as I was concerned, that was the sort of thing that made Joe the boss, the reason you had to love the guy."

To the consternation of his fellow Cosa Nostra bosses, Joe Colombo had formed the Italian-American Civil Rights Defense League in 1969. The declared goal was to make Italian-Americans proud of their heritage, to combat the gangster stereotype that all Italian-Americans supposedly had to endure and to force the media to stop using the buzzword *Mafia* in stories about organized crime.

One of the first tactics to gain attention was protest marches at the New York office of the

FBI. Sammy the Bull was in the initial picket lines, along with Shorty Spero. "I mean," Sammy recalls, "it was crazy. We were up there at the FBI in Manhattan around 69th Street and Third Avenue and there wasn't more than twelve or fifteen of us in the beginning. I remember it was raining and the FBI was clicking cameras on all of us. That's all I needed, I thought. Who gave a fuck about Mafia in the papers? It was just asking for trouble. I felt like a fool. So did Shorty. But the boss was the boss."

To everyone's amazement, the movement caught on, culminating in a huge "unity" rally on Columbus Day, June 29, 1970, at Columbus Circle with well over fifty thousand people cheering Joe Colombo. New York governor Nelson Rockefeller accepted honorary membership in the league. Even Carlo Gambino, who had opposed the whole idea, went along. The Gambino family controlled the Brooklyn waterfront, and for the first time in history a complete twenty-four-hour work stoppage was ordered on the docks so that longshoremen could attend the event.

Within Cosa Nostra, however, concern mounted. The FBI, stung at being targeted, had counterattacked. Throughout the city, surveillance was heightened and suspected mob figures were hauled in day and night for questioning on any pretext. The normal course of conducting mob business became all but impossible. The most visible sign that something was amiss occurred when it was learned that for a second giant rally the following year, on June 28, longshoremen were not getting the day off. And that day, as he stood at Columbus Circle observing the crowd assemble, Joe Colombo was shot three times in the head with an automatic pistol. He was not killed. He had been reduced to a vegetative state, however, lingering on for seven more years before dying. His assailant, a black man from New Jersey, with a press card and carrying a movie camera, was shot dead on the spot by Colombo bodyguards.

At first, law enforcement as well as Cosa Nostra viewed the renegade Joey Gallo as the most likely mastermind of the plot. Recently released from prison, he was known to have cultivated relationships with a number of black inmates.

"Obviously," said Sammy, "somebody had to be behind it. This black guy was a nobody. We looked into him. He had a record, but he was small-time. He wasn't attached to any black organization or anything like that. We heard that the gun was hidden in the movie camera. Could he have done that on his own? But the family decided that Joey Gallo was not responsible. He sent a message that he and his people were looking to kill Joe Colombo, they were at war, and if they caught him, they would have killed him. Joey Gallo said he'd love to claim the Columbus Circle job, that he did it—but he didn't. Junior

Persico, Shorty, all the top guys in the family believed him. Some guys thought the government had set it up to make it look like the Gallos done it. But in reality that didn't make any sense. To me, to this day, it's a mystery. The only ones who really know are the ones that pulled it off. Or maybe that black guy was just some radical nut. It can happen."

Two years later, Joey Gallo—"Crazy Joe"—was killed while celebrating his forty-third birthday with his wife, daughter, and other relatives at Umberto's Clam House in Little Italy. But it wasn't because of the Columbus Circle shooting, Sammy said. "When Joey got out of jail, he had started rubbing elbows with all these writers and movie stars, theater people and whatnot. He was going to write books and make movies and do all that stuff. He got to be like a high-society pet, and Joe Colombo had called him in to discuss this and other matters, and he refused to come. That's one of the most important rules in Cosa Nostra. When the boss calls you in, you come in. Or else. So Joe Colombo had put a contract out on him, and the new family administration finished it off even though Joe Colombo was out of it by now."

Being with the family was a two-way street for Sammy. He had the clout of the association. But he also was expected to obey orders, no questions asked. One day, with Shorty Spero present, Carmine Persico summoned him and Tommy Spero. A Long Island distributor of commercial washing machines and dryers had been discovered having an affair with the wife of one of Persico's brothers. They were to give the distributor a beating. Persico wanted an ear of the distributor brought back to him. He was very explicit about the ear. He told Shorty, "Have Tommy do the driving and talking. Let Sammy do the work."

"So off we go. We had a plan. We went in there and Tommy asked for this guy, the owner, and when he comes out, Tommy tells him he'd like to see some literature, he's thinking about opening up a Laundromat. The guy took out some brochures. I had a blackjack in my back pocket. And when the guy leaned on the counter to show us the brochures, I hit him. I clocked him on the side of the head with the blackjack. I jumped over the counter and started beating him up. There are a half-dozen workers out back. They heard the yelling and the banging around. They all come running out at us. One of them grabbed me by the shirt and I caught him in the face with the blackjack. Meanwhile, the other guy, the owner, was getting himself up. He had grabbed the edge of the counter with one hand. Now Junior in the contract had told me that I was supposed to go in there and cut this guy's ear off. I had no intentions of doing that. I mean, come on! But when I whacked this guy's hand with the blackjack, I knocked his little finger off. It came completely off. That finger went flying. It must have been the way he was holding on to the edge of the counter.

"We just about made it out of there, got in Tommy's car and took off from Long Island to Brooklyn. When we saw Shorty, I didn't get into the details. I told him, 'I'm sorry. I didn't get the ear. But I got the guy's finger. I seen it come off. I couldn't bring it back for Carmine. There were too many other guys and everything like that.'

"Carmine did find out that the finger was gone. He and Shorty thought it was the greatest thing in the world. Carmine must have told Joe Colombo because after that, instead of me waiting for the right moment to say hello to him, he would come over with a big smile and say, 'Hey, Sammy, how you doing?' "

Committing a murder—making your bones—was not a prerequisite for induction into Cosa Nostra. But more often than not, it would happen. Murder was the linchpin of Cosa Nostra—for control, for discipline, to achieve and maintain power. For made members and associates, it was an everyday, accepted fact of life. The code that could trigger a hit was very clear. If someone broke the rules, he would be whacked. Murder was the means to bring some semblance of order to what otherwise would be chaos.

In theory, a Cosa Nostra hit required a precise procedure. A case had to be made. It then had to be sanctioned by the family boss. A murder that had not been authorized invited immediate retribution. Yet time after time, transgressions occurred out of fear, jealousy, desperation, greed.

In early 1970, Shorty Spero called Sammy in. Sammy had just turned twenty-five. "Are you ready to kill for the good of the family?" Spero asked. "I got a piece of work for you. It's on record. The boss has given permission."

4

In a hit, pulling the trigger is the easy part.

THE INTENDED TARGET WAS JOE COLUCCI.

"I was stunned. He was with Shorty, like I was. I knew him real well. He was a bruiser. He had this drop-dead gorgeous wife named Camille, jet-black hair, great legs. I'd heard some rumors that Tommy Spero was coming on to her behind Joe's back. I didn't pay much attention. It wasn't my business. But I already know that fooling around with another guy's wife is one of the worst rules you could break. So this isn't making sense to me.

"'Joe is looking to whack you,' Shorty said.

"'*Me?* Why me?' I said. It's making even less sense.

"Now I gradually get the story. But the truth is that it wouldn't have made any difference. If it's put to you that something has to be done for the good of the family, that it's been authorized, you got to do it without question, without hesitation, without personal consideration. It seemed like Joe Colucci had heard the rumors, too. And he's going to make a move. He's got a plan, real devious, I had to admire it, but he outsmarted himself. Joe figures that if he asks permission to kill Tommy Spero, he ain't going to get to first base. Tommy is Shorty's nephew. So from being in the right, he's in the wrong. And that's where I come into it.

"If Joe just whacks out Tommy, it really don't take a brain surgeon for Shorty to figure it out. Joe's plan is to whack Shorty *and* me. Me because I'm somebody he has to worry about coming back at him. With both of us gone, there'll be confusion. Nobody will know what the fuck is going on. Then he can rub elbows with Tommy—'Hey, we'll find out what happened. Gee, your uncle! What a shame!'—and later on, in a couple of months, he'll take him out. And nobody's the wiser.

"Joe's big mistake is that he confides in another guy with us named Frankie. Joe needs Frankie because he can't do this on his own. He and Frankie are pals and Colucci knows Frankie don't like Tommy. Frankie asked him, 'Why do you want to kill Sammy and Shorty? If you think Tommy's fucking your wife, why them?' That's when Joe Colucci tells him, 'If I whack Tommy, it's guaranteed Shorty'll put it together in two minutes flat and Sammy will take me out in a minute flat.'

"Frankie don't buy it. He's nervous about this whole scheme. So he goes to Shorty and says how he was approached by Colucci and everything. And Shorty sees Junior Persico and reports this, and I'm told the two of them went right to the boss, Joe Colombo, and got the permission to go after Colucci. That's when it becomes a hit for the family.

"At that point, I'm getting all of this from Shorty. I said, 'Yeah, OK,' but I don't know if I'm totally buying what I'm hearing. Am I being conned? I can't get it through my head that Joe would want to kill me. Shorty tells me that Tommy is going to be in on the hit and so is Frankie.

"Now I'm close to Frankie, too, and I went and questioned him. I want confirmation. I asked him, 'Frankie, are you sure Joe said this?' He says, 'Sammy, take it from me, it's for real. I'm sick. I'm in the middle of this thing. I'm sick Joe told me. But I'm not killing you and Shorty and then killing Tommy down the road. I ain't getting involved in this plot. Suppose you and Shorty had found out I knew what Joe was intending and I never told you. Wouldn't you whack me?'

"'Absolutely,' I said. 'You did the right thing. I heard it from Shorty, but I wanted to hear it from you.'

"So I went with it.

"Personally, I think that if Joe Colucci had gone straight to Shorty about his beef with Tommy, Shorty would have understood it. Shorty was a

tough guy and a man of honor. I think he would
have turned around to his brother, Ralph, and told
him, 'Listen, what your son is doing is against our
life. This Colucci kid is right. What would you do if
somebody was fucking your wife?' I think that's
how Shorty would have answered the problem. He
would have got Joe to back off. Joe would never
get permission to kill Tommy. Joe wasn't a major
player. He was in the crew, but he's not a made guy
and he's not with somebody else's family. On top of
it, there's complications because personal family
blood is involved. They would have probably
appeased Joe, whitewashed the whole thing.
Tommy would have been reprimanded for pulling
this shit, told to cut it out with Joe's wife and put it
on the shelf. But Joe Colucci didn't go that route.
He had devised this plan and didn't give a fuck
who he was hurting in the process."

"This was my first hit. I was in charge. My hit
team was Tommy and Frankie. I told Shorty I
didn't need any more help. I was used to being in
charge. I had always been the front guy in burglaries and armed robberies. I got the gun and
worked out how we were going to do this. I felt I
had it all covered. Looking back, I can see how
lucky I was, that I missed a lot of basics. I had
plenty to learn. In a hit, pulling the trigger is the
easy part. Because it takes no brains.

"It was about a week after I met with Shorty

when we made our move. Time was important. At any second, Joe could have told Frankie to get ready to help take out me and Shorty. And Frankie could have fallen apart and warned him off.

"I set it up that me, Frankie, Tommy, and Joe would spend the night bouncing around from one club to another. That was some irony there. Here was Joe Colucci joking and drinking it up with Tommy, who was coming on to his wife, the guy Joe wanted dead. Here was Frankie, who was in on both sides of the story. And here was me, on my first hit, the hunter *and* the hunted, all at once. Just another day in the life of organized crime.

"Finally, at this one club, after dancing and kidding around with some neighborhood girls, we left to go to a cafeteria to grab a bite before calling it a night. This was when it was supposed to happen. Tommy was driving. We were in a two-door car. The plan was that Frankie and me would get in the rear seat and Joe would be in front next to Tommy. The rest would be up to me. But when we get to the car, before we know it, Joe dove into the back. There was tension. Joe was on guard. There was nothing to do except go on to the cafeteria.

"After we ate, Joe went to the men's room. I told Tommy to get Joe in conversation to give me and Frankie time to get in the back of the car. We had to get this over with. By now Joe was tired, and when we got to the car he dropped his guard. He jokingly told me to get in the backseat, but not to

sit behind him. But he was a plotter. Did he suspect anything? I started feeling edgy. Then, after
he didn't say anything more, I relaxed. By now it
was four in the morning. He had said it just to say
something. I climbed in behind Tommy.

"It's amazing to me how the details of first
events get etched in your mind. I remember everything about that night as if it were last night. We
kidded and joked as we slowly drove down the
street. Tommy turned up the radio. A Beatles song
was on. The seating arrangement wasn't exactly
what I wanted. I reached under my jacket for my
gun, which was a .38. It seemed like the music was
getting louder and more intense.

"As that Beatles song played, I became a killer.
Joe Colucci was going to die. I was going to kill him
because I had been ordered to do it and because he
was plotting to kill me. I felt the rage inside me.
You fucking cocksucker, I thought. Even if I wasn't
directly behind him, I felt invisible. I pointed the
gun at the back of his head. Everything went into
slow motion. I could almost feel the bullet leaving
the gun and entering his skull. It was strange. I
didn't hear the first shot. I didn't seem to see any
blood. His head didn't seem to move, like it was a
blank instead of a real bullet. I knew I couldn't have
missed, the gun was only inches from his head, but
I felt like I was a million miles away, like this was all
a dream.

"I shot a second time in the same spot. This

time everything was different. I saw the flash. I smelled the gunpowder. The noise was deafening. Now I saw his head jerk back, his body convulse and slip sideways. I saw the blood. Joe Colucci was dead. He looked like he was sleeping. He looked peaceful. You going to blow me away now? I thought.

"Tommy and Frankie started yelling at one another. I can't remember what they were saying. That's the only thing I can't remember from that night. I told them to shut the fuck up. I told Tommy to get on the Belt Parkway and get off at the Rockaway Park exit. We had to dump the body.

"I can't describe the anger, the violence, the intensity that filled the car. But I can still feel it. After the exit, we drove for a few minutes into a quiet residential area. We were on a side street. I told Tommy to push the body out of the car. I couldn't believe it when Tommy told me he couldn't. He didn't feel so good, like he was going to vomit or something. He was afraid to touch Joe's body. So I climbed over Frankie and out the rear passenger side window. I opened the door and put my arms around the body. I'll never forget that feeling of deadweight. I wasn't too graceful about it, but the adrenaline was still pumping. I pulled Joe's body out and dumped it facedown in the street. I got in the car where he'd been sitting and shut the door. Then I rolled down the window and shot the body three times. It lurched with each shot. There could be no doubt. The contract was carried out.

"I told Tommy to get going. He was as nervous as hell and first thing, he goes through a red light. All we needed then was to get stopped by the cops. I yelled at him to calm down. As I tried to relax, one of my hands was resting on the seat. It felt wet. I realized it was in Joe's blood. Thinking back, we should have used a stolen car. When we went over a bridge, I threw the gun in the water.

"The car was a mess. Back in the neighborhood, we washed down the inside real good. We were all scared, not like afraid, but excited. I can't really describe it. But then I felt a surge of power. I realized that I had taken a human life, that I had the power over life and death. I was a predator. I was an animal. I was Cosa Nostra.

"I stayed at Tommy's house. I took a long hot shower. I slept like a rock. Tommy's mother made us a late breakfast. She always treated me like a son. She said we shouldn't be staying out all night like this. Tommy's eyes showed shame and fear. He pulled me aside and begged me not to tell his uncle how queasy he was about touching Joe's body. I told him to stop worrying, it wasn't important. That afternoon I was hanging out on a street corner, listening as everybody around was talking about Joe Colucci being hit and who would want to kill him?

"I felt like I was in space as I listened. Like I

wasn't there. I was thinking, Am I supposed to feel remorse? Aren't I supposed to feel something? But I felt nothing, at least nothing like remorse. If anything, I felt good. Like high. Like powerful, maybe even superhuman. It's not that I was happy or proud of myself. Not that. I'm still not happy about that feeling. It's just that killing came so easy to me.

"Then Tommy found me. Shorty wanted to see us. I tried to get in touch with Frankie, but I couldn't. Shorty said we had to go with him. Junior Persico was waiting for us. On the way, Shorty said that Tommy should do the talking, it was better that he should describe what I had done."

Carmine Persico, soon to be the new Colombo family boss, was ensconced in a midtown Manhattan hotel suite. A coterie that made up his inner circle was present: his future underboss, Gennaro (Gerry Lang) Langella; Sal Albanese, a powerful captain; his brother and future *consigliere*, Alley Boy; and the man perhaps closest of all to him, his constant companion, Hugh (Apples) McIntosh, who could never be a made member because his father wasn't Italian and whose speciality was to dispatch a victim with an ice pick in the ear.

"Junior looked right at me when I walked in," Sammy said. "I might have looked nervous, because he said first off not to be nervous. Everyone there had done what was done to Joe and there was a blood bond in that room. He asked for the details.

Shorty nodded at Tommy and Tommy talked for maybe five or ten minutes. The way Tommy told it, it'd been a piece of cake. He glanced at me, but I didn't say a word. After that, Junior took Shorty into another room. When they came out, they shook hands and we left. Going back to Brooklyn, Shorty said Junior said we did a good piece of work. He told me, 'Junior loves you. He's real proud of you.'

"We all went to Joe's funeral as grieving friends. Sometime later on, me, Frankie, and Tommy were in another car. The seating arrangements were the same as the night Joe got clipped. Except in front of me now, Frankie was in Joe's seat. Tommy was driving along the Belt Parkway headed towards Long Island. We were going out to do a score. All of a sudden, as we were passing the Rockaway Park exit, Frankie said to stop, he don't feel good. He got out of the car and started throwing up on the side of the highway. When he finished, I said, 'Bro, you all right? What's wrong?' He turned to me. He was as white as a sheet. He was practically crying. He said that ever since the hit on Joe, he was scared he would be next because Joe had come to him for help.

"I was in shock. I had just killed a friend of mine because I was ordered to do it by the mob. This was the life I had chosen. Now I was watching another friend of mine tell me that he was afraid that I would do the same thing to him. I tried to soothe him. I said, 'Frankie, are you crazy? You

saved my life. I would never hurt you, no way.'
It was no use. He said, 'Sammy, in my head, I
know that, but my stomach's churning all the time.
That's all I could think of with you sitting behind me.'

"We never made the score. That was the last
time I ever saw Frankie. He just took off, out west
somewheres, to the heartland of America. This life
wasn't for him. I think about him a lot. I wonder if
he ever thinks of me.

"After the Colucci hit, Tommy Spero wound up
marrying Camille. It didn't last long. She saw him
for what he was, a total nothing, and left him for
another guy. Tommy never got made. Later on,
both his father and his uncle got whacked and the
Colombo family chased him. He was whining at
some meeting and I heard Gerry Lang slapped him
in the face. That's the worst insult you could have.
He didn't have no standing after that. They told me
he ended up half a junkie."

"I never got questioned by the police about
the Colucci hit. But I would say that this was my
stepping-stone in the mob. I mean, after the hit, I
would go to a disco or a club, I'd be waiting on line
like I always did, and I'd see a bouncer come out
and whisper to the guy running the line. Before
you knew it, the owner was saying, 'Hey, Sammy,
forget the line. Come on in. Come on. Get them

people off that table. Sit Sammy there. Sammy, what'll you have? It's on the house.'

"The first couple of times I'm thinking, What the fuck is this all about? But my reputation is out there after the Colucci hit. Rumor had it that we—Shorty's crew—had done work and that Sammy the Bull was the workhorse in the crew. So I wasn't waiting on lines no more. I wasn't just another tough guy on the street. I was getting a different kind of respect and so on and so forth. The word was that I ranked high with Carmine Persico and they had the intention someday after the books were open that Sammy was going to get made."

The next time you call my house and talk to my wife in that tone, it'll be the last time you'll ever do anything.

BUSINESS CONTINUED TO BOOM AT THE AFTER-hours club Sammy had in partnership with John Rizzo and Matty Gambino on 62nd Street and 17th Avenue.

"People were coming in not just from Brooklyn, but from Jersey, Long Island. And now the cops loved me. They didn't care whether I was a crook, a criminal, whatever. They got four envelopes from me every week: one for the division, one for the precinct cops, another for the precinct detectives, one for the sergeants. To show you how I stood with them, Lenny the Mole got pinched one time. He got caught with a gun. I walked right into the precinct, go upstairs to the detectives, and who's there but the detective I've been giving envelopes to. I said, 'Bo, what's up?' Another detective was typing up an arrest card on Lenny, who's looking real sick. I said, 'What do you want to do here?'

They tell me for twenty-five hundred, they would reduce it to some sort of bullshit misdemeanor.

"'Get the fuck out of here,' I said. I pulled the card out of the typewriter and ripped it up. I turned to Lenny and told him, 'Beat it. I'll see you at the corner.' And Lenny walked right out. Nobody said a word. The detectives looked confused. Before they had a chance to react, I said to the two of them, 'OK, listen, no pinch, forget the misdemeanor. I'll give you the twenty-five hundred.' I told them I would see them at the luncheonette, the usual spot where we used to meet. They don't question if I'd show. My name was good. Then I said, 'And I want the gun back.' They said they couldn't. No way. Lenny's got to come back. 'Come on,' I said, 'he's gone already. What are you going to do with the gun?' So that was that. I met them later at the luncheonette. They got the twenty-five hundred and I got the gun. It was all bluffing. What counted, what was real, was the money.

"It was incredible how we blew that club. It was in a factory area, but there are also residences. A couple of detectives come to me and say, 'Sammy, there's complaints from the neighbors. Noise. Cars parked all over the place. But don't worry. What we got to do is come down with some radio cars and ticket the whole block. That'll take care of the complaints for a while. You just make sure everybody stays inside and there's no problem.'

"So I'm out front that night telling the bouncers not to let anybody leave when this real tough fucking kid, Butchy, comes up the stoop. He's got the mentality of a tabletop. He had just parked and sees all the cop cars and says, 'Let me go get my car, I'll get a ticket.' I said, 'Butchy, forget about it. I'll pay for the ticket. Just stay in the club.'

"He don't listen. He runs to his car, jumps in and starts the engine. A cops says, 'Shut it off. You can't move. Stay here.' Butchy don't do it. The cop reaches in for the key and Butchy yanks him through the window and starts giving him shots to the face. Now cops come flying from all over. They drag him out and they're batting him around. Me, I stick my two cents in because I've been paying them all off. I'm yelling, 'Stop!' One cop hits me with his stick and I hit him back. The whole club empties out. There's a riot in the street. I can't believe it. Sixteen guys got pinched. Two, three cops went to the hospital.

"After that, the detectives come back. 'Sammy,' they said, 'there's no money in the world that can straighten this out. We spoke to the captain. We did everything. You're closed down. You can't open anymore. Every single time you open, we'll pinch you, everybody.' So that was the end of it."

Not long afterward Sammy had a new club. Formerly a funeral parlor, it was in a different police precinct off Fort Hamilton Parkway. "It was started by a group of guys who weren't connected," Sammy said. "So I moved in on them. If it wasn't me, it would have been somebody else. They still had a piece. They were the front guys, but I was the boss, off the record. They were happy. They didn't have to worry about the cops or wiseguys. No worries about deliveries, garbage collection, some drunk starting trouble, all that stuff. It was doing good business right away from the following I had before."

Sammy's romance with Louise Grimaldi did not lead to the marriage he had contemplated. It wasn't Sammy's idea to part with her. The problem was her exceptional beauty. "Guys were hitting on her every three seconds. And she gets the idea that she wants to date. She wants an arrangement. She wants to stay with me, but she wants to date other guys, too. Experience life, she said.

"I told her, 'What am I supposed to do, share you? I walk into a joint one night, I bump into you with some fucking jerk-off who's with you? It won't work. Live your life. Find out what's out there. Let's break up and see what happens down the road.' Then two or three months passed by and now she wants to come back. I just couldn't do it. I wanted to. I really loved her. It was just pride, that macho bullshit, whatever it was, that wouldn't let me. But like I said, I remained friends with her. Then she met some guy who was looking to marry her, sending her roses and every other thing. She called me and said, 'I still want to be with you, but he's proposing.' She probably used that to pressure me a little bit. By then, I had met Debbie. I told Louise, 'I met somebody myself that I'm real interested in. I wish you and this guy good luck. Marry him. Do whatever you want.' We stayed good friends, but that's what she did. She wound up marrying him. And I married Debbie."

Debbie was a Bensonhurst girl, Debra Scibetta. At the time, in 1970, Sammy had just gotten involved with the new Fort Hamilton club.

"One night, I'm hanging out on the corner, Bay 23rd and Bath, by where I have my apartment, with Lenny, a guy named Louie, and this girl Diane Scibetta drives up. I've known Diane for a while. As a matter of fact, she was one of the girls we bumped into the night Joe Colucci got hit. She was with three other girls. She asked if we wanted to go to Coney Island, to Nathan's, to get something to eat. Sure, why not some hot dogs? Have some laughs.

"We get into the car. There's, like, seven of us. We're on each other's laps, talking, giggling. I'm in the back when I really looked at her. I don't know her from a hole in the wall. 'Hey, Diane,' I said, 'who's this one?' She was real cute, brunette, nice figure. Diane said, 'Oh, that's my sister. Deb, say hello to Sammy.'

"I said to her, 'Where you been hiding?' and

she smiles and said she was going out with this guy and they'd just broken up. At Nathan's, we gobble down hot dogs and then Diane said, 'Come on, let's go on some rides.' We end up on this ride that's called the Hammers. You get into these little things and they swing back and forth and around. I really don't have the stomach for these rides. I think I was with Diane. The girls are screaming and I'm turning green. Those hot dogs have got to me. I'm nauseous. I'm yelling at the guy to stop the ride or I'll fucking kill him. Instead, the more the girls scream, the faster he makes it go. By the time he does stop it, I couldn't've killed him if I wanted to. I was so sick, I couldn't even look at him. I didn't throw up, thank God. But I went straight to the car. I told Diane, 'Listen, get me back to Bay 23rd.'

"A couple of nights later, I see Diane and she said, 'Is it all right if I come by your club with my sister?' I said, 'Of course, come down.' She asked me what I thought of Debbie and I said she was good-looking and all, but the truth was I couldn't remember much except trying not to throw up after that ride. Well, Diane said, she's heard about you and she thinks you're cute and this and that.

"So when they come to the club on a Saturday night with some other girlfriends, I see that they're taken care of and not bothered. But I'm watching Debbie. She looks so out of her element in that place. I mean, I'm used to seeing a certain kind of woman in there and she is not that kind of woman. She seems so fresh, so innocent. More than anything, that's what caught my attention.

"After a while, I go and sit with them. I offered Debbie a drink and then I said, 'Let's take a walk.' It was a nice summer night. I needed a breather now and then from the club. It ain't a place where I'm having fun. I mean, when I'm there, I'm working my ass off. We walk and talk. She told me about her mother, what a great mother she was, and that her father worked nights for Western Electric putting together circuit boards for the phone company. She said he was a terrific father, but very strict, that the only reason she could be out so late was because she was with Diane. By the time we went back to the club, we were holding hands.

"She told me her parents were going to be away on Sunday and why didn't I come over and she'd cook dinner. I went over with a couple of guys. They were watching some game on TV—I'm not really interested in sports, except boxing, maybe handball—and I saw her in the kitchen. She had an apron on, she looked like a little housemother, cooking away, cooking and tasting the sauce and the sausage and the macaroni. She was so different from the sluts that I'm dealing with every other minute at the club. The only one who could hold a candle to her was Louise. Then and there I realized that she was for me. And I was right. We would be like wolves who mate, that stay with one another for good. If something should ever happen to one of them, they still don't ever mate again.

"The problem was her father. I guess he asked around and heard about me and he told her to forget it, I was an out-and-out hoodlum. Besides I was a lot older than she was, eight years older. But the main thing was I was a bad dude."

There was another factor that might have influenced Debra Scibetta's father, which Sammy was not aware of. Her family never spoke about it, and only years later did she herself mention it. There was an uncle lurking in the background who was a notorious captain in the New Jersey branch of the Bonanno family, named Joseph (Bayonne Joe) Zicarelli. Among his other activities, he controlled a vast illegal gambling empire operating out of Hudson County, New Jersey. Around the time Sammy met Debbie, he was sentenced to twelve to fifteen years for paying off politicians, allegedly including a U.S. congressman and even a cooperative local prosecutor, to protect his underworld interests.

"Debbie's sick about her father's attitude. She's carrying on about it at home. We keep seeing each other on the sly. Finally, her sister, Diane, who's in this, too, said, 'Would you come over and meet our mother?' That's what I did. Her father was at work already. I had a conversation with the mother. I told her I wanted to go out with Debbie. We were just going to the movies and then a pancake house. I promised to get her home by ten-thirty, the latest. We talked for about twenty minutes and she said, 'All right, I trust you.' Then, right in front of me, she told Debbie not to say anything to her father. They were hiding it from him.

"That annoyed me. I said why did we have to hide this? For what? What did I do? The hell with this. I don't need to come to the house. Her mother said, 'Sammy, I don't want you to feel like that. Let's see what we can do.'

"So I do meet the father. He turns out to be a beautiful guy, a mild-mannered guy, totally legitimate, one of the nicest guys I ever met in my life. His whole thing was looking after his baby daughter, which is completely understandable to me. I didn't have a problem with that. I told him, 'Listen, I'll respect your wishes. Any time you want to do anything or say anything, I'll respect it.'

"That's the way it went. But toward the end of the year, we decide we want to get married. Now there are protests from both her mother and father. She's too young, she's only seventeen. At first, they're totally against it. Then they try to postpone it. Finally, they say we should at least wait until she's eighteen, which will be in May. I said all right. They told us to go book a hall for the wedding. They didn't say so, but they were figuring that we wouldn't be able to book a place less than a year in advance, and given enough time, we would break up. But it didn't work. We got married on April 16, 1971, in St. Bernadette Church, just a couple of weeks before she was eighteen.

"What happened was I went to this guy Butch, who had a big catering hall in the neighborhood, the Colonial Mansion, between Bay 22nd and Bay 23rd. Butch was my pal because I had helped him after he was burglarized once or twice. Butch was booked a year in advance, like Debbie's mother and father assumed, but he offered to do something special. Put us in on a Friday. No deposits, no down payment, nothing. It was a done deal, just like that. Debbie was beaming when we went to her folks with the news. 'We're getting married April 16th,' she told them. 'April?' her mother said. 'What did you get, a cancellation?' Then she looked at the calendar. 'What are you talking about?' she said. 'April 16th is a Friday. A Friday wedding? What's that? Who ever heard of a Friday wedding?'

"But that's what we did.

"There were about three hundred people there, a lot from the neighborhood, all the guys I hung out with, plus some old-time wiseguys. Old man Rizzo, Shorty were there. People like Carmine Persico, people at that level, didn't come, but they sent envelopes. There were a ton of envelopes. Debbie and I went to the Poconos for our honeymoon. I was twenty-six."

"I was still scoring on stickups, but I was getting less and less. Old man Rizzo had his hand in the jewelry business and he would tip us now and then on a score and I would fence the stuff with him. Another thing was that Louie Milito introduced me and Alley Boy Cuomo to this tough Jew, Michael Hardy. Hardy was a renegade, a loner. I think Louie was using him to rob cars. Alley Boy was a neighborhood guy I knew who was with the Genovese family, like I was with the Colombos.

"Now this Hardy was into dealing drugs. The setup was that Hardy would be with a wholesaler making a buy, and Alley Boy and me would bust in with guns, flashing badges and yelling at everybody to hit the floor, yelling 'Police!' like we were plainclothes cops. We got the cash, whatever it was, and Hardy kept the goods. We'd cuff them. Since Hardy was on the inside, we'd do some acting. 'Hey, you fat fuck,' we'd say to Hardy, 'where's the dope, where's the money?' Boom! Maybe I'd kick him for effect. Maybe Alley Boy and me would go back and forth about whether to take everybody in.

"Once we had the money and the dope, we'd tell them it was their lucky day, we weren't taking them in, we were going to rob them. And we'd get the hell out, leaving them cuffed on the floor. As far as I know, they never knew what hit them.

"But later on, Alley Boy and I would have some big trouble on account of Michael Hardy, as big as it could get.

"Besides the club, I was looking for other things since I'm married. Now I know this guy Jimmy Brassiere. He used to bring in shipments of women's clothes from overseas and sell them to department stores. One time he got a huge load of brassieres. That's how he got his name. Then he got into women's pocketbooks, bags, even shoes. Some are slightly damaged, the department stores won't buy them, so me and Tommy Spero took them off his hands real cheap. We sold them out of the trunk of a car.

"At first, business was only so-so. Then Tommy and me came up with the idea that if we told people the merchandise was hot, it might sell better. And it did. After that, everything flew out of that trunk. People thought they were making a big score, getting stolen stuff. We got so many orders ahead that I decided to open a store just for this. As soon as Tommy's father, Ralph, heard about it, he wanted in, too.

"I found an empty store in a real shopping area on 86th Street. It was a tiny store. I named it The Hole in the Wall. As I was a crook, we called ourselves The Hole in the Wall gang. Jimmy Brassiere supplied us. I bought denims, all kind of jeans, all different sizes. Everything was slightly irregular. We had Polo shirts, T-shirts, women's bathing suits.

We continued with the pocketbooks and shoes. All kinds of things a woman would want.

"Business just took off. Now salesmen were coming in, like from Levi jeans. Let me show you this, that. There were other salesmen representing legitimate companies. A Polo shirt guy would be there with different styles and colors. 'Hey, OK,' I'd say, 'I'll try them. Give me three dozen.' On occasion, Debbie would come in and help. So would Tommy and his wife, Camille, Joe Colucci's widow. Tommy's father, Ralph, was there. We were so busy, I hired a girl for an eight-hour day, so we were always covered in case none of us could make it.

"I'm there, too, on and off. Then one time when I was there, a lady came in and said she wanted to return something, whatever it was. I said sure, did she have her receipt? She said no, she didn't get no receipt. I asked her who sold her the item and she said it was the older man. She was talking about Ralph. It happened again. I caught him half a dozen times. I become conscious of the stock, matching up what we have and the sales receipts. He was robbing us blind, the cocksucker.

"Now Ralph Spero ain't a made guy. He never got made. But it's an awkward situation. He's Shorty's brother and I'm with Shorty. I decide it was better to sell the joint, get the fuck out. Learn my lesson and tomorrow's another day. Basically, that was what I did with people, if they turned out to be pieces of shit. I tried to avoid confrontations. If you pushed me too far over the line, then I would react. But there's enough people to shoot in the head without looking for it all the time.

"I went to Jimmy Brassiere and said, 'Do me a favor and buy the store. Or get one of your friends or the people you do business with to buy it. It's a tremendous deal. Tons of customers are coming in.' He says, 'Sammy, you got a gold mine there. What the fuck do you want to sell it for?'

"'Listen to me,' I said, 'either buy it or get me a buyer.'

"He comes back to me. He's got a buyer. 'But why are you doing this, Sammy, why?'

"'Listen, between you and me, Ralph, Tommy's father, he's in there robbing. I'm going to wind up killing him, or something else bad will happen. I don't want to be partners anymore. I don't want no beefs.' So Jimmy sold it for me.

"When she found out, Debbie said, 'Are you crazy? The store's a gold mine and it'll only do better.' I didn't respond, so now she takes the position that what's really going on is that I don't want to stop being a thief, that I've given up on leading a regular life. She said, 'Don't you ever want to start a family and become legitimate?'

"So I told her about Ralph. I don't tell her about my official relationship with Shorty—I never talked about the life with her—but I said, 'I can't be there all the time. What am I going to do? He'll say he didn't do this, he didn't do that. I want out and that's it. I don't need this.'

"So I told Tommy and Ralph that it was over. There wasn't nothing they could do. They didn't know how to take it over. Jimmy Brassiere was close to me, not them. They didn't have the contacts I had. I said, 'I'm a crook. What am I doing, selling jeans? Let's get the fuck out of this.'"

Tension, however, continued between Sammy and Ralph Spero in the aftermath of The Hole in the Wall affair. He heard reports that Ralph was complaining to Shorty that Junior Persico was unfairly favoring Sammy over his son and that when the Colombo family books were eventually opened, Sammy might be made before Tommy was. As Tommy's uncle, Shorty had to do something about it.

Then a member of Shorty Spero's crew, Ralphie Ronga, was shot dead by police during an armed robbery. "Ralphie came out of the building they were robbing," Sammy said, "and walked straight into four cops with their guns drawn. They were waiting for him. 'Freeze!' they ordered. But Ralphie wasn't the kind of guy to give up, no matter what the situation, and he didn't freeze. All four cops started shooting and Ralphie shot back, but he didn't stand a chance. What balls that guy had! We all respected him very much."

About a week later, after Ronga's funeral,

Sammy was in a saloon with several friends, including John Rizzo, Louie Milito, and Alley Boy Cuomo. When he had gone in, he had noticed a blonde drinking with a man at the far end of the bar.

"One of the guys says, 'Sammy, I think that blonde over there is making eyes at you.' I look up and the guy she's with is going to the bathroom. So they egg me on to see what she wants. I head over and she gets up and starts walking towards me. When I'm seven, eight feet away, I finally recognized her. I'm in total shock. It's Ralphie's wife. She's got this little short dress on and she's dyed her hair platinum. She said, 'Sammy, you weren't paying me any attention. Are you mad at me?'

"I said, 'Mad at you? Your husband ain't even cold yet. What are you doing with this guy?'

"'I can get rid of him,' she said. 'I'd rather be with you.'

"I said, 'You fucking cunt. Get the fuck out of here.' By now, the guy has come back and I tell him, 'You, you get the fuck out of here, too.' The guys I'm with are hearing this and they're standing up. The guy says, 'Pal, I don't know what's going on. I just met her. I'm leaving.'

"'Take her with you,' I said.

"Ralph Spero and her husband had done some time together and now Ralph was saying that I tried to pick her up and bang her. I found this out when I got home. Debbie was petrified. She said that Ralph had called and said, 'Where is your fucking punk husband? We're gonna kill him. He's trying to fuck Ralphie Ronga's wife.'

"I said, 'He said that to you?' and Debbie said, 'Yes.'

"I got him right on the phone. I told him, 'Ralph, you looking to kill me? Do it! I tell you what, I'll see you in front of your house.'

"'No,' he said. 'Junior's going to send for you tomorrow.'

"I say, 'Fuck Junior. I'll meet you right the fuck now.'

"'I ain't meeting with you,' he said and hangs up.

"I hop right in my car and race over. My gun is under my belt and I'm going to kill the guy as soon as I see him. But his wife answers the door and tells me he is gone, he had taken off. Remember, I'm like a son to this lady. I got no beef with her, so I control myself in front of her. 'OK,' I said, 'just tell him I was by.'

"The next day Shorty sends for me. I'm to be at a place on Cropsey Avenue. Louie Milito calls. 'Don't go,' he warns, 'there's a mob of guys there.' But I got to go. I *want* to go. I don't give a fuck. Then old man Rizzo got in touch with me and said, 'Let me go with you. I can vouch for what happened.'

"So he comes with me and Shorty said to him, 'John, what are you doing here?' and Rizzo said, 'I'm a witness to all of this and I want to talk to you.'

"'OK, but I want to hear from Sammy first.'

He stares at me and said, 'You were looking to fuck Ralphie's wife?'

"I said, 'Shorty, there's no way in the world that I would do that.' I told him what really happened. Old man Rizzo jumped in and said, 'I was there. And five or six other guys. What Sammy said is word for word the way it was. Exactly.'

"Shorty lowered his head. '*I knew it!*' he said. 'My brother's a piece of shit, but I'm stuck with him. Ralph has been envious ever since Junior started favoring Sammy.' Shorty kind of groans. 'I got an impossible problem. Ralph is going to look to get Sammy killed, or Sammy'll end up killing him, and if he does, I'll have to kill Sammy. John, do you think you people in the Gambino family would be interested in taking Sammy in? That way, even though it's different families, we could still have a relationship without my brother and my nephew involved.'

"John said, 'I'll propose it to Toddo. I know he thinks the world of Sammy.' Toddo was Salvatore Aurello. He was John Rizzo's skipper.

"And Shorty goes up the line on his side. By now, Junior was away. He had got fifteen on a hijacking case. They tried him five times. The final time the key witness against him was Joe Valachi. But he's still in charge. Down on Carroll Street, his brother told Shorty that they were sick about me leaving. Right in front of Shorty, Allie Boy Persico said to me, 'Sammy, to resolve this, we'd have to kill Shorty's brother and nephew. We'd love to do that, but out of respect for Shorty, we really can't do it. We give you your official release from the Colombo family. We'll always be friends.'

"Toddo sent the word up to his boss, Carlo Gambino, and now I was on record as being with the Gambino family. In a way, I was sick about this, too. I liked Shorty. All this backbiting and double-crossing was what the real Cosa Nostra was. Except I wasn't smart enough to know it then. I guess Ralph and Tommy got it pretty good because they came around sucking up to me, apologizing for creating this story. I told Ralph, 'Don't apologize to me. The next time you call my house and talk to my wife in that tone, it'll be the last time you'll ever do anything.'

"The only good thing about what happened was that I was with Toddo Aurello. He was very respected, like that old man, Zuvito, who helped my father with those union goons when they tried to shake him down."

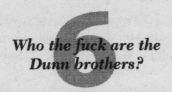

Who *the fuck are the Dunn brothers?*

SAMMY WOULD ALWAYS REMEMBER JUNIOR PERSICO as a brilliant mob figure. "He was smart and he was real smart streetwise, which don't always go together. It's true he got caught up with things from years and years ago—like the Valachi thing— but it was mostly the doings of other people and later on the tapes of other people that caused it. Sometimes, no matter how smart you are, you can't avoid getting tripped up."

But for Sammy, Toddo Aurello now became his mentor in Cosa Nostra. Aurello, then in his six-ties, dated back in the family history beyond Carlo Gambino—to Albert Anastasia.

As a Gambino family *capo,* Aurello had first presided over a social club on Bath Avenue in Benson-hurst before moving to another one on 86th Street. In both, anyone who lived in the neighborhood was welcome. Weather permitting, he would receive supplicants for his help or counsel in the yard behind the club, where he tended his garden.

The switch that had been arranged for Sammy from the Colombo family to the Gambino family—and Aurello's crew—was unusual. It gave him the sense of being valued. First thing, Toddo Aurello had taken Sammy aside and asked and received Sammy's word that he would leave Ralph Spero alone. "What's happening here is a big thing," Aurello said, pointing out that the next time, if there was any more trouble between them, it would involve two families, with all the ugly possibilities that this could trigger.

"I want you to stay close to me," Aurello told Sammy. "Come to the club every day. I want to really get to know you."

"So," Sammy said, "I used to go there in the back. I'd have on nice slacks, nice shoes, a nice little shirt, nothing fancy, but nice, and a little moderate jewelry. And there he'd be, his pant legs rolled up, wearing rubbers, watering his garden, with a cigar in his mouth. He had a whole garden. He loved that garden. This was the way it was in Italy, he said. He had tomatoes, he had fig trees. He had the whole nine yards. Everything. When he finished watering, he'd sit there and smoke his cigar and talk with people that came in to see him. He'd point to a chair and say, 'Sit there.

Make yourself comfortable,' and he'd listen to their problems, whatever they were.

"I really enjoyed being with him. What made me love him more than anything is that he just reminded me of my father. He had all them same ways. All them same mannerisms. He was small, like my father. The same build, same height. My father was one billion percent legitimate. Toddo was a mobster, but the most honorable guy you ever wanted to meet in your life. I like to think that the honesty that I got from Toddo *and* my father rubbed off on me.

"Once when I was a kid in my mom and dad's dress factory, I was doing the payroll. My father would give me the breakdown for the workers. They're piece workers, so they got from how much work they did. I'm breaking it down, so many twenties, so many tens, so many fives, and so much change, to whatever it said on the envelopes. I don't seal the envelopes until I'm finished. I do the whole payroll and I have about five hundred dollars left. I do it all over again. Same five hundred again. What could I have done wrong? Finally, I tell my father, 'Dad, there's five hundred dollars extra. The bank made a mistake. I think they overpaid you when you went for the money.'

"We do it a third time, together. Same result. I am psyched. To me, it's like a score. It's like money from heaven. But my father says, 'We can't keep it. It would not be right.'

"*Not right!* I'm thinking. Who gives a fuck? I said, 'Dad, it's a bank. They got billions of dollars. Who cares? They probably won't even pick it up.'

"'No,' he said. 'The girl who gives me the payroll money works for a living. She didn't do anything wrong. She just made a mistake, but she could be fired.'

"So he calls up the bank and the bank president is over to our house with the girl, and the president says, 'Oh, Mr. Gravano, you're a good man, an honest man. I appreciate this very much. We've been tearing our hair out all day trying to account for these funds.' The girl's got a grin from ear to ear. She hugs my father. 'Gerry,' she says, 'I would have lost my job if it wasn't for you.'

"I was sick! We didn't even get a reward. I think the bank guy said something about my father being rewarded in life. But that's how honest he was.

"Not that I took the legitimate road, but I was fairly honest in my dealings with people. When I gave my word, I kept it. Later on, I did have a reputation all through the mob as being honorable, as being trustworthy with money.

"Toddo was an honest man within the life. It may be hard to understand that. He was a gangster and a crook, but to us he had honor. You hear the expression about honor among thieves. Well, some thieves do have honor among other thieves. A good part of them don't, but some do.

"So I think I picked that up from Toddo, too. Sitting there in the garden listening to him, he'd be so wise. A lot of times, I thought he was like a witch. How the fuck did he know how this or that would turn out? But he did. It was amazing. Like, he'd always know when to pull out of a deal—right before the bust.

"So one day I finally asked him how he did it. He told me, 'You know what it is, Sammy? In my position, a hundred people a day come to me with different problems. You see that roof over there? Say, you ask me what would happen to you if you jumped off it. If I've never seen anybody jump off before, I don't know the answer for sure. But if I've watched a hundred people jump, maybe I've seen ninety-two of them break an ankle, crack a hip, sprain their knees. Eight of them are in real good shape. They don't get hurt. Now person one hundred and one comes to me and says, 'I'd like to jump off that roof.' 'Don't do it,' I tell them. 'You'll break your ankle. You'll hurt yourself.' I know now that ninety-two percent of the time, I'll be right. I'm not that smart. I know from my age and from the amount of people who ask me for advice what the outcome will be. I've done it over and over. Someday you could be in the same position. You'll see, this will come naturally to you. I think you have all the right qualities.'

"One time, I was sitting and watching Toddo

watering his plants when one of his people tells him there's a guy inside who wants to see him. I get up to go inside myself, when he says, 'No, no, Sammy. Stay. Sit down. I want you to sit and learn. Just keep your mouth shut and listen.'

"So this guy, a sharp guy, comes out and tells this whole story about another guy. He's got a beef against the other guy. I don't remember what it was. Toddo listens without saying anything. Then, when the guy is finished, he tells him, 'All right. You know what you do? Sit tight. I'll get back to you in a day or two.'

"After the guy leaves, Toddo starts puffing on his cigar. He leans back in his chair and looks at me and says, 'Assume you were me right now. What would you do?'

"I said, 'I'd get a couple of guys with some bats and send them over and break this other guy's legs. I'd break everything he's got.'

"'Good,' Toddo says. 'You got balls. And you're young and you're stupid.'

"I said, 'Why am I stupid?'

"'I'll show you why. Come back here tomorrow. I'm sending for the other guy.'

"The next day I'm back there. I can't wait to hear this. Toddo calls for the other guy to come out. He's real friendly to the guy. He tells him that so-and-so has seen him and told this story. 'Tell me your story. What do you have to say?'

"The guy gives a totally different story. And

Toddo says, 'All right. I'll get back to you. Don't worry about nothing. I'll straighten this out.'

"When the guy's gone, Toddo asks me, 'What would you do now?'

"I said, 'I don't know, Toddo. I'm confused. After that first guy's story, I would have opened up this guy's ass. But his story is completely different. Like night and day. I don't know.'

"'Good,' he says. 'You know those things attached to the sides of your head? Those ears? Use them. Remember that in life. Listen with both ears. You listen to one story. You listen to the other one. Someplace in the middle is the truth. It's up to your own brains and knowledge to determine what to do, if you know the background of the people who are involved. Don't ever react to anything in life—legitimate or illegitimate—by listening just to one side. You got plenty of time to react. Listen to both sides. Think about someplace in the middle and make up your mind. Then react. Then you do what you want.'

"I never forgot that. It was the best lesson I ever heard in my life. Because there were so many things later on I would hear that steamed me up. I'd just say, 'All right. I'll think about it.' And guys would ask me, 'Ain't you mad?'

"'Sure I'm mad. But let's see what happens after I know the whole story. Let's see if I'm still mad.'"

Toddo Aurello would speak to Sammy about

the wellsprings of Cosa Nostra. Since Sammy wasn't yet made, he spoke in generalities. But the existence of the mob was no secret in Bensonhurst. By then, Joseph Valachi, a soldier in the Genovese family, had broken the code of *omerta*, revealing for the first time not only the family structure of an American Mafia but its actual name and how it was organized across the country. While Valachi's front-page revelations gripped the public at large, Bensonhurst barely gave them a second's thought. So what else was new? Sammy was eighteen at the time. "What I heard on the street," he remembered, "was that it was mostly an embarrassment for the Genovese people."

Aurello told Sammy that it had all started in Sicily with peasants who had united to fight French occupation and oppression, and that in the United States it remained an independent, second government that cared for and protected its own, that America, in fact, was an enemy state. It had been, said Aurello, a society that prized honor.

There was nothing formal about these sessions. "We'd just be schmoozing," Sammy said. "Something would spark something and Toddo would drift off into the old days and get into Cosa Nostra, what it meant, how in the beginning these were people who loved and respected family, had a little integrity, had honor and who helped their fellow people in the community.

"And there were little hints from him that this was starting to deteriorate not only in Italy but here in this country, how made guys were more and more in bars with women, wearing these fancy clothes, showing off, doing this and that. He mentioned that maybe this had started with Al Capone becoming such a public figure with all the things he was doing and that wasn't what we were all about, how we were supposed to conduct ourselves.

"Once he told me that Carlo Gambino had spotted him in some restaurant with a girlfriend, whatever, and Carlo had called him over. In Italian, Carlo said, 'Where's your wife? What are you doing with this *putana* in a place like this where you're seen by people who know you and your wife? Don't you have any shame? Don't you have any pride? Don't you have any respect for your wife?'

"Toddo didn't take offense. He thought Carlo was right and he was wrong. If you couldn't be loyal to your wife and your children, how could you be loyal to Our Thing. He wasn't talking about somebody who just goes with a woman on the side. Every man, I think, does that at one point or another. But you don't flaunt it. Put some shade on it. Like your wife could walk into a beauty parlor and other women are going to be there laughing behind her back. You put her in this position. You're the one who belittled her.

You want to sneak away somewhere, sneak away. Toddo would reminisce about that time he bumped into Carlo and would see that it was part of his own deterioration.

"It was the same thing with Joe Colombo going public, going on talk shows, marching and rallying against the FBI. He thought it was a tremendous mistake. I mean, he didn't doubt Joe Colombo's motives were good. But if reporters want to write *Mafia*, so be it. Trying to stop them from using that word just makes them credible. We can't win that kind of controversy, so why bother?"

Around this time, in 1972, Sammy saw *The Godfather*.

It was a validation of everything he believed in.

"I left that movie stunned. I mean, I floated out of the theater. Maybe it was fiction, but for me, then, that was our life. It was incredible. I remember talking to a multitude of guys, made guys, everybody, who felt exactly the same way. And not only the mob end, not just the mobsters and the killing and all that bullshit, but that wedding in the beginning, the music and the dancing, it was us, the Italian people!

"The mob end was so on the money, it was crazy. It was basically the way I saw the life. Where there was some honor. Like when Don Corleone, Marlon Brando, says about the drugs,

sure, he owned these people, but he would lose
them with that. It wasn't like gambling and certain vices we do, loan-sharking. His thinking and
what he said was how the life was supposed to be.
Even when Michael says about killing the police
captain, that he wasn't just a captain, he had
crossed the line into our world. That is true. In
Cosa Nostra, it's an unwritten rule. You don't kill
newspeople and you don't kill cops. But we
wouldn't think twice about killing a cop or a news
guy if they had come in with us. It happened in
Philadelphia, when the boss down there, Nicky
Scarfo, had a judge killed. That judge took money
for a situation and then double-crossed Nicky and
Nicky blasted him. Nicky was right. Fuck that
judge!"

As with Shorty Spero, a portion of every score
Sammy made was shared with Toddo Aurello.

Financially, life was a roller coaster for him.
One week he'd be flush with cash. Two weeks
later, he would be dead broke. Neither he nor any
of the mob associates of his age saved any money.
Their safety net was another score. Cash left his
pocket at a dazzling rate buying clothes, out on
the town night after night, grandly picking up
restaurant and club tabs, handing out huge tips,
champagne and filet mignon at the Copacabana
nightclub, a favorite watering hole in Manhattan

for wiseguys. "It was let's go to the Copa," Sammy said. "Fucking kids, all dressed up like jerk-offs, running around, doing a little gambling, doing a little of this and that and I'm broke again and it's macaroni and ricotta at home or spaghetti, *pasta e olio*, with the oil and the garlic."

But then Sammy confronted a new reality. He was now the father of a baby girl, Karen, and Debbie would soon be pregnant with a son, Gerard. His epiphany came when he and Debbie actually had to open up baby Karen's piggy bank to buy enough food for dinner. He decided to dramatically change his ways. He relived memories of childhood summers spent at the cottage his parents had bought near Lake Ronkonkoma on Long Island, which had become their permanent home. "I remembered that it was just great times there. I had a dog. One year my dad and mom got me a goat, a baby goat named Rosie. I made a lot of friends with the kids out there, and some kids from the neighborhood, from Bensonhurst, would come out to stay with us. We had company and stuff all the time."

He would move in with his parents, who were delighted, and transform the attic into living quarters for him, Debbie, and Karen. One of his sisters, Fran, had married a man named Eddie Garafola, who was a partner in a small Long Island construction business, specializing in plumbing, and Sammy arranged to work for him.

"This was in '74. I'm with Toddo, but I told

him I was tired. I was packing it in. I said I was going to try to make a new life with my wife out in Long Island. I was going legitimate. But I told him that I was still with him. If he needed me for anything, all he had to do was call.

"Toddo wished me luck. 'Go ahead,' he said. 'See if you can do it. If I need you, I'll call. If you need me, I'm always here. You're with me.'

"So I finish up the attic into an apartment and I'm working for my brother-in-law, Eddie. I'm making peanuts. I don't think I'm making a hundred a week. I'm killing myself, working my ass off, and I ask him and his partner, Dominick, for a raise. They have a meeting. They needed this big meeting to give me a raise? Finally, Eddie comes to me and says he's talked it over with Dom. The best they can do right then is to give me ten cents an hour more. Ten cents an hour? I go home and I'm devastated. I'm sick. I can't believe it.

"Without me knowing it, Debbie calls up her uncle Danny, an Irish guy. He's married to one of her aunts. Her aunt's Italian, but he's Irish. He's out in Long Island, but closer to New York, like around Amityville.

"My wife says, 'My uncle Danny wants to talk to you. Ring him up.' I called him and he says, 'I spoke to Deb. I hope you're not mad. I heard you were working and how much you're making and the kind of raise you were offered. There's somebody I can talk to.'

"I told him that I would appreciate anything he could do. But I said whatever happened, I'd be OK. I didn't want to reveal nothing. I mean, I got a little mad at Debbie. 'Don't ever tell anybody our business unless I know about it,' I said.

"The next day her uncle called me back. He's set up an appointment for me with this guy Mike Perry, an Irish guy who's in housing construction. He calls me in and says, 'Could you work one day before I make up my mind what I'm going to pay you?' 'Sure,' I said. Their work was carpentry. Other people did the plumbing, the electrical work and so on. What they did was the framing and putting in the plywood, the sheeting. The plywood would go up on the roof and I spent the whole day nailing it down. I went home with blisters all over my hands because I wasn't used to this. Mike Perry called me up that night and said he would start me at a hundred and seventy-five a week, and as I learned, he'd give me raises.

"*Mamma mia!* I can't fucking believe it. My brother-in-law and his brother-in-law, this Dom, are giving me a hundred a week and offering me a ten-cents-an-hour raise. I think it was a Saturday that I did the one day's work for Mike Perry. Sunday I see my brother-in-law and I said, 'You and Dominick can take that ten cents an hour and stick it up your ass and the job, too.'

"'Oh, why are you being like this?' Eddie says. 'We'll do something down the road.'

"'Down the road, my fucking ass. We're finished,' I said. 'You do your thing and I'll do mine. Good luck with your business. I'm not mad, really, maybe a little insulted with the ten cents, but adios.'

"The problem I have is that Mike Perry's people move from one place to another. After a couple of weeks, a month, whatever, you're in another spot, and I don't have no car. He says to me, 'I have an extra car.'

"And I'm breaking my ass. Like if I worked nine or ten hours, I don't think about asking for overtime. By the same token, when I work only six hours, if it's a short day, he still gives me a full day's pay. So there's a relationship there. Debbie's uncle Danny has got a union job in the city, but on weekends, if he wants to pick up some side money, he works for Mike. So I see him a lot. He's a great guy. After about eight months, Mike raised me to two fifty a week, a seventy-five-dollar raise. I'm looking ahead to a real good future, maybe going into construction on my own."

After about ten months working for Mike Perry, Sammy received a phone call that would forever alter his life.

The call was from Alley Boy Cuomo.

"*Compare,*" Cuomo said, "I got bad news."

"What?"

"The cops are looking for me and you." Cuomo said that he did not yet know all the details. "It came out of the precinct in Coney Island. They're looking for us for a couple of murders."

"What murders? What are you talking about?"

"I tell you, I don't know. But you gotta come in. We got to get together."

"When I hang up, I told my wife, 'I got to go into Brooklyn. There's a little bit of a problem.'"

Indictments had been handed down and arrest warrants issued. Sammy and Alley Boy were wanted for the double homicide of two Coney Island brothers named Dunn.

"Who the fuck are the Dunn brothers?" Sammy asked.

Cuomo replied that he didn't have the slightest idea.

The twists and turns of the case as it began to unfold were Byzantine. Their accuser turned out to be the Jewish hoodlum Michael Hardy, with whom Sammy and Alley Boy had once posed as plainclothes cops to shake down drug dealers targeted by him. Louie Milito had provided the introductions. Apparently, Hardy had continued to work for Milito's car-theft ring. He then had a falling-out with a member of the ring named Larry Martieri. Hardy claimed that Martieri owed him $5,000. When Martieri refused to pay, Hardy kidnapped one of Martieri's associates. When Martieri still would not come up with the money,

Hardy first clubbed the associate nearly senseless, shot him, then shoved a gun barrel up his rectum, ripping it open, and finally tied him to a shower-head and left him writhing under a stream of scalding water.

Somehow, the associate survived. Martieri enticed Hardy to a meeting where he was arrested by the police on kidnapping and assault charges. In an effort to make a deal, Hardy offered the Brooklyn D.A., Eugene Gold, an irresistible catch. It was as if part of Sammy's past had returned to haunt him. The prize Hardy promised to deliver was a notorious Colombo family *capo,* Dominick (Mimi) Scialo. "I couldn't believe it," Sammy said. "This is the same fucking Mimi who killed my pal Jimmy Emma, back when I was with the Rampers."

The 1969 murders of the two Dunn brothers, Arthur and Joseph, owners of a local automobile body shop, had remained unsolved. Hardy's story was that he had been present at a Coney Island pizzeria with Scialo and Martieri. According to Hardy, Scialo was complaining to Martieri that one of the Dunns had defaulted on a loan. He quoted Scialo as saying, "I want him hit straight out." He swore that Martieri volunteered that Louie Milito had these two boys "Alley and Sammy, they're pretty good," and Scialo said, "All right."

Sammy would only learn all of this in bits and pieces. As soon as he discovered that there were warrants out for their arrest, he and Cuomo fled to Florida.

"Me and Alley Boy took off in his car. We need time to find out what's going on here. Now we're in touch with Louie Milito and he fills us in a little. For some reason, Louie's name is never mentioned yet. He don't even think he's part of this pinch. Down in Florida, I keep asking Alley Boy if he knows anything about these Dunn brothers and he swears to God he don't. So that's why we came back, we turn ourselves in. We didn't kill nobody, so what the fuck. What are we on the lam for?"

Still, it was a dangerous situation. "A frame can be a lot worse than something you actually done," Sammy said, "because you don't know what they're gonna throw against you." Sammy was held in the Brooklyn House of Detention on Atlantic Avenue. Bail for him, Cuomo and Martieri was set at $100,000. By now, Hardy had included Milito in the conspiracy mix. His bail was $75,000. Mimi was also indicted. But he was nowhere to be found. The presumption was that he was evading arrest. "What we heard and believed strongly was that Mimi and his guys took out the Dunn brothers, really took them out, so when this Hardy makes up his bullshit story, he knows some of that but changes the players to get back at Larry Martieri. He hates Larry, which is the cause of all this."

Sammy was then twenty-nine, married, and a new father. He was also facing life in a state penitentiary. Even granting the possibility of parole, it meant minimally twenty years behind bars. "This D.A., this bum Eugene Gold, who would get caught molesting some kid, don't give a fuck about anybody except Mimi. He sees big headlines with Mimi. And this assistant D.A. comes to me and he says if I flip, if I testify against Mimi, I get a total walk. I'm out of the whole thing. Now I don't exactly love Mimi. I mean, I'll never forget it, he killed Jimmy Emma. But I told that assistant to fuck off. I didn't do nothing and I ain't testifying to nothing.

"What me, Alley Boy, and Louie have to think about is Mimi. He was such a bad guy. We know that whenever he gets arrested, he'll kill everybody in the indictment so he can fight it alone and shift the whole case around. We're a little worried, being as we're in the same indictment with him. So we made a pact in the can that soon as we get out, we'll kill Mimi ourselves. We ain't waiting for him to do something. We'll whack him. It wasn't until after we got out of Atlantic Avenue that we find out Mimi ain't with us no longer on this planet. He ain't on the lam, he's dead. We heard that the Colombo family did it because he was deep into drugs."

Sammy finally made bail, putting ten percent down. Toddo Aurello supplied the money. "It was practically a regular loan," he said. "Toddo only charged me one point."

Michael Hardy continued to embroider his story. "He's got Louie Milito at a meeting with Mimi and Larry Martieri negotiating for twenty-five hundred each for me and Alley Boy for the hit. He's got us all at another meeting, with Mimi ranting that we were only supposed to whack out one Dunn brother, I forget which one, not both, and he's got me saying what the fuck did he want us to do? The other brother had walked in right in the middle of everything."

Once back on the street, Sammy returned to Long Island. "I told my mother and father I had to go back to Brooklyn. I told this Mike Perry there's no way I could work for two fifty with the expenses I got now. I gave him a kiss on the cheek. I said, 'I appreciate what you did, but I'm out of here.' I told that to Debbie's uncle Danny, too. I don't have a pot to piss in. Nothing. My mother-in-law and my father-in-law take me, my wife, my daughter in. We lived with them in their five-room apartment. My sister-in-law was still there. We were in one little bedroom. We slept on mattresses on the floor.

"To pay the lawyer, to pay back Toddo—that ten thousand sounds like nothing now, but it was a lot then—I'm out every single night, seven days a week, robbing and stealing with Alley Boy. I'm trapped. Every time I see my lawyer, I say, 'Here's a thousand, here's five hundred, here's fifteen hundred.' And the word is out on the street that Sammy the Bull's a good kid, a strong kid.

"Me and Alley went on a robbing rampage for a year and a half that was unbelievable. We robbed everything that wasn't nailed down. We went trunking—which is when you open up a car trunk and take everything in there. We had connections to get rid of golf clubs, even bowling balls, tires, rims, you name it. We didn't leave nothing."

Three times while Sammy was out on bail, he was arrested for criminal possession of a weapon, for possession of burglary tools, possession of stolen property and attempted petty larceny. In two of these cases, he copped misdemeanor pleas. The third was successfully appealed. The criminal justice system was in such disarray that none of these arrests and court appearances affected his bail status on the murder charges. Indeed, only one of them—an arrest in Manhattan—even wound up being listed on his rap sheet.

Sammy's legal fees ate up all of his nightly robbery profits. "I have lawyers going on three different cases at once. And in the murder case, I'm having to pay for an investigator, too. My lawyer fees were killing me. Plus, I was trying to take care of my family. We were still living with my in-laws at the time. Debbie and my little girl and I, the dogs, the cats—Debbie always had animals around—were crammed together in my sister-in-law's room. She was sleeping on the couch in the living room. On top of everything, I didn't even have a car."

He had to find a way to obtain some kind of steady income. "Old man Rizzo told me that a friend of his had this luncheonette and was selling it. Me and Alley Boy went in it together. Toddo loaned us the money, again for just a point. Next door there was a tailor shop that was going out of business and we took the lease. We made it into a convenience store where you could get some groceries, cigarettes, some ice cream, eggs, butter, milk and cheese, all that stuff you would use every day, ketchup, mayonnaise, mustard. I got some carpenters, did some wood paneling, a dropped ceiling. There was already air-conditioning. I wheeled and dealed with various companies. The milk company I made a deal with put in a refrigerator. The ice cream outfit gave the freezer. I made a deal with Wise Potato Chips. They provided racks and displays. We started doing good business."

The defense attorneys, meanwhile, managed to get separate trials for the four available defendants. "By then," Sammy said, "even the great Eugene Gold, that fucking pedophile, whatever, knew that Mimi, who was going to get him all that publicity, was long gone.

"But I was starting to wonder if maybe I had

killed the Dunn brothers. Hardy's story was so detailed. The meetings, times, the dates. It sounded real. Innocent or not, I figured I was in deep-shit trouble. But then one day, during some preliminary hearing, Hardy was talking about how we all left some meeting and got in my white '72 Lincoln, and my father-in-law says, 'Sammy, you didn't even have a car then.' Sure enough, I had bought it used a couple of years after all this was supposed to have happened and I could prove it. I started feeling a little more optimistic at that point."

The first to be tried was Martieri. He was acquitted after the defense pointed out one inconsistency after another in Hardy's story. The following week the Brooklyn D.A.'s office moved to dismiss the charges against Sammy, Alley Boy Cuomo, and Louie Milito.

If Sammy's childhood dyslexia was instrumental in turning him toward a career in crime, the indictment for murdering the Dunn brothers sealed it permanently.

"That pinch changed my whole life," Sammy said. "I never, ever stopped a second from there on in. I was like a madman. Never stopped stealing. Never stopped robbing. I was obsessed. I had been looking to pull away, going out to Long Island with my wife, raising a family, going to work and maybe going into my own business as soon as I got on my feet a little bit. Maybe it wasn't meant to be. But that Dunn brothers thing glued me to the mob, that's for shit sure. And then Toddo Aurello proposed me to be made in the Gambino family. So that was it."

Sammy's a friend of ours.

7

IN OCTOBER 1976, CARLO GAMBINO, WHO HAD been in ill health for some time, finally succumbed to a heart attack at age seventy-four. Given his slight frame, droopy eyes, banana nose, and upturned fedora brim, he had seemed an unlikely organized-crime don. But his nineteen-year reign as a family boss was exceptional in its longevity. And even though another famous mob boss, Joseph Bonanno, had once characterized him as "a squirrel of a man, servile and cringing," he had the last laugh. Under his aegis, the Gambino family became the most powerful in Cosa Nostra.

After succeeding Albert Anastasia, he quickly neutralized possible internal family unrest by appointing as his underboss one of Anastasia's most loyal followers, a crusty, pug-faced gangster

of the old school named Aniello (Neil) Dellacroce.
He also kept Anastasia's brother, Tough Tony
Anastasio (the original spelling of the name), in
charge of Local 1814 of the longshoremen's
union, which enabled the family to control the
Brooklyn docks. And when Anastasio died of nat-
ural causes, he appointed Anastasio's son-in-law,
Anthony Scotto, a *capo* and passed on to him
leadership of the local.

Carlo Gambino desired to take the family in
new directions. While the Valachi revelations may
have left Bensonhurst unmoved, they gave new
impetus to the federal government's prosecution
of the mob under Attorney General Robert F.
Kennedy and also led to a powerful new legal tool
passed by Congress in 1970 called the Racketeer
Influenced and Corrupt Organizations Act (RICO).
Although the mob members would never abandon
such standbys as loan-sharking, illegal gambling,
hijackings, and narcotics trafficking, Gambino
favored a more sophisticated effort to dominate
the construction industry, trucking, food distribution, garbage disposal, even to infiltrate Wall
Street, all immensely lucrative and all far less
likely at the time to attract the headlines usually
associated with more obvious mob activities.

Gambino was especially adamant about narcotics trafficking and the unwelcome public attention it provoked. All he had to do was to look at
Vito Genovese, who died in prison while serving a

lengthy narcotics conviction. Even though it was generally believed in Cosa Nostra that Genovese had been framed, the message from Gambino was crystal clear. Death was the penalty for anyone in the family dealing in drugs.

Gambino's reliance on personal family relationships, replete with marriages of in-laws as well as cousins, reflected his inbred, secretive ways, his profound wariness. The Gambino and Lucchese families had traditionally shared power in New York's garment industry. In former times, they had extorted protection money from manufacturers to safeguard against the extreme likelihood of hijackings. That had changed. Now control was exerted with a stranglehold on the industry's trucking. Nothing moved except in trucks owned by the two families through front companies. Garment manufacturers, comforted by this new stability, to say nothing of the guaranteed soundness of their kneecaps, immediately acquiesced and passed on the cost to the unsuspecting American consumer.

Don Carlo saw to it that a son, Tommy, received a proper Christian Brothers education at Manhattan College. He was then assigned to oversee the family's garment industry interests.

As he neared the end of his life, married to his first cousin who was also the sister of a *capo* named Paul Castellano, Gambino chose Castellano to be the new family boss, bypassing his expected successor and underboss, Neil Dellacroce.

Sammy, of course, attended Carlo Gambino's funeral. He had only met him once. "I was with Toddo somewhere and he introduced us. Toddo and his crew was backing Paul Castellano. Carlo was still the boss, and he was going with the boss's wishes. Toddo said something like 'This is Carlo Gambino. This is Sammy.' It was hello and hello. I don't think he really knew who I was. He may have heard the name. I don't know how sharp he was. But he gave me the courtesy of saying hello and that was it.

"What I heard was that he was pretty sick for a while and everything wasn't right with him, that he was losing it. There were problems. Like you owed him thirty thousand and brought it to him, and three days later, if you saw him again, he'd be saying, 'Where's the thirty thousand?' That's not him. He wasn't no shakedown guy. He was just getting old and senile and fucked-up and sick. He must have known it. That's why he made Paul the acting boss maybe a year before he went. Neil was in jail on an income tax rap. Then when Carlo died, he wanted Paul to be the boss and Neil was still in jail."

It was not a sure bet that Castellano would be ultimately accepted. Within the family, there was a Castellano faction and a Dellacroce faction, and no final decision was made until Dellacroce was paroled from prison about a month after Carlo was buried. On November 24, 1976, a meeting of the family captains, with both Castellano and Dellacroce present, was held at the home of a *capo* named Anthony (Nino) Gaggi, who was supporting Castellano. The Castellano faction was taking no chances. Dellacroce was known to be as tough as they come.

According to FBI sources, Gaggi had stationed his nephew Dominick, an ex–Green Beret sharpshooter, at an attic window where he could survey the front of the house. The nephew's instructions were that if he heard shots, he was to gun down anyone who ran out of the house. But there was no confrontation.

Toddo Aurello would tell Sammy that Dellacroce was a real hoodlum. He could have told Castellano that he didn't give a fuck what Carlo made him. *He* was still the underboss. He would put it to a vote. "But Neil didn't even do that. He said, 'I know this is what Carlo wanted. I'm just out of jail. I've been away for a while and I don't know basically what's going on. I'm happy with my position. If you don't want me to be your underboss, fine.' And Paul said, 'No, I want you to continue with me.' That was the deal. No arguments. No nothing.

"The ones who would be sick about this were John Gotti and his pal Angelo Ruggiero. John was close to Neil and if Neil was the boss, the power would be over there. I think it was very obvious from day one that Paul didn't have any love for John. And especially Angie, who always had a reputation for drug-dealing."

In 1975, the year before Carlo Gambino's death, the membership books of the families, closed since 1957, were finally reopened. To be eligible, your father had to be Italian. "I guess the public could say mob guys were racist because they just strictly deal with Italians," Sammy said. "But I think they're the most unracist people in the world. They're just greedy. The only color they care about is green, the color of money. They do their thing. They don't give a shit about any nationality, any religion, any anything. Nothing. They're not really racist or prejudiced against anybody. It came from Italy, Sicily, staying tight with your own. Years and years ago, you had to be Italian on both sides. Then it became that you only had to be that on your father's side. Not your mother's. Because they say you are what your father is, you carry his name. Like John Gotti's wife is part Russian Jew. So his son, John Junior, got made, right? He's part Italian and part Russian Jew."

There was a long waiting list of associates, and each family was initially allotted ten new members. The names were then submitted to the other families for comment. The following year the families were permitted to replace made members who had been lost through attrition. For the next group, later the same year, Toddo Aurello proposed Sammy. Aurello had been particularly impressed by the way Sammy conducted himself while under indictment for the murders of the Dunn brothers.

Aurello had overheard a Gambino family member belittling Sammy for the robbery spree he'd been on to make ends meet during that period, saying that it was demeaning for a family associate to be acting like a crazy street kid. Aurello sharply rebuked him. "What are you talking about?" Aurello said. "Sammy acted like a man. He stood up to his responsibilities. He did what he had to do. I don't want no more of this."

The first Sammy heard about being proposed came from Sal Albanese in the Colombo family. "Sally told me, 'Sammy, I hear good things about you. I saw your name on the list. Don't say I told you, but Toddo proposed you to become made.' Then, when Toddo speaks to me, I find out that he wasn't intending to propose his son, Charlie. I said, 'Toddo, guys are making their sons.' I wasn't thinking about all the trouble I had before with Ralph Spero, whether I was going to be made before his son. It wasn't anything like that. I told Toddo, 'I know Charlie all my life. He's a good kid. If you don't do it, you'll embarrass him. He hangs around, he's in the clubs.' Sally Albanese talked to Toddo as well and we convinced him. Charlie's gonna be made.

"So the time comes when Toddo tells me to be at his club the next day. 'Dress up,' he said. And me and Charlie show up in suits.

"Toddo took us to this house in Bensonhurst, Frankie the Wop's house, I can't remember the street, it was the only time I was there. We go into the living room on the first floor. A bunch of other guys are there. They're calling one guy at a time to go to the basement. I'm as high as a kite. I mean, this is the biggest day of my life, especially at that point. Finally, I'm told, 'Sammy, we want you to come down.'

"I'm nervous as hell, but happy nervous. I walk down the stairs—and again, I'll never forget any of this as long as I live—the stairs are squeaking. They're wooden stairs. It's like I'm in slow motion. I hear every one of those squeaks. I walk down nice and easy and when I get to the bottom, I turn and I see into the room. It was very dim. Really smoke-filled. There's a big long table. At the head of the table is Paul Castellano and sitting next to him is Neil Dellacroce. And next to him is the *consigliere,* Joe Gallo—not those Gallos—Joe N. Gallo. Toddo was sitting there. People who I know are captains, like Jimmy Brown, are all there. The guys that were called down before me are sitting at the table, too.

"There's an empty chair next to Paul. I'm told,

'Just go to that chair by Paul.' Paul said, 'Sit down, Sammy. Sit down here.'

"Paul stares at me and said, 'Do you know why you're here?' This is the only thing that Toddo has told me, what my answer should be. 'No,' I said.

"Then Paul asked, 'Do you know everybody here?'

"'Yes, most of them.'

"'Do you like the people here?'

"'Yes.'

"'Do you know that this is a brotherhood, this is a secret society?'

"'Yes,' I say.

"Paul said, 'In this secret society, there's one way in and there's only one way out. You come in on your feet and you go out in a coffin. There is no return from this.'

"'I understand.'

"He said to me, 'Would you drop all loyalties to everything and keep this brotherhood number one, the first thing in your life?'

"'Yes.'

"'Would you kill for us?'

"'Yes.'

"Paul said, 'Which finger would you pull the trigger with?'

"I pointed to my index finger. Toddo got up and came over. He motioned me to stand up. Paul stood up. Neil stood up. So did Joe Gallo. Everybody else stayed sitting.

"Toddo pricked my finger with a pin until the blood was coming out. He was my sponsor. He put my blood on a picture of a saint and put the picture in my hands.

"Paul said, 'We are going to burn this saint.' He lit it with a match and it caught on fire. I ended up with blisters all over my hands. I was supposed to jiggle the picture like the other guys did, but I was just standing there in such amazement, I got so involved in the whole thing, I was concentrating so hard on the oath, that I didn't feel any pain when I forgot to do it.

"As the picture is on fire, Paul told me that if I divulged the secrets of our life in any way, shape or form, my soul should burn in hell like the saint burning my hands. I had to repeat this to him.

"Paul said one or two things in Italian—still, today, I don't know what he said. Then he told me to crush the burnt picture. I crushed it in my hands and the ashes fell into an ashtray. Neil or somebody told me, 'Kiss Paul on both sides of his face.' Afterward, I went around the table kissing everybody and came back to Paul. He told me to sit down again.

"Everybody else at the table stood up and held hands. They called it a 'tie-in.' I was the only one not holding hands. In Italian, Paul said, 'In honor of our brotherhood, I untie the knot,' and everybody let go. I wasn't sure what was going on. But then I was told to stand and join hands in the circle and Paul said again in Italian, 'In honor of our brotherhood, I tie the knot.' So now I'm tied in with them.

"At this point, Paul turned to me and said, 'You are a member with us. You're now a friend of ours.'

"He said that a lot of rules and regulations would be explained later. I found another place at that table. Then they called another guy down. That's when I noticed all the white blisters on my hands.

"When they were finished giving everybody the oath, Paul explained that this was a family. We were the Gambino family. Introductions were made. Paul was the *representante,* the boss, of the family. Neil was the underboss, Joe Gallo was the *consigliere.* They introduced the men who were captains. We were told how to introduce one another. If I introduced somebody as a friend of mine, that's all he was. But if I'm with a made member and we meet another made member, I would be introduced as a friend of ours. You needed that third party to do this, so there wasn't any way to break into that circle.

"Paul explained that there were five families in New York. He named them and who the bosses were. He said that there was a smaller family, the DeCalvacante family, in New Jersey. He said there was another family in Philadelphia and many more outside New York, which he wasn't going to get into right then.

"He said that there was a commission, which was the ruling body settling disputes amongst the families and deciding policy, and that on each commission seat there was a boss.

"He told us that the man we answered to was our captain. He was our direct father. You do everything with him. You check with him, you put everything on record with him. You can't kill unless you get permission. You can't do anything, basically, until you get permission from the family. You don't run to the boss. You go to your captain. That was the protocol. Your captain will go to the administration of the family, which is the boss, the underboss, and the *consigliere*.

"Paul said, 'You are born as of today. Any grievances you have, anybody you have disliked from before, don't bring it up. As of today, it's over with.'

"He also said that there is no God. We don't have allegiance to any country. Our immediate family, like our wives and children, is secondary. Our Thing—'this thing of ours,' he said—is first, the only thing in your life above everything. You want to believe in God? You want to believe in your country? You want to believe in your own family? That all comes way after this.'

"He said, 'Anytime you are sent for by the boss of your family, you must come in. If your child is dying and has only twenty minutes to live, and your boss sends for you, you must leave that kid and come. If you refuse, you will be killed. When the boss sends for you, it precedes everything else. This is the one time you don't check with your captain. You don't tell him that the boss sent for you and what should you do? The reason is that your immediate superior, your captain, may be the target. Maybe I want you to kill him. Ninety-nine-point-nine percent of the time, that will never happen. If I tell you to tell your captain, go ahead. If I tell you not to, you don't. I'm the boss. I'm the father of the family. *I am your God.*'

"Then after that, different captains spoke about different things, other rules and policies. They talked about honor. You couldn't go with each other's wives and daughters. You couldn't raise your hands against one another. All these things meant the death penalty.

"I bought this all one hundred thousand percent. I really felt that I belonged to a brotherhood that had honor and respect. All the things I looked for in life was in a good part of that oath. A lot later on, I got to learn that the whole thing was bullshit. I mean, we broke every rule in the book. Like, at one of the trials, a lawyer asked me, 'How could you break the oath of *omerta*?' I said, 'There's a hundred rules. We broke ninety-nine of them. This was the last rule. It wasn't that hard anymore.' But back then, in the basement of that house, I was a true believer in every way, shape, and form.

"We all stood up and untied the knot again. We ate. We had a little party, a little celebration.

"Then we went—Toddo and myself and Charlie Boy—to Toddo's club. Frank DeCicco's father, Boozy, was waiting there. He was a made member in Toddo's crew. He knew what was going on. His son, Frank, was already made in the first batch. And except for Toddo, there was nobody in the mob I would become closer to than Frank.

"Anyways, at the club, Toddo called Boozy over and said, 'Sammy is now a friend of ours.' It was the first time I was ever introduced like that. Chills just went up and down my spine. Lots of times, before I was made, I'd be with Toddo and maybe the way I was carrying myself, some old-timers who came down to see Toddo would say to him right in front of me, 'Sammy's a friend of ours?' and Toddo said, 'No, Sammy's a friend of mine.' Now I realized for the first time what Toddo was doing. It never meant anything to me up to that point.

"So Boozy is congratulating me and then some other guys there, who weren't even made and not supposed to know, came by and said, 'Hey, Sammy, good luck. It's great.' I played it real quiet and low-key, not recognizing what they were saying. That was part of the deterioration Toddo had talked to me about. We're supposed to be a secret society, and then you get made and everybody and his mother in the neighborhood seems to know about it.

"But Toddo stayed with the tradition. He said, 'Eventually, when you go to weddings and wakes and other places, over a period of years, you'll get to know a good portion of the people. But you got to remember, you have to know that a guy is made before you can introduce him to another made guy. And you can't go over to another made guy and introduce yourself as made. You need a third made guy to make the introduction, to say, "This is so-and-so. He's a friend of ours." We can never break that circle. If they find out that you did, you'll get killed.'"

In less than two years, Sammy would learn precisely what his blood oath to Cosa Nostra, his commitment to the life, entailed. He learned this from Frank DeCicco.

If Toddo Aurello was Sammy's father figure in Cosa Nostra, Frank DeCicco was his big brother. Twelve years older than Sammy, he was active in construction and labor racketeering and early on had been earmarked as having boss potential. He was initially in the crew of James (Jimmy Brown) Failla, who supervised the Gambino family's hammerlock on the collection of commercial garbage in Manhattan and Queens. To keep abreast of DeCicco's progress, Paul Castellano reassigned him to the crew of Tommy Bilotti, an unrivaled Castellano confidant. Even though Bilotti was a captain, he chauffeured Castellano everywhere he went and hardly a day passed that the two did not meet. DeCicco also was one of the few made men equally at ease with both the Castellano and Dellacroce wings of the family.

"I knew Frank from way back from around Bensonhurst," Sammy said. "Everybody respected him. So did I. It wasn't any one thing. We just gradually got tighter and tighter over time, especially after I was made. I can't ever remember Frank lying to me once or giving me bad advice."

The crisis Sammy faced centered on Nick Scibetta, the kid brother of his wife. "He was a good kid, nice as you could want, growing up," Sammy said. But then the drug culture sweeping the country snared him. He started doing cocaine. And to make matters worse, he began drinking heavily. There were car crashes and arrests for drunk driving.

Louie Milito phoned Sammy to report that somehow Nick had ended up in a gay nightclub owned by John Rizzo. A major brawl had erupted. The police had been called. "I got down there right away and got him out of the joint before the cops started pulling people in," Sammy said.

Another incident involved the son of Tony Jets, a Gambino family associate. Nick and the son had gotten into a fight and the son had beaten him up. Nick went to the police and the son was arrested for assault. "He was being marked as a rat," Sammy said. "But I made Nick change his story, so the charges were dropped and that settled that."

In still another incident, Nick had apparently insulted the daughter of Georgie DeCicco, Frank DeCicco's uncle. "Now Frank didn't get into this, but the girl's father went bananas. He goes to Toddo. He wants Nick roughed up. I step in and say I'll take care of it, let me handle it. I talked to Nick and I slapped him in the face pretty hard. But it was better than him getting his arms and legs broken.

"There are other situations with the kid. I'm trying to figure out what to do. Maybe get him the hell out of Bensonhurst. But unbeknownst to me, Paul Castellano is hearing about all this. It's being put on record with Paul—the drugs and the drinking, the thing with Tony Jets's son, Georgie DeCicco's daughter, and so on and so forth. Paul decides he ain't tolerating this no more. It reflects on the family, he says.

"Paul grabs Frank DeCicco and tells him to get Sammy's crew and to whack out the kid. And he says to be sure not to tell me nothing about it.

"Frank gets in touch with Louie Milito and Stymie, who ain't made yet, and tells them, 'This is what we got to do. This is what the boss wants.' Stymie is Joe D'Angelo. He would become like my Luca Brasi, Don Corleone's guy in *The Godfather*. There wasn't nothing he wouldn't do for me. Him and Louie say to themselves, 'How can we do this behind Sammy's back?'

"They get together with Frank and tell him this. Frank agrees with them. He goes to Paul and says, 'This is wrong, not telling Sammy.'

"Paul finally says OK. 'You have a meeting with Sammy. Tell him what my orders are. If he doesn't go along with this, I want him killed on the spot.'

"That's when I first found out from Frank himself about what's going on. When Frank finishes, I tell him, 'Fuck Paul! I'll take Paul out first.'

"Frank looks at me. 'Come on,' he said. 'You go to war with Paul and you're a dead man, guaranteed. Louie and Stymie will be killed. Stymie, for sure, if he goes with you, which he will. And in the end, your brother-in-law will still die anyway. So what good would it do?'

"I couldn't talk to Toddo about this. Paul has purposely kept him out of the loop. This piece of work is off the record. If I talk to him, he's involved, too. Besides, I pretty much knew what he'd say: 'The boss is the boss.'

"I said to Frank I wished that he never told me. He said, 'Think about it. How could we live with ourselves without telling you? How could we look you in the eye?'

"So now I got an option. It's to die with Nicky. I chose against Nicky. I took an oath that Cosa Nostra came before everything. I never thought it would come down to this. But it did. I was devastated. I was thinking of my wife and my in-laws, what good people they are, and how devastated they would be.

"I was hoping that it would be like he just disappeared. It would be better for his mother and father. They knew he was a crazy kid. Maybe he had met somebody, some group of people, and run off.

"The bottom line is that I let it happen. That makes me just as guilty. I didn't know his body would be chopped up afterward. That's not me. I mean, when Junior Persico told me to bring back that guy's ear out on Long Island, I wasn't about to do it, order or no order.

"The cops found his hand somewheres. There was a memorial. I figured my job was to comfort the family as much as possible. What else could I do?"

Did you ever meet this John Gotti?

8

AS SOON AS SAMMY THE BULL GRAVANO WAS OFFI-
cially a Gambino family soldier, he was authorized
to have associates, as he had been for Toddo
Aurello.

Aurello made the suggestion. He told Sammy,
"Take Joe Paruta with you. I'll release him to you. I
know he wants it. I've watched you two."

"I was real happy to hear this. Everybody called
Joe the 'Old Man.' He was only about fifteen years
older than me, but he already had white hair and
looked kind of decrepit. He was tough and loyal.
Old Man Paruta would kill for me as quick as he
would get me a cup of coffee. Over the years, there
was nothing I couldn't ask of him.

Aurello also released another associate in his
crew to Sammy—Vinnie Oil. "Old Man Paruta and
Vinnie were always together. They were partners in

bookmaking and shylock operations. The difference was that Vinnie knew how to make his money grow. Paruta? He gambled away every dime he ever earned on the ponies. There wasn't a day he wasn't at the racetrack, whatever track was open, rooting for some nag that don't come in. But I couldn't have two better guys beside me.

"The story I loved best about Old Man Paruta was one Frank DeCicco would tell. It seems that in his early days, Frank was going on a robbery with some guys. And for this particular score, they needed a lockpicker. Somebody told Frank that Paruta was just the person they were looking for. Frank was surprised. He said to Paruta, 'How come I haven't heard this before about you?' Old Man Paruta just smiled and said there wasn't a better lock guy around than him.

"So they're in the place and Frank nods at Paruta, who steps forward and what he does is, he kicks in the door. 'See, what did I tell you?' Paruta says. Frank was stunned. He couldn't stop laughing. And if that ain't enough, Paruta holds out for his end of the loot. His reasoning is that they never would have got inside the place without his talents. So you know a guy like that is all right."

Shortly afterward, Sammy took another associate, Joe (Stymie) D'Angelo. "When I look back, those two guys—Stymie and the Old Man—were extra special. They never let me down.

"Stymie had this bar in Bensonhurst called

Doc's. He's basically on his own. One day Old Man Paruta comes to me and says there was some bad beef at Doc's between Stymie and Hughie McIntosh, one of Junior Persico's top guys—a guy who would be made like that if his father, not just his mother, was Italian. Stymie was likely to be killed. Paruta says what a shame this is, they don't come any better than Stymie. Paruta was really telling me that Stymie would die unless I got involved.

"I send for Stymie and ask him does he want me to get into the McIntosh situation and would he want to be with me, be part of my crew? Stymie has heard a lot about me and he loves the idea. I get in touch with McIntosh. I know him from my days with the Colombo family. I tell him I heard there was some problem with him and Stymie. Does he know that Stymie's with me? Is there some way I could help resolve this problem?

"Right away, McIntosh's attitude changes. 'No,' he says, 'I didn't know that. Hey, it was a bullshit dispute. I forgot about it already. Tell Stymie to forget it.' He says he respects Stymie for standing up to him. 'He's a man's man,' he says."

Despite his new status, Sammy was still saddled with debts, paying off the rest of his legal fees for the murder and burglary cases. He was asked to come in on a couple of hijackings. "I think one was a load of shrimp and another was aluminum, but hijackings weren't my thing. In the back of my head always was getting into business." As a made member, he could borrow money from major mob loan sharks for a point or a point and half and reloan it for two or three points. He also had a small gambling operation. He was getting by but wasn't getting ahead. "I wasn't accumulating any capital," he said.

And he had new financial obligations. Debra's father put a $20,000 down payment on a house in a new development on Staten Island that had a suburban feel to it. Ownership was in her name and her father's. Everyone agreed that it was a far better place to raise children than an apartment in Brooklyn. The rent Sammy was to pay would cover carrying the mortgage as well as taxes and insurance. "I was scratching my head on how the fuck I was going to handle the rent, plus there was unfinished interior work, no furniture, no landscaping, nothing."

A tipster saved the day for Sammy. "I used tipsters all the time when I was doing stickups," he said. "Tipsters are guys who point you to where you can make a score, but they don't want to do it themselves. They don't have the balls, whatever. Anyway, he comes to me and says there's this other guy he knows down in Florida, in Miami, that's dealing shit—marijuana—buying and selling, and he keeps a lot of cash in his place.

"So I get a couple of guys I know from around

the neighborhood—not guys from my crew, I mean you could say this involves drugs, even if we're just robbing money—and we drive down there.

"It don't take no rocket scientist to pull this off. The tipster goes to the guy's place and tells him he's got somebody coming—me—that's big in this shit. I walk in and there are introductions. I have my gun down by my ankle in case he pats me down.

"The guy, I think he's part Spanish, says, 'Are you buying or selling?'

"I said, 'I can go in any direction. I'm always looking to buy. But right now I have some good shit I'm looking to sell. You got any money?'

"He says, 'No problem.'

"Now the tipster jumps in and says, 'I can vouch for that. He's got plenty of money.'

"Finally, the guy goes to the bathroom. I whisper, 'Is the money here?'

"'Yeah, yeah.'

"When he comes out of the bathroom, I got my gun out. 'On the floor,' I say. I tell the tipster, 'You, too, on the floor.' He says, 'What the fuck are you doing?' I said, 'Shut the fuck up.' And to make it look good, I kicked him in the face.

"I opened the front door and let in the two guys outside. We tied them up. We go through the place. We find about two hundred thousand. We leave both of them there. The tipster got ten percent, twenty thousand. The three of us cut up the rest amongst ourselves. I believe I gave Toddo ten thousand from my end. I just told him I made a score. He don't know anything about this and he don't ask. That's the way it is. You don't ask. So I got fifty.

"I told Deb, 'We're in good shape. I'm giving you a little money. Put it on the side, so you can pay the rent and there's no problem with your father. I'm going to do some construction for the house and we'll buy some furniture and things.' Coming out of an apartment into a house like we were, we got some things, but really hardly nothing."

Around that time, Sammy opened up a new after-hours club in Bensonhurst, The Bus Stop.

"This guy, Mackie DeBatt, had a bar there. He introduced me to his son, Mike, who was in college playing football, a college down south, Wake Forest, I think. Mike would eventually be with me, like his father was.

"Now Mackie dies and he owes everybody and his mother money. Everybody closes in on his family. They speak to the wife and tell her she's responsible. The son comes forward to protect the mother and now he's responsible.

"The widow comes to me, 'Sammy, please help us.' I get involved at that point. I get the wolves away from the door, get all the people off their back. Mackie also owed me money. I took over the bar, closed it down and got rid of the liquor license. I remodeled it. So I'm in business. It ain't a big joint, but I fixed it up nice. At the start, I'm there making sure everything is going good. I got a bartender. I got a waitress. I'm the bouncer.

"One night early, the bartender and the waitress are there. I'm sitting, talking to Tommy Spero, who wants to see the club. It wasn't crowded. We're just about open. A couple of customers come in and order drinks. A little while later, a bunch of bikers walk in, ten or twelve of them. I step outside with Tommy to get a breath of air. Then the bartender comes out and says, 'Sammy, there's a problem inside.'

"I go up to the lead biker. He's a mountain of a guy. I say, 'What's the problem?'

"He said, real nasty, 'There's no fucking problem. This is our place. We're taking it over.'

"I look around, and again, there's a lot of them. And none of my guys are around. It's too early. So I decide to try and use my head, try and avoid a confrontation with them. Which, if there is one, I know I'm definitely going to lose.

"I try conning him. I say, 'Look, I'm the owner here. You could be my partner. You can come by tomorrow and we'll go over everything.' I'm thinking how different things will be tomorrow.

"'Fuck tomorrow,' he says. 'I don't need no partners. I own the whole place.'

"As we're talking, the conversation basically moves outside. He's standing in the street and I'm on the sidewalk and he's still towering over me. I'm five five, he must be six four, two forty or fifty.

"I start to realize I'm in big trouble. I can't talk my way out of this. There's nothing I can do. It's getting more and more intense. A couple of the other bikers have come out and they're laughing and making remarks.

"This guy tells them, 'Hey, this is the fucking punk who owns the joint. This is our joint from now on.' He looks at me and said, 'When you come in here from now on, you got to pay.'

"My mind is racing a hundred miles an hour. My conclusion is that I'm gonna go down, but I'm taking him with me. I make like I'm looking down. I key in on him and I throw a vicious punch. I hit him and he goes fucking flying backwards. But when I go to rush at him, my leg slips off the curb. The curb is like four or five inches high. My leg comes down all crooked. My ankle is busted. From my ankle going like that, I fall to my knees. He's almost up on his feet again. I try to grab him when he's halfway up and hold him down. But I can't. He's as strong as a bastard. These other bikers are hitting and banging away at me.

"Tommy has come running out and they throw him away like he's a rag doll. The bartender comes out and they clock him right away. It's just over-whelming, what's happening. Cars are stopping, blowing horns. People are screaming from the windows. It felt like it lasted three hours. Probably, it was more like three or four minutes. There are sirens and these bikers take off.

"Tommy Spero grabs me. 'You OK?' I say I think so, I think I busted my ankle. Tommy takes me to a hospital before the cops get there. That's when they tell me officially, after the X rays and all, that the ankle is busted in three places, two places on one side, one place on the other side. They put on a cast and they tell me to go to a specialist. These kinds of breaks are bad. I could break the ankle again. So anyway, I go to a doctor and he resets the ankle and gives me another cast about up to my knee. I'm on crutches and the ankle hurts like hell.

"I'm hobbling around and I am steaming. By that time, my guys are around. Louie Milito drives me to see Toddo and Toddo makes an appointment with Paul Castellano. We meet in the backyard of Jimmy Brown's club on 86th Street.

"I tell Paul what happened and he said, 'What are you looking to do?'

"'I'm looking to kill all of them, if I can. Especially that one guy.'

"Paul said, 'Go ahead.' He said he would authorize more men if I needed them.

"I give my guys a description of this guy and we start scouring the whole neighborhood for him, asking questions, where he might be hanging out. I'm with Louie Milito and this kid Danny is driving. And a couple of days later, lo and behold, there he is getting out of a car that's double-parked around

West 10th Street and King's Highway. There's another guy with him and they're going into a house. It's getting dark, but I recognized him.

"Louie said, 'Let's get the guys.' But I said, 'We don't have time. He's double-parked. He's going to come out and we're going to lose him.'

"We race back to the club and me and this Danny get pistols. Louie has a sawed-off shotgun. We get back and sure enough, the car's still there. We double-park down the block. About fifteen minutes later, they come out.

"I'm in the backseat. Danny's driving and Louie is in front with him. I said, 'Louie, they know me, but they don't know you and Danny. I'll duck down and when Danny pulls up to them, you ask that guy for directions, like you're lost or something. And when he comes toward you, I'll blast him.'

"By then, I guess he knows who he fucked with and he's a little nervous. Anyway, Louie rolls down the window and says, 'Hey, pal.' That's as far as he gets. The guy—we found out his name was JoJo— turns around and runs up the block like a bastard. He don't wait for nothing. He just boogied out of there. He must have seen something in the car. Louie jumps out and throws a shotgun blast at him. He hits him. I'm leaning out of the side of the window and I'm shooting at him with a pistol, but I miss him. We see the guy stagger, but he's still running.

"The problem is that Louie doesn't have the right shells. It was so spur-of-the-moment that when we went to get the guns, the only shells that were there for the shotgun were birdshot, not the double-o buckshot we would normally have used. We didn't realize this until the whole thing was over and we checked out the shells that were left over. Louie had kept saying, 'I hit him, the mother-fucker. I know I hit him and the motherfucker didn't even go down.'

"Now I see the other guy coming right at Louie. I don't think he runs at Louie to attack him. I think he's so scared and confused, maybe stoned, that he don't know where he is. I yell to Louie and Louie turns around and hits him a shot in the chest from a couple of feet away. The guy topples over. Louie lowers the shotgun to his head and gives him a full blast. Then we went around the block trying to locate JoJo. We knew he was hit and maybe he flopped down somewhere, but then we heard the sirens and drove off.

"The next day another appointment is made with Paul. I told him we killed one guy, but the other one, the main one, got away. Paul gives me the strangest look. His eyes are, like, popping out of his head. He says, 'You went on this hit like that? With crutches? And a cast on?'

"'Well, yeah, Paul. I couldn't get out of the car. I threw a couple of shots from out the window at the guy running away, but it was too far and I couldn't aim too good. It was Louie that did the work. He got the guy in the shoulder and took down the other guy.'

"'All right,' Paul said, 'when you catch him, you still got permission to whack him.' Then he said, 'You know, if the law had come down on you, you could never have gotten away. You didn't stand a chance.'

"Afterward, Toddo told me Paul had said to him, 'What's with this Sammy, going out on a hit in his condition? I thought he would just assign his people to the contract.' 'What can I tell you?' Toddo said. 'He's got the balls of a fucking elephant.' Toddo said Paul kept shaking his head, like he couldn't get over it.

"To tell the truth, I didn't even think about being ballsy. I was so fucking hot with this guy. I mean, if Louie would have put him down, I would have jumped out, crutches and all, with the pistol and run over and shot him in the fucking head personally, myself.

"By now, we know a lot about this JoJo. Information was coming in. He was supposedly a Golden Glover with the idea of becoming a pro and ends up a biker. He was from the neighborhood. It turns out that Old Man Paruta's sons know him, know where he lives. But they say he took off. He's out of the state. So I relax. I tell them, 'Don't worry. He'll be back. When he is, let me know and we'll take care of him.'

"It's a long time, maybe a couple of years, before he does come back. He reaches out for Paruta's kids and asks that they sit down with their father. He knows their father is connected, but he doesn't know he's with me. He says he had this trouble with Sammy the Bull and he knows he's a marked man. He wants Paruta to talk for him, and Paruta says, 'Sure, you're good friends with my kids, I'll talk to this Sammy for you. Just take it easy. Go about your business. Stay low-key and I'll reach out for Sammy.' Paruta's sons obviously knew their father was bullshitting him. The kids know Paruta is with me and everything that means.

"So Paruta comes to me. He says, 'That kid JoJo is back. He came to me through my kids. He wants me to sit down with you and resolve this issue. Do you want me to take him out?'

"'Let me ask you something,' I said. 'You gave your word, your kids gave this kid their word that he'd be OK?'

"'Yeah, more or less.'

"I asked what he was like.

"'Sammy,' Paruta says. 'He must be down to a hundred sixty. He's shot to the socks. His face is all hollow. He's been living the last couple of years like it was a horror. His eyes keep shifting around.'

"I said, 'You know, Joe, your kids gave their word. You gave your word. People will know this, probably. So I'm giving him a pass. We had a fight. He did what he did. His friend got clipped. He's living a life like you said. He paid the price. Go back. Tell him you resolved it. It's over. Tell him I won't do nothing.' And till today, as far as I know, he's still alive.

"I go see Paul. I tell him what happened. I say, 'I'm recalling the contract. I'm not doing it. I'm letting it go.'

"Paul says, 'That's up to you. It's a manly thing. You think you can trust him?'

"'Trust him!' I said. 'He's been on the lam all this time. He's scared to death. He's just happy it's over.'

"Paul says, 'All right.' And basically, that was that."

"Now, getting back to the time before this biker incident, I'm just back from the Florida robbery. I'm doing construction on the inside of the Staten Island house, fixing it up. I'm putting in tile floors. Me and Deb are buying furnishings. There's a living room, dining room, kitchen, bedrooms in the back.

"I'm getting along OK and then one day my mother calls. My dad has had a stroke two or three months before and he's incapacitated. Right away, I'm thinking he took a turn for the worse.

"But it isn't that, she says. It's my brother-in-law. Eddie Garafola. 'Come down right away. There's a problem.' So I shoot out to Long Island.

"When I see her, she starts crying and everything. 'What's the matter?' I said.

"'Eddie went broke again,' she says.

"'Mom,' I said, 'so what? He goes broke every other week. He swindles somebody, he's broke. Don't even worry about it. He's back in business three weeks later.'

"'No,' she tells me, 'this time, Sammy, it's different. In this business he started, he put up his house, the furniture, the car, the jewelry, as collateral. They're taking everything from him. Your sister and the kids are going to be on the street.

"'Sammy,' she says, 'what could we do? Could you lend him some money so he could get another house? Are you in a position to do that?'

"Well, I'm thinking of this community where Deb and me are living. They're still building houses. I told my mother that if she wanted, I would loan Eddie and my sister some money to buy a house there. The down payment would be about twenty thousand.

"She says, 'Sammy, *please*.' Then she says that if I would do that, she and my dad will sell the house at Lake Ronkonkoma to help them get back on their feet, help with the mortgage, buy furniture.

"I'm heartbroken when I hear this. I know how much my parents loved that house. I beg her not to do it, but she's determined. So what can I do?

"When I went back home, I told my wife, 'Deb, we have to stop buying furniture. We'll lose our deposits on some of the things we bought. And we got to stop work on the house.'

"'*Why?*' she says. 'What's wrong?'

"I explain the story and she says, 'That bum! Isn't he ever going to stop?'

"'Deb, don't make me more sick than I am,' I said. 'I don't need it. We're just going to stop everything. I'm not seeing my sister on the street.'

"She understood. 'Sammy,' she said, 'forget about it. The hell with the furniture. We'll live like this.'

"I fork over the twenty thousand for a house which was called a 'mother and daughter' and has a bullshit little apartment down below. That's where my mom and dad end up. My dad's half out of it and my mom is making the best of it, feeling God knows what, but at least I get to see them more often.

"So everything in our house is half done. Half the floor is tiled. I renege on half the furniture that was on order. I lose the furniture and they keep the deposits. I'm basically broke again."

Sammy was still in his cast when he first met John Gotti. At the time, it meant very little to him.

Gotti had recently been released from the Greenhaven state penitentiary, along with his boyhood pal Angelo Ruggiero. Both were with a Gambino family crew, operating out of Ozone Park, Queens, next door to JFK airport. The crew specialized in hijacking tens of millions of dollars in goods—from designer clothes to gourmet foods—being trucked out of JFK. The captain of the crew was an old-timer, Carmine (Charley Wagons) Fatico, who was extremely close to the family underboss, Neil Dellacroce.

In 1972, a nephew of Carlo Gambino's, Emanuele (Manny) Gambino, was kidnapped. Early the next year Manny's body was discovered. The family eventually determined that the kidnapper was a wild Irish hoodlum with an apparent death wish from Manhattan's West Side named James McBratney. The contract to kill McBratney—slowly— was passed to Dellacroce, who turned it over to Fatico. He picked three men from his crew, Gotti, Ruggiero, and a third hit man, Ralph (Ralphie Wigs) Galione.

One night, McBratney was tracked down to a Staten Island bar. The plan was for the hit team, equipped with fake police credentials, to go into the bar, pretend to arrest McBratney, get him outside and, as scripted, the rest would be history. McBratney, however, refused to leave quietly. In the subsequent melee, Galione pumped three bullets into McBratney, killing him. Witnessed by so many bar patrons, this wasn't quite the kind of clean hit that Carlo Gambino had envisioned, and Galione himself was killed, just in case, facing an open-and-shut murder prosecution, he might talk. Gotti and Ruggiero went into hiding but were finally located by the FBI, acting on an informant's tip. With the actual shooter now dead, both pleaded guilty to a reduced charge of attempted manslaughter.

"I read in the papers and stuff that Carlo had paid a hundred thousand ransom for the nephew," Sammy said. "But what I heard myself was that he didn't pay nothing. He told his family, his personal family, 'If I pay now, every one of our kids and nieces and nephews are susceptible to this.' I believe the FBI was even told the kid wasn't kidnapped. Their help wasn't wanted.

"Later, the story would be that Carlo ordered John Gotti to take the fall, to plead guilty. That's bullshit. Carlo wouldn't tell them, him and Angie, that. If you're with us, nobody has to say you got to take the fall. I mean, you got pinched and there's a million witnesses, you got three options: go to jail and keep your mouth shut, run away, or talk. What they did was they gave John as much help as they can. They got one of the best mob lawyers around, Roy Cohn. And Cohn pulled some strings and did whatever he did and John and Angie copped out to the attempted manslaughter. Cohn plea-bargained it down to four years, of which they served about thirty-odd months in prison, in Greenhaven. At that time in John's life, it was nothing.

"Anyway, I'm in this after-hours club that belongs to Frank DeCicco with my busted ankle and my crutches. John comes in with a little entourage of guys. And Boozy, Frank's father, says to me, 'Did you ever meet this John Gotti?'

"I said, 'No.'

"'Well,' Boozy says, 'he's a good kid and he's going to be a friend someday with us, take it from me. Let me take a minute and introduce him.'

"So Boozy brings him over and I said, 'Hey, John. How you doing? You just got out?'

"'Yeah,' he says, 'I did some time.'

"We have a drink and talk about this and that, I don't remember. He was dressed nice, but nothing like he dressed later on when he was hitting the papers. I think a black turtleneck, black slacks. Frankie has a big crap game in the back room, which was why, being the fucking degenerate gambler he was, John was there. And he excuses himself to go shoot dice.

"Afterward, I'd see him at weddings and wakes, things like that. On occasion, I would see him at the Ravenite, Neil's club on Mulberry Street, when I went to play some pinochle with Neil. He's on another planet as far as I'm concerned, Ozone Park, in Queens. He's into hijacking. That's not my thing.

"The next thing I remember about John is that he comes into Doc's with some fellows. Stymie owns Doc's, but Stymie is with me, so it's my bar, too. I was using it as my club. I'm not there, but my guys told me that he was really hot and bothered about something, something about some girl with his nephew. I never got to the bottom of it. I didn't have to. John was acting real arrogant. Getting hotter and hotter. Out of line.

"One of the guys says, 'This is Sammy the Bull's place, we're all with him,' and John says something about how that don't mean nothing. Stymie backs away quietly with two or three other guys and they all load up. I think they would have clipped him on the spot if he continued his arrogance. But all of a sudden, he must have sensed something. He calms down and he's smiling. He says, 'Sammy's my buddy. I love Sammy. Give him my regards.'

"When Stymie told me he had loaded up, I said, 'What'd you do that for? He's a friend, close to being made.'

"And Stymie says, 'Sammy, we don't give a fuck who anybody is. If they're not gonna respect you in your place, knowing it's your place, we're dropping them. They're going.'

"I start to laugh. 'You're right. Fuck who they are. They don't do the right thing over here, knowing *who* we are, drop them. That's our fucking rules, anyway. That's our life. They want to disrespect the fucking life, we will abide by the rules and take them out.'

"We didn't have any actual business dealings. He's way over in Ozone Park. I didn't grow up with him or Angelo or any of the other guys around him. But over time, I get to know him pretty well. Certain crews in the family were called workhorse crews, the ones who got the contracts. There was Toddo's crew, which was me, and Charley Wagons's crew, which was him. There was Frank DeCicco's crew, Nino Gaggi's, and Roy DeMeo's. Those were the crews that got the most respect. If our family ever went to war with another family, we're in the front lines, fighting and killing. We're the strength of our family. This thing we have isn't business. It's Cosa Nostra. So we got very friendly with each other. When my dad finally died, John showed a lot of respect. He came to the funeral with about fifteen guys."

"I'm starting to come back a little. My clubs are earning. I'm doing my shylocking. But I'm still in the hole because of my brother-in-law, Eddie.

"Then Eddie came to me. He wants to be with me. And he wants to be my partner in business. I ask him, 'What about your brother-in-law, Dominick?' He wants to drop his partner of twenty years! 'It would just be me and you,' he says. 'Don't worry about it. Dom and me ain't partners anymore.' That tells you what kind of a sneaky, scurvy scumbag he is. I liked Dominick, even though he was in with Eddie offering me that big ten-cents-an-hour raise. But Dom is Eddie's business and Eddie's got a hook in me, being married to my sister. I figure he's sure to fuck up again, and how many times can I come to his rescue?

"He may be a swindler and a cheat and all that. But I give him credit for one thing. He knows business. I think if I keep him under my thumb, don't let him run crazy, this could work. So we open up our plumbing company. We start wheeling and dealing and eventually I take over a drywall company.

"That's when Paul Castellano takes another kind of interest in me. He hears more and more that I'm getting into construction. He sends for me and says, 'What are you doing, Sammy?'

"I said, 'Nothing, really. I got this little plumbing company and I'm into drywall and stuff.'

"'I hear you're meeting with union guys. I hear you're doing good with the business.'

"'Yeah, Paul,' I said, 'we're starting to win a few contracts. It could be good.'

"'Good, good,' he says. 'You need entree into the unions, the contractors, anybody, you let me know. We own them all. I'll help you.'

"And he did. The better I did, the better it is for the *borgata,* the family."

Paul just loved construction.
That was his true pet,
the construction industry.

ONCE PAUL CASTELLANO LEARNED THAT SAMMY had formed a plumbing partnership with his brother-in-law, he promptly availed himself of the company's expertise. While Carlo Gambino would have applauded the direction that Castellano was taking the family, he might have been less enthralled with Paul's taste for opulence. For all of his power, Don Carlo lived and died in an unpretentious Brooklyn residence. Paul, however, as the new family boss, had constructed a $3.5 million mansion on the highest part of Staten Island, exclusive Todt Hill, which commanded a spectacular view of the Verrazano Narrows Bridge arching over the entrance to New York's Upper Bay.

Castellano's problem was that the house was so big, the water pressure fell off dramatically on the upper levels. "We had our people come and take a look at the system," Sammy said. "They advised putting in a secondary station with an extra pump. When the water got so far and hit this spot, it would be repumped, so you got the pressure out of the showers that you wanted. Paul was real happy with the result."

With its grand portico, wiseguys started calling the mansion the White House, an analogy that Castellano did not find displeasing. The elaborately landscaped grounds featured an Olympic-size pool and a manicured boccie court. The interior furnishings, rococco and heavy on brocade, may have bordered on the vulgar, but the marble was Carrara and the inlaid floors and notched moldings reflected exquisite workmanship.

"When he showed me around," Sammy said, "you could see he loved this house. He was real proud of it. If he wanted a place like this, there's nothing wrong with that. If he could afford it, why not?"

But Castellano's mansion on the hill perfectly symbolized a growing reclusiveness that over time would ultimately prove to be his undoing. By effectively abandoning his presence in the family's social clubs, he began to lose touch with the pulse of the streets, with a rank-and-file engaged in traditional hijackings, loan-sharking and bookmaking—the nitty-gritty of mob life that he cared so little about. He saw himself as a man of substance with far-flung business interests. This led to a widening division between the so-called Castellano and Dellacroce factions in the family.

Castellano, ironically, never had any notable personal difficulties with his underboss, but he would with those who had allied themselves with Dellacroce, especially John Gotti. Carmine Fatico, Gotti's aging captain, had expressed a desire to reduce his activities, and Dellacroce appointed Gotti the crew's acting captain. Although Castellano didn't hesitate to use Gotti on a hit contract, he considered Gotti no more than a thug.

Almost as if he needed a perverse reminder of the wellsprings of his strength, he constantly kept at his side a *capo* he had appointed named Tommy Bilotti. They made an incongruous pair. The boss, Paul, with his imposing Roman nose, a big man some six feet two, envisioning himself increasingly as a captain of industry, a member of the capitalist establishment, a man who favored satin dressing gowns and velvet slippers at home, who in public wore conservatively cut business suits and who carried himself with studied dignity—and Bilotti, who was Castellano's main liaison with the violent side of Cosa Nostra, a foul-mouthed, bellicose, not overly bright hoodlum, with an ill-fitting toupee that he believed no one knew about. He had started out as Paul's driver and bodyguard, and despite his elevated status still served essentially in that capacity with the doglike devotion of a pet pit bull.

Castellano himself was the son of a Bensonhurst

butcher and small-time racketeer who, along a stretch of 17th Avenue, controlled the sale of tickets for the Italian Lottery—a popular game in the 1920s among Italian immigrants, with the winning number drawn in the old country.

Young Paul quickly demonstrated an ineptitude for street crime. In 1934, he was arrested in Hartford, Connecticut, for an armed robbery that was right out of a Keystone Kops comedy. He and two pals were on their way to a July Fourth celebration in Massachusetts. Passing through Hartford, they suddenly decided to stick up a clothing store. The cash register turned out to be empty. As they were relieving the owner of the contents of his wallet, customers walked in through the front door, which they had neglected to lock. With Castellano waving a pistol, the trio escaped in his car, the license plate of which was immediately noted. The take for each amounted to $17. Arrested back in Brooklyn, Paul refused to name his accomplices and was sentenced to a year in jail. He served three months and returned to Bensonhurst with the reputation of being a stand-up guy.

Paul's father was an early member of Cosa Nostra. But it was under Carlo Gambino that Paul began his rise in the family's ranks. Nothing better jibed with Carlo's inbred instincts than their close-knit familial relationship. Carlo was married to Castellano's sister, and Paul was married to Carlo's sister-in-law. In 1957, Carlo Gambino did his brother-in-law the honor of taking him along to the great Cosa Nostra conclave in Apalachin at which, among other items on the agenda, Carlo's ascension as a new family boss was to be confirmed. There Paul would be able to mingle with such Cosa Nostra powers beyond New York as the Buffalo boss, Stefano Magaddino; Chicago's Sam Giancana; Nick Civella from Kansas City; Cleveland's John Scalish; the Florida boss, Louis Trafficante; Philadelphia's Joseph Ida; and journeying all the way from California, the Los Angeles boss, Frank DeSimone, and the San Francisco boss, James Lanza.

Castellano was one of those who, in trying to escape the state police roadblock, stumbled unsuccessfully through the surrounding woods and brambles until he was finally detected wandering along a country lane, his overcoat torn, tie askew, his shoes mud-caked. But despite the ignominy of the event for Cosa Nostra's overlords, it was not without benefits for Paul Castellano's reputation. At age forty-two, he was one of the select few to have been present. And it didn't have to be whispered about. It was right there on the public record for the edification of anyone who did business with him.

By then, with his butcher's background, he had launched a moderately profitable wholesale meat operation. With his growing clout, he built this into a much larger enterprise called Dial Meat Purveyors,

Inc., that specialized in the distribution of poultry to more than three hundred local retail butchers. He had his eye, however, on a much larger arena—the supermarket chains. And he soon had two of them completely under his thumb. One was the Key Food Cooperative, on the board of directors of which sat a Gambino captain, Pasquale (Pat) Conte. The other was the Waldbaum chain. It wasn't Castellano's business acumen or competitive pricing that got him prime shelf space. When the immensely wealthy owner of the Waldbaum chain that bore his name was asked by a presidential commission on organized crime how he could have knuckled under to the Mafia, he replied, "Don't forget I have a wife and children."

Paul had turned over Dial's day-to-day operations to two of his sons, Paul Jr. and Joseph. Because his long-range goal was legitimacy, neither son was inducted into Cosa Nostra. Nor was a third son, Philip, whom he set up in a Staten Island cement company, Scara-Mix.

Dial's amazing success did not require analysis by business-school academics. Should an independent butcher complain about Dial's prices, the upshot was no deliveries from Dial—or anyone else. If, say, a poultry producer elected not to use Dial, he would soon find that his chickens were missing from supermarket displays and promotions. And if supermarkets did not go along with Dial's recommendations, they could find themselves being picketed by the United Food and Commercial Workers

Union, whose leadership enjoyed a cozy relationship with Paul Castellano. No extortion threats per se were made. They didn't have to be. As in the garment industry, it was a fact of life—and in the end, the costs were simply passed on to the consumer.

In 1976, Dial had approached America's chicken king, Frank Perdue, about distributing his product in New York. Perdue refused. Perdue later told FBI agents that the reason he gave was that he simply didn't have enough chickens to go around.

Within a year, however, Perdue was in business with Dial. He explained to the FBI that he had checked around. "Joe and Paul Junior seemed like honest, hardworking guys," he said.

"It didn't have anything to do with the problems you were having getting your chickens promoted in the Waldbaum's and Key Food chains?" Agent Joe O'Brien asked Perdue.

"Look," Perdue said, "business is business. If you're asking me was there coercion, were there threats, the answer is absolutely not."

But Perdue would discover that Castellano had a long memory. Perdue subsequently had severe union problems. His processing plant in Virginia was nonunion, and the United Food and Commercial Workers Union began an all-out boycott campaign against his chickens. Even the Dial connection did not seem to help him in the supermarkets.

He admitted to the FBI that he turned to Castellano directly to "get the union off my back."

How, Perdue was asked, was Castellano supposed to help him?

"Because," he told O'Brien, "he's the Godfather."

Perdue was noncommittal about any aid he got from Castellano regarding his union troubles. And in the end, after a lengthy and acrimonious fight, the Virginia plant voted to remain nonunion.

But, said Sammy, Castellano had turned him down flat. "Paul told him that when he first had tried to buy Perdue's chickens, Perdue said he didn't want to do no business with a gangster. Paul said, 'I resent that you come to me for this. What makes you think that I can control the union? I think you've got the wrong guy.' When it came out in the papers and stuff, it sounded like Paul was trying to shake Perdue down. But that wasn't true. Perdue was being the cute, scheming businessman, looking for union favors. I think Paul could have benefited from this if he wanted, but he didn't. Paul didn't sit for this Perdue. He threw him out."

Now, twenty-odd years after Apalachin, Castellano received his captains at the mansion. Joe N. Gallo, the family *consigliere,* was in regular attendance and, as always, Bilotti was ever-present. The underboss, Neil Dellacroce, was not. If Castellano was literally king of the hill, Dellacroce remained in the valley, holding forth at the Ravenite social club on Mulberry Street.

Castellano would preside over these meetings, usually at a large table in his massive kitchen. There, he discussed and reviewed the status of the Gambino family's interests in the Brooklyn docks; the garment industry; the marketing of pornographic films, magazines and books; produce and meat wholesale distribution; garbage collection; road-building contracts; Italian bread distribution; linen and liquor service to restaurants and nightclubs; trucking; payola in the promotion of records; stock frauds; fraudulent bankruptcies; the family's participation in the bid-rigging of concrete-pouring contracts in which no work could begin on any contract in New York worth more than $2 million without Cosa Nostra approval; and the family's hold over various locals of the building trades unions, including the painters, carpenters, laborers, mason tenders—and the teamsters.

"Paul just loved construction," Sammy said. "That was his true pet, the construction industry."

Over time, as Sammy's involvement in construction grew, an aging Toddo Aurello, clearly headed toward retirement, advised him that in construction matters, he should deal directly with the boss.

Sammy would often find Castellano seated on a balcony of the White House, in his robe and slippers, reading the *New York Times* and the *Wall Street Journal*. "I thought he was the best thing since sliced bread," Sammy said. "He was smart, business-wise. He knew how to control people. He was a genius at it. He had that mannerism, that way about him. He was extremely articulate. Matter of fact, Fat Tony Salerno from the Genovese family once was at a meeting we had. Fat Tony was listening to him and he said, 'Paul, you talk so beautiful. I wish I could talk like that.' So he was very, very articulate, very, very smart, very, very rich and he looked to be very, very fair. We all thought he was going to run a real good show.

"The only thing was that he wasn't a gangster and he didn't understand gangsters. He didn't understand what the fuck it was to be broke, to have to go out and rob and do certain things. He didn't understand what a gangster was all about, obviously. I mean, he didn't really understand gangsters like John Gotti and Angie Ruggiero, or me or Frank DeCicco, anybody who is a real hoodlum or gangster in that sense of the word.

"Like for Paul, John Gotti was into hijacking. He was a thug. But you can't be a thug forever if you want to get ahead. Somewhere along the line, you have to learn to be a racketeer as well. You can be both. Gangsters can have certain rackets they control because they have street knowledge. A racketeer could have all kinds of rackets because he's smart, but he can never be or understand what the fuck it is to be a gangster. He don't know what it is to rob tires. He don't know what it's like to sit in your in-laws' house with one room for you, your wife and your kids and you can't pay rent or buy a car. Paul don't know these things.

"One time, later on, I'll never forget it, we're up at the house—there's me, Frank DeCicco, John Gotti, I think Nino Gaggi and Roy DeMeo, whatever—all the guys in the family who regularly killed for Paul, the guys Paul sent out when he wanted somebody hit.

"And Paul says, 'You know who the true tough guys are?'

"I think Frankie was the one who says, 'Who, Paul?'

"He says, 'The cops. They go on these domestic disputes and things and they never know what they're up against.'

"You could have heard a pin drop. He's telling this to *us*. He's sitting there with guys who you send out to do a piece of work, piece after piece of work, whacking out other guys here, there and everywhere, and you have the balls as a boss to say to us that the true tough guys are cops?

"As we walked out, Roy DeMeo, the guy who killed Paul's daughter's boyfriend because Paul asked him to, said, 'Next time he's got a hit, he should send in the fucking cops!'

"Paul was so out of it, saying a true tough guy is really a cop. That's not a gangster talking. You don't tell a gangster something like that. Maybe Paul thought it was a big deal for a cop to go in with thirty thousand other cops and helicopters and SWAT teams because he don't know what it's like to kick in a door and go in shooting without a bulletproof vest and without all that training. Cops were our enemy. Gangsters would never consider the enemy better than them or more ballsy. I mean, cops got a license to carry a gun. They got radios. In three fucking minutes, you're not fighting one cop, you're fighting all of them. They've got the whole government, everybody, on their side.

"When I broke my ankle with that biker, the first thing out of Paul's mouth was 'Sammy, what were you doing in there? You're a made guy. You don't belong in those clubs anymore. This is beneath you.'

"I said, 'Paul, it's my club. I'm trying to put things together. I was dead broke. I'm starting to make a living there. I'm making sure things run right.'

"Now I'm supposed to be a racketeer, Paul wants me to be a racketeer, but I'm still a gangster in my heart. I'm a gangster in every inch of my body. I not only own this club, but I'm every fucking thing in it, in the middle of everything. Paul don't know what that is. He never went through major hard times. He started out as a butcher in his father's shop and then they started branching out.

He was extremely wealthy right off. He was a captain for like a hundred years. He was a captain under Anastasia. He never knew what it was really like to go out and rob, what it was like when I would come home and look at my wife and have to say, 'Deb, what's the matter?' And it'd be that the landlord called again. Son of a bitch! Three hundred is due on the rent and I couldn't pay it. I gotta figure out what I can do. I don't want to take out another fucking loan because I know, sooner or later, with all these loans, that I'm going to have to go rob again to pay them off. That's the cycle you get into.

"Paul has no idea what it's like to break open the piggy bank of one of your kids to eat. What we would eat was that fucking pasta with ricotta night after night. It's not that I didn't like it. But every fucking night! I remember I'd come home and say, 'No more ricotta, *please.*' Deb would say, 'No, tonight I made pasta with garlic and oil,' and I'd say, 'Oh boy, that's good, that's great.' You know what I mean? Paul never knew what that was like.

"That's what Paul's downfall was. He didn't have enough gangster in him. Even with Frankie DeCicco, when there was a business partnership we wanted to go in, Paul says, 'Frankie? Frankie's a gambler. He's a street dog, Sammy.' This was Paul's mentality.

"As time went on, in mob matters, he went with decisions that were more and more stupid. He would be fed dumb information by Tommy

Bilotti. If he had kept Frankie DeCicco close by and listened to him, what was going on, maybe he would still be alive.

"But, in the beginning, like I said, we thought he was the best thing since sliced bread. One thing, I learn a lot from him. In business, in construction, he knew what he was doing. As a businessman, he was a genius. And when you got into construction, like I did, you were right in with him. But if you weren't making money for him, he'd see you every once in a while and he'd be, you know, courteous and stuff, and that was it. It was weird.

"The more I was in construction, the more Paul got interested in me. He was helping me. He was watching to see what kind of a guy I really was business-wise. I guess he liked what he saw because he started calling me in more and more. I wasn't out controlling anything for him. It wasn't like I was his guy. I was one of his errand boys, whatever you want to call it. There were a bunch of us. He would use Tommy Bilotti, Frankie De-Cicco, myself, Funzi Mosca, even this Joe Watts—Joe the German—who could only be an associate because only his mother was Italian. Whenever Paul felt he could use one of us, he'd call us in.

"There'd be a beef with the carpenters on a drywall job and Paul would say that Sammy's doing drywall with Vinnie DiNapoli and the Genovese people, who control the carpenters. So he'd send for me to straighten this out with Vinnie. When he wanted to use Funzi Mosca for messages and whatnot, he used him.

"The more he used me in different areas, different things, the more we worked together. To jump ahead, down the line I did a job, a HUD job, for minority housing, and I had with me this contractor. I knew Paul was always complaining about taxes, all the taxes he had to pay, and in these negotiations with the contractor, I asked, 'Who's buying the shelter?'

"'Oh,' he says, 'I didn't sell it yet.'

"'How about I show it to Paul?' I said.

"Paul just loved it. I thought the shelter was going strictly to him, but he put in with him his sons and Tommy Gambino and DiB—Robert DiBernardo—who handled the teamsters and ran the pornography.

"This contractor went nuts. 'Look at all these names,' he said. He was sick. 'What did you do to me? Sammy, my God, this is going to ruin me. The feds are going to be all over me.'

"I started laughing. He says, 'Yeah, Sammy, you can laugh. But I sold this shelter. The government's going to be right into my office.'

"'Why do you give a fuck?' I said. 'You sold it through lawyers and shit, all legal. Why should you care?'

"He says, 'But look at the signals I'm sending. Look at the people Paul put in on this. Pornography people. People running the garment industry.'

"But Paul loved me for this shelter I set up for him. That job is federally funded. Everybody's paying the piper and there's Uncle Paul and all those heavies who are in that big money position and they're saving millions in taxes."

With Paul's blessings and the family's union connections, Sammy and Eddie Garafola were soon winning one plumbing subcontract after another.

When Sammy went into drywall construction as well, he entered into a partnership with Joe Madonia, who was not in the mob. Madonia's company was Ace Partitions. It operated as one of the subcontractors for Louie DiBono, a made member in Pat Conte's crew in the Gambino family, the same Conte who sat on the board of directors of the Key Food Cooperative. DiBono owned one of the largest drywall companies in the city. On major construction projects, DiBono would get the drywall subcontract and subcontract it out again to a company like Ace Partitions. "We would come in with nonunion labor and do the actual work, which was called lumping," Sammy said.

Madonia was delighted to have Sammy at his side. It not only meant more subcontracts, but DiBono could no longer push him around at will or set arbitrary deals. "We had maybe a hundred carpenters in the beginning," Sammy said, "and before you knew it, we had at least two hundred working full-time sometimes.

"Sure we had an edge, but I insisted on good people, first-class work. A lot of guys would say, 'Fuck it, we got the job, that's all that counts.' But it isn't. They don't understand. You turn in enough shoddy work and no matter how much muscle you have, a builder or a general contractor ain't going to keep doing business with you. A general contractor would hear that Ace Partitions was up for the drywall work and he'd say that was great. No problem."

In the building trades, the key to nonunion labor was Cosa Nostra control of union shop stewards, many of whom were made members or had put sons or relatives in as stewards. On average, a subcontractor using union labor might expect a profit margin of 15 percent. With nonunion workers, even with payoffs, the profit was 30 percent or more.

If all else failed, there remained the Gambino family's control of Local 282 of the teamsters, so absolute that if the other New York families needed teamster assistance, they had to share the proceeds with Paul Castellano.

Cosa Nostra had traditionally been in the driver's seat with the union. In America's heartland in the 1970s and into the 1980s, Cosa Nostra families in Cleveland, Chicago, Milwaukee, and Kansas City had utilized teamster pension funds as a private bank to finance the takeover of Las Vegas casinos, from which they skimmed millions upon millions of cash dollars.

But in New York, other millions were at stake in the city's bedrock industry, construction. Paul Castellano owned the local's Irish president, John Cody, who was richly rewarded, so much so that he eventually wound up being convicted on racketeering and income tax evasion charges. This was of little consequence to the family, which promptly saw to the selection of its choice as Cody's successor, another 282 officer named Bobby Sasso.

Ideally, a builder would pay off Local 282 not to have a teamster foreman at a construction site gate. That way, nonunion workers and drivers could roll in at will. The usual payoff was $40,000. As law enforcement began to zero in on the local, however, this arrangement was altered. A foreman would be assigned to preplanned sporadic duty, and the cost dipped to $20,000 or $10,000.

Sometimes, though, a developer would not go along at all and other leverage would come into play. "Let's say we're dealing with a Donald Trump, not really Trump but somebody like him," Sammy said. "I'm just using him basically as an example. I'm going to bid on the drywall work on this project and Mr. Trump says no, he's dealing with his own people. He's a hundred percent union. So a guy from 282 goes over and whispers in his car, or his general contractor's ear, that it would be very advantageous to him to hire this certain drywall company. He still don't want to do it. OK. Fine.

"I get my lazy-ass nephew, who never worked a full day in his life, that I've made a teamster foreman, and I tell him he's going to be doing a full eight-hour day on the job. He's going to stay at that gate. I say, 'Every truck that comes in, you're gonna check if it's a union company number. Number two, you ask the driver to let you see his union book. You walk over to the shanty. You call up. Is his union dues up to date? OK, they are. The guy is straight as an arrow. Now you come out and you check his tires, the brake lights, the this, the that. And you're gonna do this like a snail and by the book.'

"So what happens is this huge construction project has forty or fifty trucks lined up waiting to get in, with my nephew, the snail, at the gate.

"Now Mr. Trump catches the drift real quick. He calls up John Cody, or later, Bobby Sasso, and he says, 'What are you doing?'

"Say it's Bobby. Bobby says, 'The foreman is doing his job. What's the matter?'

"'He's killing me. The job, instead of being a year or two, it'll be five years. I'll never get done. I borrowed big money. I'll lose my shirt. Help me with this.'

"Bobby says, 'Listen, I know you got this other project ready to go and I'm sure there's a drywall contract there. Maybe this time you'll take my advice and give it to the company I recommended for this one.'

"'Yeah, yeah, anything.'

"Boom! Now I tell my nephew, 'All right, just show up for two or three hours and go home. And stop breaking balls.'

"All the while, this seventy-million-dollar project has been stopped dead in its tracks and there ain't a fucking thing anybody can do about it. Mr. Trump, whatever, can call the feds, which he knows is a waste. They'll come down and they'll find this kid at the gate who's just doing his job. What could Mr. Trump say? I didn't threaten him. I didn't beat him up. I never even met him.

"So he knows he's boxed in. Lo and behold, he goes along with the program. And this situation might not happen again."

Sammy's nights of eating pasta and ricotta were over.

Along with his thriving start in construction, he opened another successful after-hours club called 20/20. He also ran, through fronts, the Plaza Suite, a large and very popular discotheque in the Gravesend section of Brooklyn adjacent to Bensonhurst. His personal take from the Plaza Suite alone was $4,000 a week.

Now that he could afford it, the time had come to enjoy life. And he bought a 30-acre country home, which he turned into a horse breeding and training farm for trotters, near the village of Creamridge, in rural New Jersey, midway between Staten Island and Philadelphia. "I never brought any business with me," Sammy said. "I just wanted to get out of the city and all that stuff. I would get off the turnpike on 7A and about a mile or so down the highway there was a sod farm. I would just stop and park, unwinding from the city, smelling the sweet cut grass. I became like a different human being.

"Just being there was the best time of my life. Back in Brooklyn or Staten Island, if my wife had said, 'Let's take a walk and talk,' I would think she was crazy. I would never do it. But on the farm we would always take walks after dinner. My driveway down to the road was maybe eleven hundred feet and we'd go down it and then along the road. On the other side was this huge breeding farm, a two-hundred-and-fifty-acre farm. Some of the horses would see Deb and the next thing you know, there were forty or fifty horses coming over the meadow to her. It was really a gorgeous sight with the sun going down, the air so clean and clear. They all knew her. They would line up at the fence as we walked by. She always had a bagful of apples and carrots. It was really something watching them react to her.

"Deb seemed to have this special thing with animals. We had cats, wild cats, that lived in the barn. She had dogs. It was incredible how good all the different animals got along under her. I'll never forget one time when my brother-in-law, Eddie, came to the farm. I take a walk with him and as we're talking, he suddenly turns around and says, 'Holy shit, look at that!' I look and I see there's a chicken, a rabbit, and a cat all eating out of the same bowl at the same time. I wished I had a camera. Who would have believed this?

"I got the chickens and the rabbits for the kids. It was around Easter. I went to this slaughterhouse in Brooklyn. I had my kids and one of my nieces with me. I figured on getting a couple of chickens and a rabbit or two to keep on the farm for them. Now I'm talking to the guy to get this together. Before I know it, the kids had wandered back to where they were slaughtering. I turned and saw the expression on their faces and I ran over and grabbed them. They said, 'Daddy, they're killing all the chickens.' I said, 'I know. Sometimes they have to do that so people can eat.' I wasn't getting anywhere. They were all teary-eyed. My niece went to one of the cages and said, 'Uncle Sammy, let's save this chicken.' Now I pull the kids away and I say, 'OK, pick out the ones we want to save.'

"I end up buying twenty-two chickens and six or seven rabbits. I told the kids, 'I can't fit any more in the truck. What we'll do is I'll come back and buy them all.' I winked at the guy and told him, 'Listen, don't slaughter no more of these chickens or rabbits. I'll be back.' The kids are happy. Of course, thank God, they forgot about this. They're little kids, and on the farm they have those twenty-two chickens and them rabbits and the other animals to occupy them. I mean, there must have been fifty thousand chickens in that place."

Sammy named the farm Bar Ridge. He brought in his construction crews to remodel the original house. He had paddocks and stables built. He duplicated the racetrack in nearby Freehold. "I got hold of the blueprints to the track and had my people make a replica of it. I contracted with the people who maintained the Freehold track and they would come in every two months with graders and stone dust and do my track.

"My trainer lived right on the farm in a little trailer I got for him. There were two other trainers that we rented stall space to and the use of the track. The draw, really, was the track.

"I used to get up early in the morning, make myself a cup of coffee and sit on the porch in a robe watching the horses work out and clock them. The house was on a hill and the track was down below, so I had a good view. Guys from New York—a lot of mob guys are horse-betting degenerates—would come out and sit with me. 'Sammy, this is heaven what you got here. Where's that horse running? Is this a jogging day or a training day?'

"My trainer's name was Joe Luciano. He was teaching me how to jog the horses in a sulky. He'd be right with me, saying, 'Sammy, take it easy. Pull the reins.' Do this. Do that. One day, after two or three lessons, I say, 'Joe, why don't you jump off? Let me take it alone.'

"'No, Sammy, this horse is too expensive.'

"Voom! I pushed him off and went with the horse. Joe was sick. But I knew what I was doing. When the horse is going clockwise, which is the opposite of a real race, it realizes that this is just for jogging. It don't go crazy. If you turn him around the way he normally races, now you got a problem because he'll think it's time to go and you can get into trouble. But just jogging, it was a real thrill.

"I named my racing stable after my kids, Karen and Gerard. I called it K-Rod. We raced at Freehold and the Meadowlands. Deb and me would go to the different tracks, have dinner, and watch the horses. Deb would bet, but she didn't care really whether she won or lost. Being an animal lover, she just loved the whole thing.

"For me, that farm was the highlight of my life. It was a retreat from the mob, from everything. I got the kids ponies, so they could learn to ride. I got little minibikes for them. It was like a resort all our own for me and my family.

"We'd have friends from the city for cookouts, barbecues. When the kids got out of school, which was June 19th, I think, Deb and I would move out for the entire summer. I would go out on Friday and stay until late Monday afternoon, or even Tuesday. And then I'd commute the other days. To tell the truth, I never wanted to leave it."

But the reality of Cosa Nostra was never far away.

Sammy always retained a special feeling for Louise Grimaldi. And he had warm memories of her streetwise father, Little Louie, her two older, computer-oriented brothers, and her younger brother, Johnny, who remained on the Bensonhurst streets and who early on apparently had developed a cocaine habit.

"After me and Louise broke up, we still stayed real good friends. Her kid brother came to me. He was in big trouble. He was arrested for shooting a cop in a bar. I knew that bar. The bartender was related to a made guy. I grabbed him and we fixed it so that the cop was drunk and pulled out a gun and whoever shot him, shot him in self-defense. The bartender will say he don't believe it was the kid, Johnny Grimaldi. P.S. The kid was acquitted.

"But then he gets into a fight in some disco and stabs, of all people, one of Carmine Persico's sons. Right off, the Colombo family puts out a contract on him. Louise's father, Little Louie, who had connections, is smart enough to keep the kid from being seen too much while he's trying to talk to people and whatever. I told Louise, 'What do you want me to do?' She says, 'Nothing right now. My father's trying to do something, but my brother thinks he's being followed.'

"'Louise, listen to me,' I say. 'Tell your brother to take off, go on the lam. Get the fuck out of the neighborhood. Let your father continue talking and tell him to come see me.'

"The father did his best. He went to some of the Colombo people. They all bullshitted him: Don't worry, it'll be all right. There's no problem. There's no this, there's no that.

"I'm sick about it. I go to Toddo Aurello for advice. How can I get into this? He told me that the only thing to do is to say Louise is my girlfriend and I'm close to the family and can't we work this out and force a sit-down with the Colombo people.

"I never got the chance. Later I would find that they knew I was seeing Louise, that Sammy the Bull was at the Grimaldi house. The guys on the hit were told to continue doing what they were doing but definitely don't hurt Sammy in any way, shape, or form. Keep Sammy out of this. Avoid Sammy. Don't get near him. In other words, Junior, the Colombo family, don't want a sit-down with me. They don't want to save the kid's life.

Because that's what I would have asked for and they knew it.

"What happened was a week or two later, I got a message from Louise to come right away. I go to see her and she's walking up the block toward me in tears. I'll never forget it. 'What's the matter?' I asked.

"She said, 'They found my brother. He's dead.'

"My heart went out to Louise. I, you know, could feel her pain. I hugged her and tried to comfort her. There wasn't nothing I could do.

"I went to the funeral. When I told Little Louie how sorry I am, he said, 'They didn't have to do this to my son.'"

*Now deception is at the core of a
clean mob hit. It's absolutely essential.
It knows no bounds.*

10

ON SEPTEMBER 19, 1980, THE BODY OF A REPUTED
high-ranking member of the Philadelphia family
named John (Johnny Keys) Simone was discovered in a secluded, wooded area in Staten Island
with a gaping gunshot wound in the back of his
head. It was not the first time a body had turned
up in Staten Island that was the obvious result of
an mob execution. The mystery was what Simone's
body was doing so far from home and why the
body was without shoes.

Sammy had the answers.

For decades, the Philadelphia family had been
a model of stability, first under Joseph Ida and
then the boss who succeeded him, Angelo Bruno.
Carlo Gambino and Bruno had been very close.
Both had become bosses at approximately the
same time and both had seats on the Cosa Nostra

commission. So close was the Gambino/Bruno friendship that the Philadelphia vote on commission matters was usually sent in via the Gambino family and almost inevitably took the same side. After Don Carlo's death, Paul Castellano continued this relationship. FBI surveillance observed him dining with Bruno in New York as well as in Philadelphia.

Mob dynamics in Philadelphia changed with the emergence of legalized casino gambling in neighboring Atlantic City. Bruno, wealthy, getting on in years and fearing the federal attention it would bring him, had little interest in Atlantic City. This not only caused unrest in the family but it created a vacuum—the plum of construction deals, of moving in on union organizing, gambling junkets and casino service operations—that especially attracted the Genovese family.

Bruno was shot to death in March 1980. "For the record," Sammy said, "the Genovese family had manipulated a Philadelphia family member, Tony Bananas, to murder Bruno. Then they sacrificed this Tony Bananas. Right away, there was a commission meeting, and to cover themselves the Genovese people volunteered to track down Angelo Bruno's killer. And soon after, Tony Bananas was found in the trunk of a car."

But peace never returned to Philadelphia. The anarchy was such that Bruno's successor as boss, Phil Testa, was blown apart by a remote-control bomb, packed with roofing nails, that had been placed under his front porch, a method of assassination strictly forbidden under Cosa Nostra rules.

The continuing battle for control of the family pitted the family *consigliere,* Nicky Scarfo, against another faction now being led by a powerful *capo,* John Simone.

Sammy's involvement in the hit on Simone began with a completely unrelated event. "It just shows you," Sammy said, "the reality of an all-out mob, *any* mob, war, how complicated it gets, all the twists and turns, all the plotting and deception driven by greed and the quest for power, all the murders!"

For Sammy, it began when Toddo Aurello said, "Take a ride with me up by Paul's." Two aging members of Aurello's crew, Nicky Russo and "Pal Joey," operated in New Jersey. "Toddo told Paul that this Nicky Russo's son was killed in some dispute by a Frankie Steele, who headed up a powerful Irish gang over there. Russo naturally wanted to avenge his son's murder. One night down around Philadelphia, he comes on Steele, who is alone in a car. He took a shot at Steele and misses. Steele comes back at him and shoots Russo in the leg. When Steele moves in to finish him off, his gun jams. He starts beating Russo on the head with it. He's gonna beat him to death. Somehow Russo manages to get in another shot and hits Steele in the stomach.

Steele took off and Russo is still alive by the skin of his teeth.

"Toddo told Paul that Russo and Pal Joey are old guys. They can't win. They are outnumbered, outgunned, and out-everything. They need help.

"Paul listens and says, 'All right.' He looks at me and says, 'Sammy, you want to go on this?' I said, 'Of course, Paul, whatever you want.' He tells me to choose anybody I need. Paul said, 'Whack him out and anybody in his gang who gets in the way.'

"I go down to Jersey and meet with Nicky Russo. But Steele wasn't stupid. He wasn't making it easy to find him. I knew he'd been shot and I had all the Philadelphia-area hospitals checked out to help get an address. But there was no record of any hospital admissions. Then I found out that he had made a visit to an undertaker to remove Russo's bullet. Jesus, I thought, this guy has balls. But the most important thing I found out was that some made guys in the Philadelphia family got him to the undertaker. Steele is hanging out with them. This changed everything. If and when I find him and start shooting, suppose he's with a wiseguy? I won't know who's who. I could take some made guys out and this could cause big trouble.

"I report this to Paul and he agrees. In the Philadelphia war, Paul has sided with Nicky Scarfo. He tells me to notify Scarfo of what was going on. I explained the situation to Nicky Scarfo and he says, 'Sammy, let me do this. Tell Paul I'll take care of the problem.' And he does.

"This still don't satisfy Nicky Russo. He says that Steele had a baby son, or a baby brother, I forget which, and he wants the kid killed, like they do in the old country. I told him, 'You got to go back to Paul on this one. I am not killing a baby. I don't give a fuck about what they do in Italy or any of them antique bullshit ways they have there. Not only am I against it, I'm not doing it, period. I ain't killing no kid.'

"When Paul is told about this, he becomes real irritated with Russo. He tells him that it's over with. Steele, the guy who killed his son, is gone. Enough is enough. Case closed.

"I figure that's it. I go back to my business. But before I know it, I'm up to see Paul about some construction stuff. He is fuming. The veins in his neck are popping out. His face is as red as a pepper. He's just been to a meeting of the commission, which has already voted to back Nicky Scarfo in Philadelphia, and he's told that Scarfo is protesting that his main competition, that this Johnny Keys—John Simone—had been seen huddling with a made member of the Gambino family over in Jersey. And who is it but Nicky Russo and Pal Joey. Scarfo assumed the worst. The Gambino family is secretly supporting a bid for power by Johnny Keys. Talk about how being in Cosa Nostra distrust breeds distrust!

"It's a major, major embarrassment for Paul. The commission sanctioned a hit on Johnny Keys and gave the contract to the Gambino family.

"Paul wants to see Russo. Toddo and me bring him to Paul's estate. We're out by the Olympic-size swimming pool he has in back. Russo saves his life by convincing him that his meetings with Johnny Keys was innocent. He said they had been friends for a hundred years. He swears that anything they had to do with each other was purely social. No family business was ever discussed.

"Now, deception is at the core of a clean mob hit. It's absolutely essential. It knows no bounds. And Paul has learned that Johnny Keys had reached out to an old friend, the boss of the Cleveland family, for support. But the old friend betrays him and reports the overture to the commission. The Cleveland boss is advised to pass the word to Keys that Paul was interested in being on his side against the Scarfo faction.

"Paul is still fuming. He looks directly at me. It's like Toddo is hardly there. He says, 'Sammy, you're in charge. I want this done right.' I should use Louie Milito and whoever else I wanted.

"He told Russo to go back and to repeat to Johnny Keys what the Cleveland boss said, that Paul is looking for ways to help him. But he is going to have to deal with an emissary straight from Paul. Russo is to cite his advanced age and that his memory isn't as sharp as it was. Russo is

old. He has to have a cane to get around because
of that bullet from Steele. Paul wants a younger
set of ears and a mind that remembers everything. So he's sending a newly made member, not
especially ballsy but a good talker and listener and
a good relayer of messages. The name of the go-
between is Sammy Gravano.

"Russo will do this to perfection. But right then
he's dying to get this Keys hit over and done with
as quickly as possible. His meeting with Paul has
left him nervous and flustered. Getting the hit
done will prove his innocence.

"Russo says to me that he can set it up right
away. His plan was going to be very simple. Him
and Pal Joey meet with Johnny Keys a lot at this
ice cream place in south Jersey called Friendly's.
They always sat in the same booth in the back.
Now Keys don't know me and he don't know
Louie. The idea is that the two of them will be
waiting in a rear booth where they usually are,
and I'll be sitting near the front door at one of the
fountain stools with my .357 magnum. Louie will
be in a booth halfway between where I am and
they are.

"They'll wave to Keys when he comes in. That
will be my signal. As he walks by me, I get up. I
follow him and shoot him as he's walking toward
Russo and Pal Joey. Then Louie Milito will jump
up, take out a sawed-off shotgun he has hidden
under his coat, fire a couple of shots in the ceiling

and yell at everybody in there to hit the floor. And Louie and me would stroll out to a waiting get-away car.

"It sounded good, but you never know. I wanted to check this out from every angle. 'Let's do a dry run,' I said.

"The minute I was in this Friendly's, I saw it would be a disaster, it wasn't doable. There was a whole bunch of people in there. Families. And lots of kids. There was no way I was going to jeopardize them. And I'm not going to shoot the guy in front of a bunch of kids. I told Russo the plan was nuts.

"The first meeting between myself and Johnny Keys took place right after that. It was at a luncheonette in the Trenton area. He was ecstatic to be with Paul Castellano's messenger. I was treated to an in-depth recital of all the events preceding, surrounding, and after Angelo Bruno was murdered. He was direct. He wanted Paul's approval in his quest to gain control of the Philadelphia family.

"He talked to me alone in the luncheonette. But I saw that he arrived with bodyguards, who stayed outside. He apologized for this and said he hoped that I wouldn't take any offense. He apologized for frisking me, but there was a war going on and he had to take precautions. He apologized again for being armed himself and showed me his gun.

"I could see he desperately wanted to believe that I was Paul Castellano's eyes, ears and mouth. But it was obvious he was also careful and shrewd. And I wasn't careless, either. I didn't have a gun on me. I didn't know what to expect at this first meeting, but I did know I wasn't going to hit him then. When he was sure I was unarmed, he visibly eased. We talked some more. I told him that we should plan another meeting after I reported back his messages to Paul.

"There had to be another meeting if I was to lull him into a complete sense of security. When I left that first one, I told Louie Milito and Stymie, who I also picked for the hit, that this guy was very sharp. We are going to have a tough time here.

"The next meeting was at a very public bar and restaurant in Jersey. He followed the same security procedures and searches as he did the first time. Of course, I was unarmed. He came with bodyguards. This meeting was to put the icing on the plan's cake. So I brought him welcome news. I looked him straight in the eye and told him that Paul Castellano has decided to back his bid to take over the Philadelphia family. I really laid it on thick. I said that the Gambino family support was not limited to moral support. Paul's pledge of support included money, guns, and Gambino family shooters.

"Johnny Keys was, like, delirious. He got almost

speechless as I went on to tell him that Paul Castellano was going to get the commission's backing for him once Nicky Scarfo was dead. I was on such a roll that I couldn't stop. I had more good news. I told him to think of a real secure place for another meeting because Paul Castellano wanted a once only face-to-face meeting with him. At this meeting, Paul would confirm everything I had just related.

"I watched Johnny Keys as he tried to come up with a suitable place. Suddenly his face lit up. He announced that he had the perfect place. It was a country club he belonged to around Yardville, near Trenton, just off the turnpike from New York. Nobody there would recognize Big Paul. I told him that sounded good. I would get back to him.

"Nick Russo was against the country club. He knew where it was. He thought it was too public, plus he warned me about the club's own security staff. I made Nicky Russo take me there, so I could check the place. I argued the other way. The site was good because Johnny Keys would be comfortable there. He had picked it himself. He would drop his guard completely. I contacted him and said the country club would be fine. But I told him he couldn't have his goons around him when he was meeting with Paul Castellano.

"According to the arrangements made amongst us all, me and Nicky Russo and Pal Joey met with

Keys in Yardville before going on to the club. The three of us did not have guns, but I had hidden one deep under the front passenger seat of the car we were in. Keys joined us. Pal Joey was doing the driving. I was up front with him. Keys got in the back with Russo. He went through his usual litany of apologizing because he was armed. He was concerned about Paul's reaction. I soothed him by saying that Paul understood a war was going on. Once again, he apologized for having to frisk us, which he did, patting us down. But I could see that he didn't have no bodyguards with him. Nobody was tailing us.

"This country club had a big parking lot. The clubhouse was some distance away. As we pulled into a parking space, I saw the van parked between us and the clubhouse. In that van I had Louie Milito and Stymie. My crew was in place. As we got out of the car, I looked at my watch and told Keys that Paul should be arriving any minute. I was still unarmed. I hadn't got the chance to grab my hidden gun.

"We walked toward the clubhouse, taking a path that would lead us past the van. We walked in pairs. I was with Keys. Pal Joey and Russo were ahead of us. It looked like nothing appeared out of the ordinary to Keys. But he was keeping his hand on the butt of the gun that was under his coat. And he kept looking around. As we got to the van, he turned his head toward it. Something had attracted his attention. I had slowed down, so I was a half a step behind him. All of a sudden, he said, 'Hey, Sammy, that van's engine is running.'

"He looked back at me, concerned. I leaped right at him and wrapped him in a bear hug. I had caught him by surprise. He didn't have time to react. I was holding him so tight that he couldn't move his arms. For sure, I didn't want him bringing up his gun.

"All this was happening real quick. But in my mind, it was like slow motion. I felt a tremendous surge of power and confidence. This was going to work. The van's side door opened and Louie and Stymie came out and the two of them grabbed Keys's legs. We all lifted together and Keys was in the van. Out of the corner of my eye, I saw a few people on a putting green looking at us kind of curious, like they were wondering what was going on. But it was over so fast, they didn't know what was going on.

"Now my mind wasn't in slow motion. Keys was on the van's floor. It wasn't graceful. I was still holding on to him. Stymie was on top of me, holding down both me and Keys. It was like the three of us were one person. Louie gets in the driver's seat. Pal Joey is next to him.

"I yell to Stymie that Keys is still trying for his gun. Stymie pried his thumb from the butt. He nearly broke it and we got the gun. Louie takes off. The van jumps the parking lot curb, goes right over part of the club's lawn and out onto the street. Nicky Russo is left behind to bring back the car we came in.

"When we finished tying Keys up with heavy plastic ties, I was feeling pretty smug. Everything looked like it was working according to plan. The original idea was to kill Johnny Keys at an isolated spot near the club. Then Pal Joey reached into his pocket and realized that he still has the keys to the car Russo was supposed to drive away. The car is stranded in the lot and the gun I had hidden was in it. I knew that bystanders had seen our moves, so there were potential witnesses. We had to get Russo and the car out of there.

"I had Louie stop the van. We let Pal Joey out. I gave him specific instructions. He was to make his way back to the country club as best he could, meet up with Russo and get the car out of the lot. They should go to Russo's home and wait for a call from me to determine if everything was clean and there weren't any problems that would cause more changes in the plan.

"After Pal Joey left the van, we got on the turnpike and headed for Staten Island. Along the way, Johnny started having some sort of seizure. He claimed he was having a heart attack. I had to bend close to him to hear him whisper to reach into his jacket pocket for his nitroglycerine pills. He begged me to put a pill in his mouth. 'Don't let me die from a heart attack,' he said. He knows we're going to kill him and he is saying something like this? That's when I realized that we were dealing with a real man's man here!

"His stature got even bigger in my eyes when we got to the toll plaza at the exit for Staten Island. I naturally assumed that he would start some sort of commotion to get the attention of the toll booth cops, to try and save himself. I was convinced of this. I whispered to Stymie to be prepared in case Keys tried to pull something. But I was wrong. Johnny didn't try a thing. He didn't refuse to try and help himself because he had given up all hope. It was because he was true Cosa Nostra. This was a family matter. There would be no police.

"We get to Staten Island without incident. We drove to a gas station that some guys with Louie Milito own. We lay over there. The hours go by. I'm calling Russo's house. I'm not getting an answer. I got to know that they got away. Because if they're pinched, they'll be pinched for murder if I kill Keys. He ain't dead yet and I would have gone to Paul and said, 'Things got fucked up. Guys have got pinched. It's your decision what to do now.'

"It was the longest wait in that gas station—I don't know, ten, twelve hours. Johnny Keys don't know what's delaying things. He figures he's been kidnapped to be killed. As a cover, I explain that a decision was being made by the bosses about whether he is to live or die. Each time I left the van to telephone the Russo home, I told him I was phoning the bosses to see if a decision had been reached.

"Johnny Keys was a cousin of Angelo Bruno. During that long wait, he lashed out against the Genovese family. He blamed it for all of the troubles the Philadelphia family had gone through, the war that was raging, all the troubles that not only came to him but to the whole family. How he now knows it was the greed of the Genovese people that caused this. How the Chin—Vincent Gigante—had conned this Tony Bananas that the commission sanctioned the hit on Bruno. How the Chin conned the commission by volunteering to do an investigation and taking out Tony. It was brutal the way Tony went, shot in the arms and the elbows first. You could feel Johnny's hatred as he talked about how this life we led was being poisoned. How many more good people would die? But there in that van he continued to act like a man.

"He asked that, if he lost with the bosses and was sentenced to die, that a made guy do it, a friend of ours. He said he always promised himself and his wife that he would die with his shoes off. If the decision came against him, would I take them off? 'Of course,' I said. I never asked him what the reason was. The more we talked, the more impressed I was. I really respected him.

"When I sent Louie and Stymie out for food and coffee, he tells us to hold the sugar for him! Afterward, I heard a noise outside the van. I drew my gun. Maybe a cop was nosing around, checking out the van that was parked there so long. He must have guessed what I was thinking. He whispered, 'If it's a cop, shoot him before you shoot me.' His resolve shook me up. It was like at the toll booth. There would be no police involved in family business. But it wasn't a cop. It was Louie and Stymie coming back from the food and coffee run.

"Louie and Stymie told me later that during one of the times I was trying to phone Russo, Johnny said to them he underestimated me all along. He said this was the first time in his life that he was caught unaware of a plan hatching around him. I'd completely sucked him in. He told them that he'd been responsible for about fifty hits himself, but that Sammy did the best piece of work setting this up he ever saw.

"I finally did make contact with Nicky Russo. Him and Pal Joey were safe. I told them where we were and to come. I was outside the van when they showed up. They said there was a lot of confusion back at the country club. Nobody was exactly sure what happened. Pal Joey was able to return and drive Russo away without any problems.

"This was bad news for Johnny Keys. I went

back into the van and told him that the 'decision' had come back against him. He had lost. He had to go. Like the man he was, the man I had come to understand him to be, the man I'd learned to respect over the past hours, he accepted this without comment. Me and Stymie and Louie— none of us—were happy with what was to come. I felt terrible that a man with such balls had to be hit. But this was Cosa Nostra. The boss of my family had ordered it. The entire commission ordered it. There was nothing else I could do.

"We drove to a section of Staten Island that had a back road running along a wooded area. We stopped the van. I remembered his request about his shoes. I took them off.

"Pal Joey went to grab him and pull him out. He kicked out at Joey right in the chest. He said, 'I'll walk out on my own. Let me die like a man.' He took five or six steps away from the van. Without a word, he lowered his head, quiet and dignified.

"I nodded at Louie Milito. As requested by Johnny Keys, he would be killed by a made member. Louie put a .357 magnum to the back of Johnny's head and fired. The shot immediately leveled him to the ground. He died instantly. He died without pain. He died with dignity. He died Cosa Nostra.

"I sent Russo and Pal Joey back to Jersey. Louie, Stymie, and me drove away in the van.

There was total silence in that van. Nobody spoke a word.

"The next morning it was all over the news that John Simone's body was found by two sanitation workers.

"I went to see Paul Castellano. He knew that the original plan was for the hit to be down in Jersey. I told him why it had to be changed. I explained everything that happened.

"Paul smiled and put his arm around my shoulder. He said he was proud of Sammy the Bull.

"I had to tell Paul that I was literally sick about this. We had just killed a guy who was the epitome, in my opinion, of our life, everything we were supposed to be. I looked Paul straight in the eye. 'This is one hit I'm never going to be proud of,' I said."

That Uzi was pointed right at me.
My body completely tensed up
like it was a piece of steel.

AFTER SAMMY TOOK OVER THE PLAZA SUITE IN Gravesend, just east of Bensonhurst, it became one of the most popular discotheques in Brooklyn.

The disco, housed in a building belonging to Sammy, was originally owned by four business-men, who formed a corporation in 1979 called Enjoy Yourself, Inc., and obtained a liquor license. Two of them immediately had silent partners, a soldier in the Genovese family whose street name was Salty and a captain in the Colombo family, Vinnie Sicilian. Intimidated by this turn of events, the other two shareholders brought in Sammy for protection and support. This, in effect, granted him a fifty percent interest in the disco.

Unhappy with what he considered to be sloppy management, Sammy decided to take over the whole operation and got rid of the four original owners. "I just bullied my way in. I said I was going to make them an offer they couldn't refuse. I didn't have to explain. I imagine they all saw *The Godfather.* I had a sit-down with Vinnie Sicilian and Salty. I told them that this doesn't do anything to their end. 'What you were getting, you will continue to get, but those other guys are out,' I said. They went along with it. All they cared about was their end. Matter of fact, they got more from me than what they got before. And everybody's happy. Every week I would send one of my guys to each of them with an envelope. They loved it."

Unlike his earlier club ventures, Sammy, now immersed in his construction projects, was not on the scene every night. "I got rid of the bouncers, who weren't doing their job, and put in guys with me, like Mike DeBatt and Tommy Carbonaro, known as Huck, who were also working my after-hours club, the 20/20. I have my own professional manager, Joe Skaggs. I bring in new bartenders and I hire good working neighborhood girls as waitresses. Everybody who was in there are people around me, or people who knew people who were close and loyal to me."

The Plaza Suite, located on the second floor, was more than 5,000 square feet. The decor was burgundy and gray. There was a long bar to the right as you came in. Banquettes surrounded the dance floor. In the rear there was a separate lounge area, a sort of VIP section.

Long lines curled around the block. The wait to enter was frequently an hour or more. Some nights it was simply impossible to get in. The music was basically deejay, but there were live performances as well. Sammy had "oldies" nights that featured, among others, Chubby Checker. On weekends, he would have first-rate attractions like The Four Tops, whose 1981 hit single, "When She Was the Girl," reached number one on the *Billboard* charts.

Sammy divided the ground floor of the building—2937 86th Street—in half. Part was devoted to his construction headquarters, with his private office and space for his brother-in-law, Eddie Garafola, and clerical help. The other part contained display space for a carpeting and hardwood flooring company he had started to complement his various construction bids.

"It was a sweet deal," Sammy said. "And then it all went crazy. It was incredible."

One day, in the late spring of 1982, Joe Skaggs came to Sammy and told him, "There's this guy. His name is Frank Fiala. He's been in here. He's a multimillionaire. He's got a Rolls-Royce. He's got private planes. A helicopter. A yacht. I don't know what else. He wants to rent the place for one night, an off night, on a Wednesday. He's giving himself a surprise birthday party."

"I forget what Joey said he'll pay. It was a lot. Around thirty, forty thousand, I believe. Something tells me this is very weird. The guy must be stark raving mad, throwing himself a surprise birthday party. What kind of person is that? But I said, 'Joey, you're the manager. I really don't care. Do what you think is best.'

"Joe must have been a little unsure himself. We've never done nothing like this before. He said, 'No, Sammy, I want you to be involved. I need your approval.' My brother-in-law, Eddie, and Louie Milito are with me in my office listening to this, and when they hear what the guy wants to pay to rent the joint, they're all for it."

Much of what Skaggs told Sammy was factual. Fiala was a millionaire several times over, who was then living in the Flatbush section of Brooklyn. His estranged wife resided in Virginia Beach. He owned two Cessna airplanes, one of which seated seven, and had two pilots on salary to fly them. He possessed a Mercedes, an Audi, and a Cadillac limousine. And he did have a new Rolls-Royce, for which he paid $85,000. Since he desired immediate use of the Rolls-Royce, he threw in an extra $4,000 to have the showroom's front plate-glass window removed, so he could drive right out in it. Besides the cars, he had a 41-foot yacht. A familiar figure at Plato's Retreat, a fashionable sex club in Manhattan, he also was in the process of purchasing a helicopter he had been leasing on a trial basis.

Fiala, just short of his thirty-seventh birthday at the time, had arrived in the United States as a fourteen-year-old immigrant from Czechoslovakia. Ostensibly, his wealth stemmed from his ownership of a Brooklyn-based manufacturer of marine parts and supplies, where he had begun as an apprentice. What Sammy did not know was that Fiala had another source of income. He was a major cocaine trafficker. Eventually it would be discovered that in a feud with two rival Colombian dealers, Fiala not only had them murdered but their children as well.

Sammy saw Fiala at a meeting Skaggs set up. Milito and Garafola were present as well. Fiala did not know who Sammy was and addressed Skaggs. He reiterated how much he adored the Plaza Suite. No other place would do for his party, which he described in grandiose terms. There would be at least three hundred guests. He would take care of the catering himself. The surprise was that none of the guests would know in advance that it was his birthday. A feature of the party would be a raffle. Among the prizes would be a Rolls-Royce, a top-of-the-line Triumph motorcycle and a vacation trip on a luxury cruise ship through the Caribbean islands.

Fiala grew more expansive. He announced that he wanted to redecorate the Plaza Suite for the party. "He was telling Joey," Sammy said, "that he would put up another ten, twenty thousand, to do it for just this one night. He said he's going to rip this down and put that up, paint this, whatever."

Sammy signaled Skaggs that he wanted to speak to him in private. Skaggs excused himself and Sammy followed him out of the office. Garafola and Milito tagged along. Sammy told Skaggs, "Joey, throw this bum out. Number one, he's nuts. Number two, he ain't touching this club. It's gorgeous. Forget about this. We don't need it.'

"But my brother-in-law's right in there saying to me, 'No, no, Sammy. This is found money. Let him have the party. Maybe we can rig the raffle, win the car and the motorcycle and the boat trip. We'll rig the whole thing.'

"So I finally go along with it. I said to Joey, 'Tell him he can have his party. He can have his raffle. But it's gonna be rigged. And absolutely no redecorating. He can't touch a thing.'

"Joey comes back and says, 'No problem. He has agreed to everything.'"

Preoccupied with his construction contracts, Sammy started hearing disturbing reports. Fiala was around the Plaza Suite all the time. He was taking Plaza Suite employees on airplane rides. He was in the disco constantly at night, doing cocaine himself, handing out bags of coke. "I hear he's like the Pied Piper," Sammy said. "In a week, he's got everybody and his mother following him around. I'm really starting to lose my patience with this guy, but Eddie and Louie are saying to go along with it. We got everything to gain, there's no downside. But I'm still getting more and more nervous. I hear that he's talking about how his party is the party to end all parties. It's going to be wild, all the weirdos and freaks that will show up.

"A night or two before the party, I sit down with my guys and I tell them, 'Listen, he's saying he's having three hundred people in there. If half of them are like this maniac, we could have a serious problem.'

"I said I wanted Stymie and my other main guy, Old Man Paruta, to be there. I told Mike DeBatt and Huck to get everybody together. They're there because they're the regular bouncers, but I want more of my people around. If there's three hundred of them at the party, I want at least twenty of us, my friends, there, too. That should make it even, if there's a problem."

Sammy decided to be on hand himself the night of the party. The first thing he noticed was that the only visible raffle prize was not a brand-new Triumph but a broken-down, filthy motorcycle of uncertain vintage, clearly not in working shape. And instead of the heralded three hundred guests, perhaps eighty at most had arrived. "I look at Eddie and Louie and I say, 'This is a scam. This guy scammed us. It's a joke.'"

Then Joe Skaggs, the Plaza Suite manager,

approached Sammy and informed him that the check Fiala wrote to rent the disco had bounced. Skaggs said that Fiala was claiming that it must have been a banking mistake. He promised he would take care of it.

"So I said to Eddie and Louie, 'See what we did? We let our greed override our brains. And I'm part of it. This is a total scam. As long as there's no more problems, don't worry about it. We got beat. We got roped in. It's not the first time and it won't be the last time. But let's use this as a good example for the future. Let's just get through the night.'"

Appalled, Sammy watched the highlight of the party: Fiala, seated in a chair in the middle of the dance floor, had his hair cut and his head shaved by two statuesque blondes. "I can't believe what I'm seeing," Sammy remembered. "They're shaving him bald while all these crazies are screaming and jumping up and down. Then the next thing I know, they've ordered in the food, Chinese food, a truckload of it. There are no utensils. People are eating with their hands. There's cartons all over. It's a mess. My stomach is literally turning. I'm in knots, but I'm trying to get through this night.

"Now Mike DeBatt comes over and says, 'Sammy, he's got a gun. He had it in an attaché case. He just took it out. He's got it in his belt.'

"Mike's a huge guy, huge, a college football player, and I said, 'Go over to him. Tell him very,

very polite that we're not allowed to have guns in the place. Tell him to put the gun back in his case and let's just have a nice time.' Mike DeBatt does that and this Fiala puts it away. Then when he ain't looking, I send Stymie over to grab the case and put it in one of our cars outside.

"I send out for some guns for my guys. I tell Old Man Paruta, 'See them three guys around him? If there's a beef and they come out with anything, if they move in any way, shape, or form to put their hands in their jackets or pants, anything like that, shoot them.

"Who knows what could happen next? I've had it. My patience has gone. It's maybe two A.M. I have somebody call him over to the table I'm at and I say, 'Listen, Frank, you don't owe me nothing. But the party's over. Get rid of your friends.' I keep my voice very calm, very easy. I tell him again he don't owe me nothing.

"He starts taking medals out of his pocket, military medals. He starts talking about military things, what these medals are for. What the hell is this? He says, 'You insult me.'

"I told him, 'You can stick your medals up your ass. You want out of here with your life? Listen to me. Get your friends out *now*. You had your party. It's finished. I'm telling you, let's don't end it like a funeral.' He mutters a few more things, I forget what, but him and the rest of them are gone. I said to my guys, 'We learned a good lesson here.'"

• • •

Two days later Joe Skaggs approached Sammy and said that Fiala was so aggrieved that he wanted to buy the Plaza Suite and the building as well. The cost did not matter. It was the only way he could save face and live with himself.

Sammy replied, "Joey, tell him the place ain't for sale, OK?"

Skaggs then handed Sammy a bagful of cash from Fiala. It covered the amount of the bounced check. Skaggs reported that Fiala had said the mistake was made by his accountant, his bank, "or something." At any rate, Fiala was now fully paid up.

"Good," Sammy said. "The place is still not for sale."

The following day Skaggs returned with the news that Fiala was unwilling to take no for an answer. He was offering a million dollars. The property by itself, considering its location, was worth less than $200,000, if that. The Plaza Suite, of course, was a success, with a considerable cash flow easily hidden from the Internal Revenue Service. But a million dollars was a million dollars.

Despite his misgivings, Sammy said, "I have to admit that it rang my greed bell when I heard that million-dollar figure. A million was always a magical number for me. And when my brother-in-law heard it, he said, 'Sammy, you got to be crazy not to sell. Give it to this maniac. What do we care. You can always open up another disco.'

"I have my lawyer, who is also my accountant, check this Fiala out. He told me, 'Sammy, he's a nut, but he's for real. He's negotiating to buy a radio station. He's a multimillionaire. He's Czechoslovakian. He does have a yacht, planes, a Rolls-Royce, a couple of other major cars.'

"So I meet with him. He still don't really know who I am. I guess he figures I'm connected, but just how he isn't sure. Probably he doesn't care. I'm starting to think maybe he's putting too much of his product up his nose."

Fiala proposed to Sammy that he write a check for $100,000 as a down payment to be held in escrow. He would then pay $650,000 under the table in cash. At the closing, he would hand over a check for another $250,000, which together with the escrow check would be recorded as the sales price for tax purposes.

"He writes out the escrow check. Now we got to deal with the six fifty under the table. First off, he wants to give it to me in gold. He wants me to fly to Czechoslovakia or Yugoslavia, wherever the fuck he's from. I feel he's looking to whack me. I definitely ain't going to no Communist country, for shit sure. So that's out. Next, he wants to meet me at some private airfield in Jersey. I'll pull up in a limo and he'll have an armored truck there to give it to me. Sounds like James Bond shit to me.

He's still talking gold. What am I going to do with six fifty in gold? I told him I won't do that, either. Then he says, all right, he'll have me go to this bank he has accounts in and I'll get it in green. To show you what numbnuts we are, me and my brother-in-law go down there with suitcases. But it turns out we have to sign for the money. We walk away. The suitcases are still empty."

Sammy finally devised a way to resolve the problem. He had a friend, Joe Ingrassia—Joe the Checkcasher—who ran the Bensonhurst Check Cashing Service. Ingrassia had many contacts in the money transfer business. One of them was an armored car service he used that carried large cash payrolls. A certified bank check for $650,000 from Fiala went to a dummy account Sammy set up. The check was subsequently deposited in the account of the armored car company. Ingrassia next went to the company and picked up the cash—in hundred-dollar bills—for Sammy. The transaction was completed on Friday, June 25, 1982.

Even before this occurred, as soon as the escrow down payment by check had been made, Fiala, to Sammy's intense annoyance, had started acting as if he already owned the Plaza Suite.

"He's walking around with his head shaved," Sammy said, "and wherever he goes, he's got this entourage with him, I mean, twenty or thirty people, lots of girls, the Pied Piper. Of course, they're looking to get coke. It's totally unbelievable. He's got them all mesmerized. It's insane. Bizarre. I find out he's bringing people, painters, carpenters, to remodel the place. I put a stop to this. I said, 'Frank, you ain't doing nothing here until you own it. Till after the closing.'

"I can't make this up, what he's doing. He goes flying in his helicopter over some other neighborhood discos, discos that made guys own, part of my competition, with a bullhorn and he's yelling, 'Don't go there! Go to the Plaza Suite!'

"A captain in the Genovese family contacts me. 'Sammy, what are you doing with that helicopter?'

"I laughed. I told him, 'Bo, I ain't doing nothing. We're dealing with a nut who's looking to buy my joint. He did this. I had no knowledge of it. You think I would do something like that? Put a helicopter up while your customers are standing in line, yelling at them with a bullhorn? You know that isn't me. But come to think of it, maybe I should keep the joint and do that myself.'

"He laughs, too. We're good friends. 'Yeah, but the guy ain't with you, is he? 'Cause we'll open up his ass if we catch him.'

"'Nah,' I said. 'Do what you want. He definitely ain't with me. I'm taking no responsibility for him.'

"To keep tabs on him when I'm not around, I have Mike DeBatt play up to him. He tells Fiala that he wants to continue to work for him as a bouncer, how I always underpaid him. And now I know Fiala doesn't have a clue who I actually am. He's saying to Mike behind my back, 'Fuck this Sammy. Fuck this punk. When I take over, I'm doing this, that.'

"I hear this and I'm gritting my teeth. I tell myself business is business. Take it easy. Be quiet. Let me just get through this. Then, after that, so what? We're through with him and I got the million. I'll just swallow a little abuse. Be smart. It don't mean nothing. There'll be another time."

The closing was scheduled for Monday, June 28. On the previous Friday night, after Ingrassia had gotten the cash from the armored car company and Sammy had left for his New Jersey farm, Sammy learned that Fiala had already physically moved into his private downstairs office. Not only that, but Fiala had ordered work to begin breaking through an office wall for a staircase leading directly to the Plaza Suite, so he would not have to use the 86th Street building entrance and walk around the block to enter the disco. He had brought in Doberman guard dogs. He had armed men patrolling the premises. "I heard they were Czechoslovakian, whatever," Sammy remembers. "They didn't speak English. It started to look like a concentration camp."

This ultimate affront enraged Sammy beyond redemption. He told Eddie Garafola, "I can't take it no more from this bum." Accompanied by

Garafola, he arrived on the scene. He asked some of the girls on his staff if they were all right.

"Yes," they said.

"Where is he?"

"He's in your office. He's moved in. He's put in a lot of his stuff."

Sammy, followed by Garafola, stormed into his office. Fiala was standing behind Sammy's desk, smirking. He idly spun Sammy's chair around to sit in it. A brace of Dobermans growled menacingly.

Sammy ignored them. "Frank, what do you think you're doing?" he rasped. "This don't belong to you till the closing. Get the hell out of here."

Fiala reached into a desk drawer and pulled out an Uzi. He ordered Sammy and Garafola to sit down. They sat.

"Eddie turned white as a ghost, pure white," Sammy said. "That Uzi was pointed right at me. My body completely tensed up like it was a piece of steel. I figured the bullets are coming the next second.

"But this Fiala didn't pull the trigger. He said, 'You fucking greaseballs, you do things my way. You think you're so tough. The Colombians are really tough. The Colombians fucked with me and I took them out. You greaseballs are nothing.'

"I realized he's talking, not shooting. If somebody's going to kill you, he don't talk. He shoots. With that, I kind of caught my second wind. I said as calm as I could, 'Listen, Frank, take it easy. What are you getting excited about? This is a business deal. There's always little hurdles you got to get over. On Monday, we'll go to the lawyers for the closing. You're right. The deal is already three-quarters done. You want to stay in the office? Fine. It's yours, Bo.'"

Sammy watched Fiala relax and lay down the Uzi on the desk. "So we're not going to get whacked. I tell Eddie to get up and we leave. I've never been so mad in my life. As soon as we're outside, I said, 'Eddie, this fucker is going tonight. He should have killed me right then and there. He would've had a better shot with the law than with me.'"

He instructed Garafola to round up Sammy's key men—Stymie, Milito, Paruta, Mike DeBatt, Huck, Nick (Nicky Cowboy) Mormando. They were to rendezvous at Stymie's bar, Doc's.

When Garafola started to advise caution, Sammy snapped, "Shut the fuck up. I'm not asking you for advice. I'm telling you what to do. Look at that guy sticking that Uzi in my face. Look what we created here. Again, it was our greed. That party wasn't enough. Even though you told me to go ahead and deal with him, I'm the biggest jerk-off because I'm the boss and I did it. Just don't open your mouth one more time. This guy is history and it's over with."

With the interior entry from Sammy's old office

up to the Plaza Suite still unfinished, Fiala would have to exit the building on 86th Street, turn left, walk to the corner and proceed about sixty feet up a side street to the disco's front door. Some ten feet past the entrance was an alley.

Sammy stationed Nicky Cowboy in a car parked on the corner. He had a shotgun. If anyone in the group that normally accompanied Fiala drew a gun, he was to start shooting. Eddie Garafola would stand on the opposite corner of the side street. As Fiala neared the Plaza Suite, Garafola was to call out to him. Armed with pistols and wearing ski masks, Stymie and Milito would be hiding in the alley. Michael DeBatt would be at his usual post by the door. Huck was inside in case of trouble there. Sammy himself would be on the side street near the alley. At a prearranged signal from him, Stymic and Milito would leap out and gun down Fiala.

"Everybody is in place and we're waiting. Down at the corner, Eddie sees him coming and nods to me. I look at Mike DeBatt at the door and give him a nod. It's about to happen.

"Fiala rounds the corner. He has a small entourage with him, maybe eight or ten people. After he passes Eddie and is almost at the door, Eddie shouts, 'Hey, Frank!'

"Fiala starts to turn to see who's calling to him. In turning, he sees me. I am no more than six or seven feet away from him. He's looking at me, eye-to-eye. Maybe he picked up the fury in my face or eyes. You could see the puzzled expression he had. I said, 'Hey, Frank, how you doing?'

"As soon as Louie and Stymie heard me say 'Frank,' they run out of the alley. Louie gets him with a shot to the head. He flops to the sidewalk. Louie goes and stands over him. He leans down and puts his gun to one eye and blows it out. Then he puts the gun in the other eye and blows it away, too.

"There's pandemonium on the street. People are running every which way. They're screaming. Some people are trying to get into the disco. Others are trying to get out. Mike DeBatt by the door acts like he's panicking. He's yelling, 'Get down! Get down! Somebody's shooting.' He's holding the door, so nobody's getting in or out.

"I had another car, a getaway car, up the street. Stymie and Louie immediately head for it and take off. Down at the corner, Nicky Cowboy has his shotgun ready. But Fiala's people are in total shock. They ain't doing nothing.

"I walked right up to Fiala's body. I spit on him. Then I go to Nicky Cowboy's car. So does Eddie. We both had guns. We give them to Nicky and off he goes. The hit men are gone. The guns are gone.

"I'm ready to cross over to a parking lot with Eddie where our car is. But by now the cops are all over. They're telling everybody, even people on the sidewalk, not to move. We're stuck. Just then some kid starts running away, why I don't know, and a whole load of cops go after him.

"In the confusion, Eddie and me make it to the parking lot. A car is pulling into the lot with some neighborhood girls I know who are always in the Plaza Suite. I said to one of them, who I know the best, 'Listen, we came together.'

"She says, 'What happened?' and I said, 'Somebody got shot in front of my joint. I can't believe it. In case any cops ask, I was with you.'

"She says, 'Yes, absolutely,' and puts her arm around me. 'I'll be your alibi.'

"I said, 'I don't really need an alibi. But it's my place, and with something like this, I could wind up with a problem. I appreciate what you're saying.' And I kissed her on the forehead.

"So we're standing there like spectators. The cops come back dragging this kid and throw him in a squad car. An ambulance came for Fiala's body. One look and they knew he was gone. They just covered him up. The cops never came over to the lot. They never talked to me or questioned me.

"They questioned people who were still on the side street, but the best they got was that men in ski masks did it. They questioned people who were inside the Plaza Suite. They questioned Mike DeBatt, who said he was so busy at the door he didn't see anything. He said after he heard shots, he just wanted to stop people from coming out so they wouldn't get hurt and he was shouting at people outside to get down."

Sammy and Garafola left the lot without incident. The entire hit team assembled at Doc's. Sammy congratulated them on a "beautiful piece of work." The gun used to dispatch Fiala was thrown in the ocean. Louie Milito and Stymie were instructed to burn all the clothes they were wearing. Garafola was ordered to get in touch with his uncle, who was custodian of the building that housed the disco. He was to wash down the side street where the murder had taken place in case the police returned seeking forensic evidence.

According to the police, the murder occurred at approximately 2 A.M. on Sunday, June 27, 1982. A detective told reporters that "Fiala appeared to be a free-spending, eccentric, self-made millionaire, who was in the process of purchasing the discotheque." Another detective noted, "On the surface, he was a legit guy, but we're not sure. Obviously, he did something wrong to somebody." He added that federal and state law enforcement authorities would be contacted. It was reported that two Doberman guard dogs had been found in an office Fiala was using. The office was described as a "porn palace," filled with hard-core movies, books, magazines, and "sex paraphernalia."

The Plaza Suite, it was learned, did not have a

requisite operating license from the city's Department of Consumer Affairs. A spokesman for the State Liquor Authority acknowledged that actual ownership of the disco was murky at best. The original applicant for a liquor license, an insurance salesman, had apparently attempted to transfer ownership to an executive in a printing company. But because of a paperwork backlog, the transfer had yet to go through. Both men claimed they had never heard of Fiala. Employees at the Plaza Suite said that they had never seen either of the supposed owners.

Eyewitness accounts varied tremendously. There had been two masked gunmen. Or there had been four, possibly five, of them. The gunmen had burst out of a car double-parked in front of the disco. Another version had gunmen shadowing Fiala up the street, tapping him on the shoulder and shooting him when he turned around.

Admitting that they had no definitive leads, detectives were reduced to saying that Fiala's murder was carried out very professionally.

"Without question," Sammy said, "the entire neighborhood knew I did the hit. But nobody said a word."

Sammy, however, was confronting a far more serious and immediate reality: the wrath of Paul

Castellano. The Fiala hit had not been sanctioned, a mortal sin in the world of Cosa Nostra. The ultimate penalty, of course, was that Sammy could now die because of this transgression. To make matters worse, the New York *Daily News* reported rumors that the Gambino crime family had a hidden interest in the Plaza Suite and identified Castellano as the head of the family.

The next day Frank DeCicco advised Sammy, "Paul is ripping. He's saying to everybody you did an off-the-record piece of work. With him saying things like that, it doesn't look good. But I'll stay right on top of everything."

Sammy decided that lying low for a while would be a wise move. He went to his horse farm. He saw how nervous Debra was. She knew that the Plaza Suite and the building were his. She knew that negotiations were going on to sell the property and that the would-be buyer had been killed. But that was all she knew. Sammy told her that he wanted her and the children back in Staten Island for the time being while "some things" were worked out. She did not ask any questions.

"I have all my men, everybody, even guys who weren't in on the hit, come up to the farm. Our whole work crew is there. I tell them there's a problem with Paul. He's ripping. He feels I did an off-the-record hit. What I want, if it's not going right for me, if I have to make a decision, is to take out Paul first. I may go, but he'll never see it. I tell them that if anybody wants to leave, they are free to.

"They all said, 'Sammy, we'll load up. We're ready.' And five or six guys stay with me on the farm.

"I took aside Stymie—my Luca Brasi—and I said, 'If I'm killed, you say that Sammy had balls, he loved the life. This is the way he would want to die and that's it. Get even on your own, if that's what you want.'

"A couple of days later, Frankie DeCicco called me. 'How do you get guys so loyal to you? Stymie came to me and says that I should tell Paul that if he has any intentions of killing you, he better kill him, too.' Frankie was laughing when he spoke to me. He said, 'It's one thing if he's talking to me. But what if he said that to somebody else? Tell him to be careful not to be going around saying that.'

"My weasel brother-in-law starts whining that I got too much balls, that I was going to get everybody killed. And then he says that I would end up being on an island by myself. Stymie heard this and says, 'Eddie, Sammy may be on that island, but he ain't gonna be by himself. I'll be with him. So fuck you and your advice.'

"Eddie turns right around to Joe Paruta and says, 'See. You can't talk to them. They're crazy.' The Old Man, very mild-mannered, says, 'Eddie,

Stymie is wrong about one thing. Him and Sammy ain't going to be the only ones on the island. I'm gonna be with them there on that island. You gave your advice, now, all right, get the fuck out of here.'

"I said, 'Whoa, whoa, take it easy, men.' Then I told Eddie to go home, be with his wife, my sister."

Sammy would slip into the city occasionally to take care of construction projects, but mostly he remained on the farm. Nineteen days passed without a message of any sort from Castellano.

Sammy saw Toddo Aurello, who asked, "You OK?"

"Yeah, I'm OK. I don't think Paul's OK, but I am."

"Good," he said.

"I told him the situation with Paul, which he knew about anyway, and he said, 'Sammy, you're a man. Whatever your decision is, I'm behind you.' He didn't ask anything about what my decision was, or my thinking, or anything else. That's why I loved him. I really did and I still do. We didn't have a major conversation. He knew the life and so did I. There was no need for any discussion.

"After the seventeenth or eighteenth day without hearing from Paul, I was starting to feel a little more edgy. I spoke to Toddo again and he said, 'Relax. Let him stew with this. Don't worry about it. You did what you had to do. It was the right thing.'"

Finally, on the nineteenth day after the Fiala hit, Frank DeCicco informed Sammy that Castellano wanted a meeting with him and Louie Milito. It was to be at a restaurant in downtown New York.

The hour was late when Sammy and Milito arrived. The restaurant had half emptied out. Castellano was there with Tommy Bilotti at his side. "And," said Sammy, "a few other guys." Toddo Aurello was not on hand. "This was straight boss to me."

After a perfunctory greeting, Castellano got right to the point. He announced that he had ascertained the facts of the situation. He said that he had heard how Fiala threatened Sammy around 5 P.M. that Saturday afternoon and he knew what Sammy subsequently had done that night. But there had been an interval of at least seven or eight hours between the two incidents. "Why didn't you come to me for permission?" Castellano demanded. "You had the time."

"I told him the truth," Sammy said. "'Paul, I know the life,' I said. 'But what this motherfucker did to me! If you could let me talk for a minute. I know that if I had come to you, you would have given your permission as my boss, my father, as my *representante*. I know you would have. But I knew that this could blow up in our face if I came to you. There could have been a lot of heat if it don't go off right. I didn't want you to be part of the trail from five in the afternoon till when I did the hit around one o'clock in the morning. I didn't want any link between us. I didn't want you as part of this heat, if it came.'"

Castellano, jaw set, replied, "I still take this as an off-the-record move. We all could do things like that. And what kind of Cosa Nostra would we have? Do you realize right now that maybe some of us are armed? Maybe you don't leave this restaurant."

"I said, 'Paul, that's a very strong possibility. That's your decision as a boss, my *representante*. I'm not armed and Louie's not armed. You can leave and let them do it. But I don't think that will be your decision. All I thought of was you and the heat. I knew you would have given me permission after what he did to me and all the other things he was doing. Now you have another, final decision to make and I accept that.'"

Castellano scrutinized Sammy for a moment. Then he replied, "You're definitely not going to die over this bum. But I want your word from now on that you won't ever, *ever* do a piece of work unless it's approved by me, or unless somebody—and you better have the bullet holes to prove it—shot at you first and you had to kill him. Or if another friend of ours broke our rules and raised his hands against you."

"Louie was sitting next to me at the table. When Paul said what he said, Louie gives me a kick. I ignore him. I said, 'Paul, I can never give you that promise. I'm a man. If my thinking was not only to kill somebody but to protect you, I'd do it again tomorrow morning.'"

Sammy saw Castellano shaking his head. There was a hint of a smile, as if he was laughing inwardly and trying not to show it. Castellano stood up. He told Sammy to do the same. Then Castellano held him by the shoulders, kissed his cheek and said, "Just be a good friend of ours like you always have been. You can go now."

Outside the restaurant, Milito said, "Sammy, one thing this fucking Eddie has right is that you got the balls of an elephant. We were lucky in there. He was real mad at you, but he loves and respects the balls you got."

However, the curse of Frank Fiala—there really was no other word for it—continued to plague Sammy.

Although the police investigation into Fiala's murder failed to turn up any suspects—indeed, no one was ever charged—it was learned from friends of Fiala's that he was in the process of buying the discotheque from Sammy Gravano and large secret cash payments were involved. One report put the amount at $500,000. Another had it at $300,000. Fiala's widow arrived from Virginia and appeared with lawyers representing her late husband's estate. Sammy saw to it that Fiala's down payment check for the Plaza Suite was returned, which appeared to satisfy her.

But then the Internal Revenue Service began a massive investigation. Agents swarmed all over Creamridge, New Jersey, where Sammy had his horse-farm retreat.

"I had a good reputation out there," he said. "Nobody knew anything about me except that I had a nice wife and kids and was a good neighbor, a good tipper. But the agents are everywhere saying I'm a gangster and a big tax evader. I think only one guy said anything bad about me. He was a breeder. He had this yearling that was going to be sold at auction. I went to him and said I wanted to buy the horse before the auction. I would give him thirty thousand, cash. The way he told it to the agents, he made it sound like it was under the table. When I was questioned, I tried to explain what I meant about cash was that I would be paying the whole thing up front, no loans, no partial payments. Of course, this breeder could have done whatever he wanted with the money, that was his business.

"But it was a small country town, and with all the agents I became like a celebrity. Every place I went, I saw people whispering. Nobody did nothing or said nothing right out. It was all whispers. I wish the agents would have understood that I didn't do anything mob-wise out there. This is where I got away from everything, to have a different life, but what did they care? So it was basically ruined for me and my family. I could tell people were getting leery of me. Let's face it, a lot of little devils cheat on their taxes and they didn't want agents seeing them associate with me. So it was time for me to get rid of the farm. It broke my heart, but I didn't have a choice.

"There was one good memory selling the farm. I had a special cart made so you could put it behind a horse instead of a sulky. It had a steel cage around it and was really secure for the kids to ride in. When the real estate woman who sold the farm for me saw it, she asked if she could buy it for her grandchildren. I said I'd think about it. I had given her an exclusive on the farm, but when the time ran out I told her not to worry, if she sold it, she would get her full commission. And she did sell it. At the closing, she said, 'Sammy, do you remember I'd like to buy that cart?'

"The guy who's getting the farm said, 'Doesn't that belong to me? Aren't I purchasing all the equipment?' I said, 'No, if you look at the list, the cart's not there. I already gave it away.' He says, 'Who to?' and I said, 'To this lady. It's for her grandchildren.' And I told her to pick it up. I wasn't charging her anything.

"Now the agents are all over her, trying to find out if funny stuff was involved in the sale, if I got cash under the table or anything else. She said that there was absolutely nothing like that. She told them when her exclusivity ran out, I still paid her a full commission, and it was done on a handshake. She said the minute they walked out of her office, she was going to call me and tell me they'd been there and all the questions they asked. Which she did do."

As the IRS investigation continued, it became clear to Sammy that he would have to declare income on at least part of the cash he had received from Fiala. In preparation for this, he gave $50,000 to each of his two passive partners in the Plaza Suite, the Colombo *capo* and the Genovese soldier. He gave a substantial broker's commission to Garafola. He gave $10,000 to each of his men who participated in the hit. Then his lawyer/accountant, Nicholas Gravanti, gave Sammy the wrong advice. He told Sammy that it would require time to work everything out. Sammy would declare the income the following year. That's when the tax would be paid.

The IRS, meanwhile, was tracking down the original cashier's check from Fiala, tracing it to the dummy account and to the armored car company where Joseph Ingrassia—Joe the Checkcasher—picked up the cash and passed it on to Sammy.

Sammy, Garafola, and Ingrassia were indicted May 24, 1985, on charges of trying to bilk the government out of taxes on a $1 million sale of a Brooklyn discotheque. Multiple counts included conspiracy to defraud the government, attempted income tax evasion and violation of the Bank Secrecy Act, which mandated reporting any domestic currency transaction that amounted to $10,000 or more. If convicted, the three defendants each faced a maximum of twenty years in prison and fines of $530,000. Sammy was accused of secretly receiving $650,000. Garafola was alleged to have gotten $40,000.

In announcing the indictments, the U.S. attorney in Brooklyn said the case stemmed from the murder of a Brooklyn businessman, although he did not link the murder to the three defendants. Sammy then retained one of the city's leading defense lawyers, Gerald Shargel. The federal prosecutors charged that Sammy had finally paid the taxes—$300,000—simply because he knew the government was closing in on him. They also claimed that Sammy had been trying to separate himself from Fiala's murder.

On the stand, Gravanti swore that he, and he alone, was responsible for Sammy's late payment. He had misunderstood the pertinent statutes. He had made a terrible, an inexcusable, mistake. In admitting this, he said, he knew he was putting his accountant's certification on the line. But the truth was the truth.

The prosecution immediately objected. And the judge agreed, sharply rebuking Gravanti. Ignorance of the law was no defense, particularly when as egregious as this. On the other hand, the judge forbade any mention that Sammy and Garafola had alleged mob ties. It was not relevant to the case that the government had brought. Nor was the murder of Fiala. Prosecutors were limited to saying only that he had died while the sale of the disco was taking place.

When the jury adjourned for deliberations, a number of inquiries were sent out regarding Garafola and Ingrassia, who were marginal figures during the trial. "It sounds to me like they're going to get off," Shargel told Sammy.

The bad news was that, in Shargel's view, Sammy was going to be found guilty on some of the counts. He was resigned to his fate. But Shargel had underestimated himself.

In an impassioned summation, laced with sarcasm, Shargel had described Sammy as a really smart crook. What an ingenious plot! Here he was, accused of evading taxes, which in fact he did file and pay. All right, he was a year late. It was a mistake, a bad one. But how did this happen? Because Sammy listened to presumably expert advice. He relied on it. He went to his lawyer and accountant. What, Shargel demanded of the jurors, would any of them do in similar circumstances? Would they file when their professional advisers told them to? Or would they just file whenever they felt like it, completely disregarding what had been recommended?

The jury acquitted Garafola and Ingrassia—and Sammy.

The courtroom was packed with law enforcement officials. Like Shargel, they were certain Sammy would be convicted. "They were like sharks circling for the kill," Sammy said. "You should have seen their faces when I walked out."

Shargel noticed that Sammy wasn't jumping for joy, either. "What's the matter?" he said. "You won. You should be happy."

"I just lost my brother," Sammy said. "He was like my right arm."

It had happened the night before. Stymie—Joe D'Angelo—had been shot dead. Sammy got the call at home from Huck around 3 A.M. Huck tried to be careful on the phone and finally Sammy said, "Just tell me what the fuck you're talking about." Then Huck said that the shooting had taken place in a bar and restaurant in Bensonhurst called Tali's that Stymie and Sammy had bought together. "I think it's finished with Stymie," Huck said.

Sammy rushed over the Verrazano bridge. He met Huck outside Tali's. Police were everywhere. He and Huck went to the hospital where Stymie had been taken. Stymie's wife, Karen, was there, sobbing. Sammy found an ER doctor, who said, "He's gone. He was DOA."

Sammy insisted on seeing the body. "I could hardly recognize him," he remembered. He came out, tried to console Stymie's wife and had Huck take her home.

Sammy spent the rest of the night putting together the story. Apparently, a young Colombo family associate, about to be proposed, stoned and drunk, had gone into a bar, the Green Lantern, not far from Tali's. A female manager ran it for the Genovese family. She was about to close up. The Colombo associate began cursing her, demanded drinks and ended up helping himself to the cash register before leaving.

The woman knew Stymie and in tears went to Tali's to relate what had taken place. Stymie told her to calm down and go to her "friends." They would straighten this out. As he was speaking to her, the same man, still coked up, stumbled into Tali's. "That's him," she said.

"From what I found out, Stymie got up and called this guy every name in the book and told him to get the fuck out."

Within minutes, the Colombo associate returned. Stymie's back was to the door when he entered holding a 9mm. Someone yelled. As Stymie turned, the first bullet caught him in the side of his head. More bullets were pumped into him as he lay on the floor.

The next night, after his acquittal on the tax evasion charges, Sammy went to Toddo Aurello.

Toddo arranged a meeting with Paul Castellano during which Sammy explained the circumstances of Stymie's death. He wanted vengeance.

A few days later Castellano held a second meeting at the house of Tommy Bilotti's aunt. "All the main guys are there. Me, Frankie DeCicco, obviously Tommy, John Gotti. Paul said, 'After all, from what I hear, Stymie abused this guy something awful.' I could see Frankie's neck swelling. 'Paul,' he said, 'this guy took out a guy we were going to make a friend of ours. He was like Sammy's brother. You mean to say that if we curse at somebody, they may have the right to kill us?'

"So Paul backs right off and said he wanted a vote about whacking this guy no matter what the Colombo family's position was, even if it means all-out war. I said, 'He's got to go.' And everybody votes the same. Except Jimmy Brown. He's a captain, with his garbage collections and all, but he ain't no tough guy. I guess he's there as an adviser. He said, 'Paul, whatever you want is OK with me,' and Paul said, 'I'm not asking you that. What I want is what you think,' and Jimmy said, 'Oh, well, you put it that way, I'm with everybody else.'

"Paul authorizes me and Frankie to meet with the Colombo people. They have already got a strong beef from the Genovese family for what this guy did in the Green Lantern. But I have the lead. That wasn't nothing compared to what happened to Stymie.

"So we go see Scappy—Tony Scarpati. He's a captain, but right then he's the acting boss of the Colombos. He said that they have this guy stashed away. He asked if they can't keep him alive for a while. The reason? The guy owed the family ninety thousand on some deal and they wanted to collect.

"I was infuriated. I couldn't believe what I was hearing. I said, 'That's your interest? You're putting money ahead of what happened? I'll tell you what. Give me the kid. *I'll* pay you the ninety. You'll get your ninety. I want the kid and I want him alive.'

"Carmine Persico was away at this time, so I don't know if he got involved. But maybe a week later, I got the word they ended up killing the guy themselves. Some years later somebody talked, and the cops eventually found what was left of him buried on a beach somewhere on Staten Island."

"So now I only had one Luca Brasi left—Old Man Paruta. I noticed he had stopped going to the track in the afternoon like he always did. I said, 'Joe, why don't you go out there with your son and enjoy yourself.' 'No,' he told me, 'Stymie ain't here no more. I'll be with you at your side until the day I die.' And he was."

12

It was all around amongst us that people with John were heavy, heavy in drugs.

By 1981, THE NEW YORK OFFICE OF THE FBI WAS finally geared up to mount a concerted strategic assault against the city's Cosa Nostra families. Except for the initiative of individual agents from time to time, it had been an effort that had languished for the past decade.

This was largely due to a mind-set at the Bureau's Washington headquarters dating back to the number-crunching days of J. Edgar Hoover and his use of statistics to get the large congressional appropriations he desired. Quantity, not quality, was what counted. The result was wholesale arrests of small-time operators running illegal card and dice games, loan sharks, and bookmakers, with sentences suspended or jail time of a year or so at best. There was little interest in long-term investigations aimed at the organized crime hierarchy, where only a handful of convictions, no matter how important, might be obtained.

Also, two critical law enforcement tools against Cosa Nostra had been badly underutilized. One was the 1970 Racketeer Influenced and Corrupt Organizations Act (RICO). The other was the Title III electronic surveillance provisions contained in an omnibus crime bill that had become federal law two years earlier.

The problem with RICO was that the Justice Department and the FBI did not fully appreciate its ramifications, even though RICO's architect, G. Robert Blakey, a law professor at Notre Dame, tried again and again to pound home the message. And the message was that RICO was aimed at a systematic pattern of criminal activity. Any two of thirty-odd specific criminal acts—murder, extortion, loan-sharking, and so on—that could be linked to a particular Cosa Nostra family would allow the government in theory to go after that family—and targeted members of it—as a criminal enterprise in and of itself, with penalties far more severe than the old conspiracy laws that were relied upon in the past. The concept was so novel that the Justice Department was hesitant to move on it. Instead, it was being used, and not often, in cases involving mob infiltration of legitimate businesses, turning *them* into criminal enterprises.

The problem with Title III electronic surveillance, which had also been authored by Blakey, was not that the FBI lacked the most sophisticated eavesdropping devices. It was that this was the domain of the Bureau's foreign counterintelligence division, which was adamant about not giving an inch to the criminal division's needs. The objection was more than territorial. In organized crime trials, the courts might force the FBI to reveal not only what technology was being used but the techniques that had been employed. A foreign counterintelligence supervisor told his organized crime counterpart, "If you think we're giving this up for some fucking gambling case, you're fucking nuts."

But in 1979, after the appointment of Judge William Webster as the FBI's new director, there was a sea change in the Bureau's culture. Blakey's incessant lobbying paid off. Using the RICO statutes along with the increased manpower available, quality investigations, however time-consuming, were encouraged. The plan was now to document a pattern of criminal activity, connect it to a crime family and convict the family as a criminal enterprise along with its responsible members.

The views of an agent named Jim Kallstrom also prevailed. Blakey had insisted that phone taps and bugs granted by a judge for probable cause were key components to the success of RICO, and Kallstrom subscribed to it totally.

Meanwhile, the courts had begun handing down rulings that increasingly protected the integrity of sophisticated listening devices in criminal cases. Kallstrom, an ex-marine officer and Vietnam veteran, and now a no-nonsense, experienced—and patient—organized crime agent in the New York office, pressed relentlessly for the creation of a special operations team devoted to physical and electronic surveillance. He wanted not only first-class technicians but access to the latest technology and a team that was knowledgeable in the ways of Cosa Nostra that would include break-in experts and sharpshooters to cover black bag entries. And he got his way. "I'm not looking for a quick fix," Kallstrom told one and all about Cosa Nostra, "or some dumb gambling case. I want the top guys, the movers and shakers, and I don't care how long it takes."

That was exactly how Agent Bruce Mouw felt. In the renewed combat against the New York families, Mouw headed up the Gambino squad, which would be designated squad C–16. Tall, taciturn and reflective, the Iowa-born Mouw was an Annapolis graduate trained in electrical engineering. After graduation, he was assigned to the navy's nuclear underseas fleet and served aboard an attack submarine, one that would seek out and follow Soviet missile subs for weeks at a time during the height of the Cold War. It was tense and exhilarating duty. But then he was promoted and faced a desk-bound future. And the truth was that engineering had lost its appeal. He resigned his commission and joined the FBI in hopes of rediscovering some of the excitement and meaning to life that he craved.

At last his goal was achieved with the Gambino squad. He had previously been on organized crime duty in New York and had been as frustrated as Kallstrom. But now it was different. The targets had been upgraded. Given the opportunity, Mouw had chosen to go after the Gambino family. It was precisely the sort of challenge he had been yearning for. Only the Genovese family rivaled the Gambino family in power. And at that stage of the game, the Gambinos were infinitely more mysterious.

Mouw would be essentially starting from scratch. He knew that the family boss was Castellano, Dellacroce was the underboss, and Joe N. Gallo the *consigliere*. He also knew that except for Dellacroce—who had spent time in prison on an income tax evasion conviction, hardly the sort of prosecution Mouw envisioned—none of them had seen the inside of a cell for as long as anyone could remember. To his dismay, he discovered that there were no ongoing cases against any of the three.

Months were required to recruit the personnel Mouw wanted. To start compiling background on the family leadership, he assigned agents to surveil Castellano, Dellacroce, and Gallo, simply to learn what their daily routine was, where they met, whom they saw. Mouw had no idea how many crews were in the family or the identity of most of the captains, much less the soldiers and associates.

Mouw did know, however, that a made family member, John Gotti, was a swashbuckling neighborhood figure in Ozone Park in Queens, immediately north of JFK airport, who operated out of the quaintly named Bergin Hunt and Fish Social Club. He knew that Gotti was the acting captain of a crew headquartered there, which had been run by the semiretired Carmine Fatico, that Gotti did little to hide the fact that he was a connected mobster, that he was considered a celebrity on the streets of Ozone Park, and that on each Fourth of July he sponsored a huge and illegal local fireworks display without interference from the police, while his crew grilled hot dogs and hamburgers by the hundreds and ice cream vendors were brought in to hand out free cones and pops to hordes of delighted children.

It was not Gotti's swaggering ways or thumb-the-nose attitude toward law enforcement, however, that caused Mouw, as soon as the Gambino squad became operational, to designate Gotti his number one target. Gotti's misfortune was that the only reliable sources of intelligence about the Gambino family that the FBI had in place at the time of Mouw's arrival concerned Gotti.

One of these sources was a bookmaker with close ties to the Bergin crew who, hoping to hedge his own bets against future run-ins with the law, began reporting Gotti's obsessive sports gambling, especially on football and basketball. Gotti was a big-time player and a big-time loser. He always paid his debts, not out of some moral sense but because to do otherwise would bring about immediate dishonor in mob circles. Gotti resided in a modest Cape Cod–style house in the Howard Beach section of Queens, adjacent to Ozone Park. His sole recorded income at the time was a $25,000 annual salary as a salesman for a plumbing supply company. On a given weekend, the bookmaker confided, Gotti would lose that much or more.

Where was the money coming from? The bookmaker suggested narcotics trafficking. Gotti's crew was heavily engaged in heroin and cocaine. He singled out Angelo Ruggiero's brother, Sal, a millionaire heroin dealer, who was in fact now a wanted fugitive. There was Angelo himself; Gotti's brother, Gene; John Carneglia; and Anthony (Tony Roach) Rampino.

"It was all around amongst us," Sammy said, "that people with John were heavy, heavy in drugs. Personally, I don't believe John ever did it himself. But he had to know what was going on. I mean, there's Genie, his own brother, Angie Ruggiero, who he grew up with, the other guys with him—Johnny Carneglia, Eddie Lino, and Tony Roach, who not only had a reputation for drugs but was an ex-junkie. What I think is John just took the money and didn't ask no questions. I think that's what Paul Castellano did, probably a lot more."

But Mouw also had an informant far more important than the bookmaker. His name was Willie Boy Johnson. He, too, had grown up with John Gotti. His mother was Italian, his father a Cherokee Indian. He had LOVE tattooed on the knuckles of one hand and HATE on those of the other. When Gotti became associated with the Fatico crew, he brought Johnson along, using him as an errand boy and an enforcer to collect overdue loans. Willie Boy became embittered because, after he was jailed on a robbery conviction, Fatico failed to care for his wife and children during his incarceration. In 1971, to even the score after an arrest for extortion, he became a source for the FBI concerning events inside the Bergin Hunt and Fish Social Club.

Although, on the surface, Willie Boy played the obedient Tonto to Gotti's Lone Ranger, he seemed to take special pleasure in reporting what Gotti was up to. Gotti's idea of humor left plenty to be desired. And Johnson seethed with resentment as Gotti delivered derisive asides about "redskins" and "half-breeds" and often treated him as a second-class citizen.

In return for his information, Johnson received cash payments from the FBI and operated on the assumption that if he were ever caught in criminal activity, his cooperation would be taken into account. No one tried to dissuade him on this score. He was too valuable.

Willie Boy was the informant who identified Gotti as part of the hit team that murdered James McBratney, the kidnapper of Carlo Gambino's nephew.

In 1979, Johnson reported that Gotti, his brother, Gene, and Angelo Ruggiero had been formally made members in the Gambino family.

He also reported that Gotti was Neil Dellacroce's prize protégé. He relayed news of Gotti's deepening anger that, despite Dellacroce's best efforts, Paul Castellano had thus far refused to change his status from acting to official *capo* of the Bergin crew. He confirmed what the bookmaker had indicated—that heroin and cocaine trafficking was rampant in the crew. He also confirmed Gotti's uncontrollable gambling and his penchant for womanizing night after night to such a degree that half the following day was gone before Gotti crawled out of bed.

In 1980, a Howard Beach neighbor of Gotti's, a man named John Favara, who worked in a Long Island convertible-bed factory, was driving home. Suddenly a boy on a borrowed minibike darted into the street from behind a Dumpster.

Favara had no time to brake and the boy was killed. He was twelve-year-old Frank Gotti, apparently the apple of his father's eye.

Friends of Favara's suggested that it might be wise to vacate Howard Beach permanently—and right away. Even one of Favara's parish priests cautioned him not to attend the funeral. At first, Favara shrugged off the warnings. It had been a dreadful accident. It wasn't his fault, as anyone with half a brain knew. What his friends were hinting at only happened in the movies. Then he found a funeral card and a photograph of young Frank in his mailbox. A female voice phoned a death threat. The hood of his car was spray-painted with a single word: MURDERER. A woman, Favara later said, approached him in his driveway and struck him with a metal baseball bat.

After that, Favara decided to move, but he never got the chance. On the verge of closing on the sale of his Howard Beach house, he left his factory job and walked to the parking lot of a nearby diner, where he usually parked. He was intercepted by three males. One clubbed Favara and he was hustled into a van. That was the last anyone saw of him. The word on the streets of Howard Beach and Ozone Park was that he had been chainsawed to death. At the time, John Gotti was in Florida.

Not even Willie Boy Johnson could confirm the circumstances of Favara's disappearance. There had been no discussion at all about it in the Bergin crew. Gotti, Johnson told the Gambino squad, was a "rising star" in the family. There were any number of men who could have abducted and killed Favara on their own in hopes of gaining his favor.

But what intrigued Bruce Mouw more than any of the information Johnson passed on was his almost offhand remark that because of Gotti's nightly carousing, Angelo Ruggiero had become his straw boss for the crew. If Gotti was the crew's acting captain, Johnson said, Ruggiero was the assistant acting captain. And Ruggiero ran off at the mouth to the point where, behind his back, he was called "Quack-Quack." Moreover, in Johnson's presence, he had boasted that he could easily foil any FBI attempts to tap his telephone. When he wanted to talk business, he would use a Princess phone that had a separate line listed in his daughter's name.

Mouw had been searching for a weak link to exploit and Ruggiero provided this opportunity. The first case that the Gambino squad opened was titled 183A–1550. It was directed at the Bergin Hunt and Fish Social Club. Its designated targets were John Gotti and Angelo Ruggiero.

Based on what had been thus far ascertained, Bruce Mouw obtained a probable cause court-authorized wiretap on the phone of Ruggiero's daughter in November 1981. By then, Gotti had every reason to believe that being the Bergin crew's acting captain was the beginning of much greater things to come for him. As it would turn out, that Title III tap was the beginning of Gotti's undoing. It was Gotti's first misfortune that the FBI's initial sources of information about the Gambino family centered on the Bergin crew. His second misfortune was that Mouw was a bachelor with no personal obligations to a wife or children, who devoted his every waking moment to the pursuit of the Gambino family in general and John Gotti in particular. With any luck, Gotti could lead him to Dellacroce and Castellano.

One of Ruggiero's daily tasks was to rouse his captain by noon. As FBI tapes rolled, Gotti's groggy voice would be heard answering the phone. "Yeah."

"John, how you doin'?"

A grunt. A throat-clearing cough. Finally, "OK, Ange, OK."

"Time to rise and shine, Johnny boy, OK?" Ruggiero jovially coaxed.

"OK, OK, Ange. C'mon. OK."

Fifteen minutes later Ruggiero would call again to make sure Gotti was up and about. "You got your coffee?"

"Yeah, yeah, Ange."

One Sunday, during a call from Ruggiero, Gotti began a litany of the losses he was facing at that very hour. "I bet Buffalo six dimes [$6,000] and they're gettin' killed. . . . I bet New

Sammy's parents, Kay and Gerry, on their wedding day.

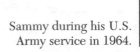

Sammy's fifth birthday, as he unwraps one of his presents: a toy gun.

Sammy during his U.S. Army service in 1964.

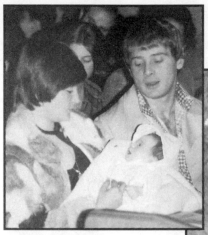

Sammy looking on at daughter Karen's baptism.

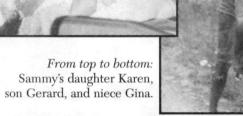

From top to bottom: Sammy's daughter Karen, son Gerard, and niece Gina.

Sammy and Debra at daughter Karen's first communion party, with son Gerard.

Celebrating the fiftieth anniversary of Sammy's parents. *Left to right:* brother-in-law Eddie Garafola, sister Fran, father Gerry, Sammy, mother Kay, sister Jeannie, brother-in-law Angelo, wife Debra.

Sammy's parents on their fiftieth wedding anniversary.

High school graduation day for Sammy's daughter Karen.

Left to right: Sammy's sister Fran, wife Debra, and sister Jeannie.

Some of Sammy's associates. *Left to right:* Eddie Garafola, Big Louie Vallario, Stymie's son Joey D'Angelo, Frankie Fabiano, and Thomas (Huck) Carbonaro.

Paul Castellano, the Gambino family boss who administered the Cosa Nostra oath of allegiance to Sammy.
(UPI/Corbis-Bettmann)

Joseph Valachi, the first member of Cosa Nostra to reveal its true name and family structure.
(Peter Maas)

Carmine (Junior) Persico at the time he was Sammy's capo, when he was associated with the Columbo family. Persico went on to become Columbo family boss and is now serving a 100-year sentence without parole.
(UPI/Corbis-Bettmann)

The body of Paul Castellano, who was gunned down as he stepped from his car in front of Sparks Steak House. *(Reuters/Photographer Unknown/Archive Photos)*

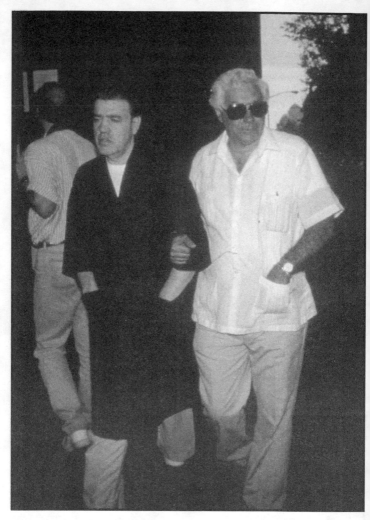

Vincent (the Chin) Gigante in his famous street attire—bathrobe and slippers—feigning insanity on his strolls around New York. *(YvonneHemsey, Gamma-Liaison)*

Aneillo (Neil) Dellacroce, the Gambino family underboss who was John Gotti's mentor. His death would pave the way to the assassination of Castellano. *(UPI/Corbis-Bettmann)*

Carlo Gambino, the Gambino family's wily boss for nineteen years. He chose Paul Castellano as his successor. *(UPI/Corbis-Bettmann)*

John Gotti speaks to an underling while Angelo Ruggiero *(right)*
listens. The bugging of Ruggiero's home gave the FBI its initial
opening against the Gambino family.
(R. Maiman, Sygma)

John Gotti, surrounded by his usual audience.
(Steve Allen, Gamma-Liaison)

John Gotti in one of his typically arrogant poses.
(AP/Wide World Photos)

A youthful Sammy Gravano on the streets of Bensonhurst.
(*Jack Smith*, New York Daily News)

Sammy being sworn in to testify before a U.S. Senate committee on the state of organized crime in America. *(AP/Wide World Photos)*

FBI agents Matthew Tricorico (*left*) and Frank Spero. They were the agents Sammy first contacted when he decided to become a cooperating witness.
(*Courtesy of the FBI*)

Special Agent Bruce Mouw, who headed up the FBI's Gambino Squad. *(Courtesy of the FBI)*

Jim Kallstrom, who ran the FBI's bugging operations against the New York crime families. He went on to become head of the FBI's New York office. *(Brad Rickersby, SIPA Press)*

John Gleeson, the assistant U.S. attorney who led the first successful prosecution of John Gotti after he became the Gambino family boss. In a secret meeting, Sammy informed Gleeson of his willingness to testify against Gotti. Gleeson is now a federal judge. *(AP/Wide World Photos)*

Federal District Judge I. Leo Glasser, who presided over the trial that sent John Gotti to prison for life without parole. *(AP/Wide World Photos)*

England six dimes, I'm gettin' killed with New England. . . . I bet three dimes on Kansas City. They're winnin', but maybe they'll lose, too, those motherfuckers."

Ruggiero then phoned Gotti's brother, Gene. Something had to be done about John's gambling. "He wouldn't listen to me," Gene Gotti said.

Then, in another conversation with Gene, Ruggiero made a slip. He asked an oblique question about a heroin deal, asking if it had gone down. "Yeah," Gene Gotti said without elaborating.

On this initial tap, Ruggiero did not talk on the phone about specific murders or drug trafficking. Still, the squad was compiling a wealth of intelligence about the Gambino family—who the players were, who was in favor, who wasn't—which enabled Mouw to start drawing up an all-important, accurate chart of the family organization.

Ruggiero proved to be a nonstop talker and an incurable gossip. Every other Sunday he would drive to the White House on Todt Hill to report to Castellano about the activities of the Bergin crew and the profits the boss could expect from the crew's hijacking and gambling operations. Back home, he was immediately on the phone complaining about Paul Castellano's high-handed manner, Tommy Bilotti at his side. He sneered that Castellano was a "milk drinker" and a "pansy." He put down Castellano's two sons, who were running the Dial poultry business, as "the chicken men" and called business advisers that Castellano had around him "the Jew club." Tommy Gambino, Don Carlo's son and Paul's nephew, who oversaw the family's interests in the garment center, was a "sissy dressmaker." Chuckling at his own wit, he conjured up an image of Castellano and Bilotti spending their evenings together on Todt Hill "whacking off." The day would come, he boasted to crew members, when John would be the family boss and he, Angelo, the underboss.

Wow! Mouw thought. He could just imagine what Castellano's reaction would be if he ever heard talk like this. And perhaps he would.

Mouw briefly considered and discarded the idea of placing either a phone tap or a microphone in the Bergin clubhouse. Wiseguys by now were alert to the fact that their social clubs had probably been wired. Any business being discussed was broached in basically unintelligible, fragmented sentences punctuated with hand signals or conducted on the street.

But when Ruggiero moved from his Howard Beach home in early 1982 to a new residence in suburban Cedarhurst, Long Island, the wiretap followed him. And now Jim Kallstrom's team of break-in experts and highly trained technicians installed a miniature state-of-the-art bug as well. They knew exactly where to put it. Thanks to Willie Boy Johnson and other sources developed once Gotti was targeted, Mouw had learned that

Ruggiero held his mob meetings in a dinette off the kitchen.

The garrulous Angelo came through. A Long Island neighbor, Robert (DiB) DiBernardo, the family's porno king, would drop by, and from the constant prurient questioning by Ruggiero, Mouw's squad got a very clear picture of both the extent and the profitability of what the family was raking in. Mouw also learned that the serious, potentially bloody rivalry supposed by conventional wisdom to exist between Neil Dellacroce and Paul Castellano was very much overblown, if it existed at all. Frank DeCicco was a visitor to the dinette. Admittedly, a racketeer/ gangster gap existed between the boss and the underboss, and DeCicco was one of the few in the family able to move easily between the two, enjoying their mutual respect. But when Ruggiero, who was a nephew of Dellacroce's, tried to convince DeCicco that his uncle had real beefs against Castellano, DeCicco wouldn't bite. To Ruggiero's unhappiness, DeCicco said that as far as he was concerned, Neil was a faithful underboss. He was old-line Cosa Nostra. He knew the rules.

Gene Gotti, John Carneglia, and Eddie Lino, who was yet to be made, sat at Ruggiero's dinette table. They all worked for Angelo's fugitive brother, Sal, whose heroin trafficking, they told Angelo, had brought in upwards of $2 million in just one six-month period. From the tone of these conversations, Mouw deduced that Angelo himself was not then directly involved in heroin.

Then, suddenly, everything changed. On May 6, 1982, almost two months to the day after the dinette bug was activated, Sal Ruggiero died in the crash of a chartered Lear jet off the Florida coast. And Angelo, as the executor of his estate, inherited his brother's drug cartel. Now the talk about heroin became quite explicit. Gene Gotti and John Carneglia would inform Angelo that they had five kilos available here, three there. This, or that, had to be done. "The guy has already paid," Gene Gotti once said. "We owe him two kilos." Other suppliers and dealers who had been part of his brother's empire would be at the Cedarhurst house, using transparent code words like "pieces of furniture" or "mortgage payments."

In his new role as a heroin trafficker, Ruggiero exhibited an uncharacteristic wariness. He not only had law enforcement to worry about but was well aware that Paul Castellano had repeatedly declared, "You deal in drugs, you die." He brought in an ex–New York City cop to sweep his home for possible taps and bugs.

As soon as Gambino squad agents learned this, the microphone was turned off. Two days later, after the sweep had been completed, it was activated again and the former cop was overheard telling Ruggiero, "Ange, I've got good news and bad news. The good news is the house is clean. The bad news is your phone's tapped."

Ruggiero could barely contain his relief. "I figured that!" he gushed. "I knew it, I knew it! Thank God I watched myself on that fuckin' phone. Them motherfuckers. *Fuck them!*"

Bruce Mouw allowed himself a small smile. Giving up the wiretap was not much of a sacrifice. The bug was what counted. Eventually it would provide probable cause to attempt to place a bug in Castellano's great house on the hill.

One bit of intelligence gleaned from this surveillance initially surprised Mouw. For all his bluster, John Gotti was deathly afraid of Castellano. When Gotti was summoned to a meeting with the boss, Mouw remembered, he returned "shaking like a leaf." And when one of these summonses occurred, usually out of the blue, Gotti would be ready to jump out of his skin. "Now what's going on? Am I in trouble again?"

Upon reflection, though, Mouw realized that Gotti had every reason to be terrified of Castellano. However tough the Bergin crew was, it was no match for the work crews that answered to Paul Castellano. For all of his desire to wrap himself in the mantle of a successful businessman, Castellano still commanded a huge army of stone killers like Tommy Bilotti, Frank DeCicco, Roy DeMeo, Nino Gaggi, a violent Irish gang called the Westies in Manhattan that Castellano used for off-the-record hits—and, of course, Sammy Gravano. But at this juncture, Sammy the Bull was nowhere on Mouw's radar screen. In Ruggiero's endless chitchat about the family, he had never once mentioned Sammy.

"At that time—in '82, '83—I was a million miles away from the Bergin crew," Sammy said. "I wasn't into drugs, into hijacking, heists, bookmaking. I was in construction. John's people, Angelo, don't know nothing about construction. I knew John did a lot of hits for Paul and he knew I did them, too. But you don't talk about them. Like Toddo Aurello once said, 'You do a hit, it's over and done with. You talk about it and you're doing it again. And it could wind up on tape.'"

Despite all the distractions of the Plaza Suite tax case, Sammy continued to broaden his construction interests. Besides the plumbing and drywall companies and his hardwood flooring and carpeting firm, he had launched a painting company. In much the same way that the Gambino family controlled Local 282 of the Teamsters, the Lucchese family controlled District Council 9 of the International Brotherhood of Painters and Allied Trades. "What I do," Sammy said, "is I get Dino, who is a guy with the Lucchese people, to go and bid the painting contracts for me. Dino gets the job and I get half the profits."

And Sammy also moved into steel erection for buildings. A relatively small company, Gem Steel, was run by an entrepreneur named Joseph Polito, "a decent guy, a cool guy." Polito's chief engineer was Mario Mastromarino. "Mario worked in steel all his life, really a top guy in his field, recognized and respected. Me and Louie Milito know Mario for a hundred years from the neighborhood. And he approaches us and asks if we could help Gem on some subcontract. And we did. He comes back and says how happy Joe Polito is and could we help out on another job he's bidding for.

"So eventually me and Louie sit down with Joe and we tell him, 'Look, you got a couple of favors from us and it benefited you pretty good. You're not dealing with morons here and every once in a while you got to pass something back.' Joe Polito is no fool. 'OK, wonderful,' he says."

The kickbacks Sammy received for steering subcontracts to Gem, resolving union problems, were not huge, averaging $15,000 or $20,000. But Sammy was content to do everything he could to engender Gem Steel's growth. He had much grander plans down the line.

Nor was that all. He would become the consultant to a fledging concrete-pouring company called Marathon. Its president, of all people, was the son of Sammy's first hit, Joe Colucci.

Concrete pouring was a cash cow and Sammy wanted in. Not a single load of concrete was poured for any contract worth more than $2 million—which is to say, every major building project in New York City—without the assent of four of the five families. Only the Bonanno family, in disgrace because of endemic heroin trafficking at the highest levels and no longer with a seat on the commission, was out of the picture.

The point man was a member of the Colombo family, Ralph Scopo, who was president and business manager for the Local District Council of the Cement and Concrete Workers Union. And, of course, there were the Teamsters. Certain concrete-pouring contractors were allowed to be part of what was called "the Concrete Club." Each of the families controlled one or more of these companies. It was the only way they could avoid sudden union problems or cutoffs in concrete deliveries. In return, there was a kickback of two percent for every contract over $2 million. With Sammy on board, Marathon was now in the club, although being the new boy on the block and still small, the amount of work it could expect was then limited.

The way the system worked was monopoly capitalism in its purest form. When bids were solicited for a project, the families decided which of the companies was up for the contract. Once the price had been determined, the other companies in the club were advised accordingly and instructed to put in higher bids.

In Manhattan, a lion's share of concrete pouring went to two companies owned by a man named Edward J. Halloran. As a result, the cost of a cubic yard of poured concrete rose to $85, the highest in the nation. Ironically, Halloran also owned a hotel on Manhattan's Lexington Avenue where the Justice Department had negotiated a special rate for its attorneys, and where John Gotti carried on many of his late-night trysts.

The reckless greed of the Concrete Club gnawed at Sammy. "It was obvious," he said. "If one of them gets a contract for, say, thirteen million, the next thing you know, after he knows he's got it, he jacks up the whole thing before it's over to a sixteen- or seventeen-million-dollar job. Now he's increased the cost thirty-three percent. So our greed is compounded by the greed of them so-called legitimate guys. They figure the families will be happy. They're still getting their two percent, only it's more now. And where are the general contractors, the developers, the builders going to go? It's a Catch-22 for them. They'll go along to the extent that it's within reason, where nobody gets really hurt, live and let live. Everything is passed on. The guy who pays in the end is the guy buying his condo and leasing prime office space. I think only one developer, Sam LeFrak, said the hell with this and went over to Jersey. But when you're just ripping them off and shaking them down that way, it gets to be another story, and eventually that was what happened. It blew up in their faces."

Sammy had witnessed similar greed with the unions. "I'm in the drywall business," he said. "But there was a time when there wasn't drywall. It was plaster. Understand, we use the unions as weapons. The only time we give a union an order is when a general contractor gets out of line. We don't control wages and bullshit like that. The plasterers' union got to be prima donnas. They were getting, like, five hundred a week way back. In comes drywall, Sheetrock. And the plaster went down to zip. Who the fuck uses plaster anymore?

"Look at the dockworkers. Tony Scotto was in charge of the local. He's a *capo* in the Gambino family only because of his father-in-law, Tough Tony, who ran it before him. He's like royalty in the family. His wife's uncle was the Mad Hatter himself, the boss of the family before Carlo. But Scotto ain't a tough guy. He lets that union go crazy. You want to unload a ship? You need forty-eight different people standing around giving orders at top wages. You got a guy on the dock for one hour? Well, you got to pay him all day. What happened is the big shipping companies went to alternate places, to Texas, Baltimore, Jersey, Philly, you name it.

"Now on the concrete, I was with Paul one time and he was asking me what I thought. I told him we were pushing too far with this. It was too much of a lock. It's not one job, two jobs, ten jobs. It's everything in the city. Every major project in the city of New York, one hundred percent controlled by us. And the prices keep getting inflated. The bubble is going to pop. Paul was a brilliant business guy. He already foresaw a lot of these things. He was basically agreeing with me, but he was saying that four families were involved, the whole commission, and he had to go with the flow. The money was rolling in. It had got to a point where it was so big, even Paul couldn't control it."

It was because of his involvement in construction, with its carefully calibrated division of spoils, that Sammy himself came close to being the object of a sanctioned Cosa Nostra hit.

Sammy and Eddie Garafola, in partnership with Joe Madonia, the original owner of Ace Partitions, continued to get most of their drywall subcontracts from Louie DiBono, a soldier in the crew of the Gambino family *capo,* Pat Conte.

When DiBono fell some $200,000 in arrears for monies due Ace, Sammy dispatched Madonia, an experienced drywall man who was not in the mob, for payment. It never occurred to Sammy that there would be a problem. DiBono, after all,

was a friend of ours, like Sammy. Financial trust
and honesty were an unquestioned given.

But Madonia returned empty-handed. DiBono
had claimed that only $50,000 was due, that there
had been a lot of back-work charges because
he had to bring in other drywall firms to redo
inferior performances by Ace Partitions. Madonia
said that DiBono produced documents to support
his position and that they were phony. Sammy's
back went up at once. If there was one thing he
insisted upon, however a job was obtained, it was
that the work had to be top-of-the-line. "It's clear
he's robbing us," Madonia said.

Sammy, with Garafola and Madonia, confronted
DiBono in his office. DiBono had a lawyer and an
accountant present. Waving assorted papers, he
began a labored explanation of how the figure
owed Ace Partitions had been arrived at.

After listening for a few minutes, barely able to
contain himself, Sammy finally ordered Madonia,
Garafola, and DiBono's representatives out of the
office. Then, leaning toward DiBono, his voice
choking with rage, he said, "Shove the papers up
your ass, you fat fuck. What do you think we are,
suckers? Don't try robbing me. There's no way
you'll ever get to enjoy the money. I'll scatter your
brains all over the wall."

DiBono shrank back. "Sammy, we'll work this
out."

Sammy stormed out of the office.

DiBono immediately contacted Conte. He told his *capo* that Sammy had grabbed him and raised his fist, that Sammy had threatened to whack him out. He wanted Conte to go to Paul Castellano and get permission to have Sammy killed. What DiBono said Sammy had done was unpardonable. It was a fundamental tenet of Cosa Nostra that one made member could never raise his hands against another. What's more, said DiBono, the charges Sammy had lodged against him were spurious.

Almost at once Castellano ordered a sit-down. Sammy knew he was in deep trouble. To make matters worse, Pat Conte was a Castellano favorite. When Castellano had sought to bring Dial's poultry products into the supermarket chains, Conte had played a key role in paving the way.

Sammy told Frank DeCicco that he had let his temper get the best of him, but the truth was, he didn't regret it. "Look," DeCicco counseled, "there was only the two of you. It's your word against his. He says one thing, you say the other. You deny it. Who can prove anything?"

"Maybe you're right," Sammy said. He respected DeCicco, and the more he thought about it, the more it seemed to be really good advice.

The meeting was scheduled to be held in the back of a Staten Island diner. At least, Sammy figured, nothing would happen there. He took

Eddie Garafola with him. But when they arrived, nobody was around.

"Then I saw this black Lincoln pull up with tinted windows, so you can't see in. Tommy Bilotti steps out of the Lincoln. He tells me the appointment has been changed. It's going to be in the basement of some house. 'Bring your brother-in-law,' Tommy said.

"Now I can't help wondering if I'm going to come out of this fucking meeting. But I went. And I'm taking Frankie's advice very seriously."

Castellano sat at the head of the table. Neil Dellacroce was there, as well as the white-haired *consigliere,* Joe N. Gallo. Tommy Bilotti took his place. Frank DeCicco was present as well. Sammy saw DiBono sitting next to Conte.

"This fat fuck, Louie DiBono," Sammy remembered, "was down there at the other end, smoking a fucking big cigar and smirking and laughing, like he's saying to me, 'Now I got you by the balls.'

Paul Castellano addressed Sammy. He said that grave accusations had been made by "a friend of ours." Sammy had raised his hands against him. Sammy had threatened to kill him. Was this true?

"I looked at DiBono, that smirk on his face, waiting to hear me whimper out of this, to dog it, lie. Probably everybody at the table was expecting something like that. I thought to myself, If I do that, nobody's going to know the truth. I said to myself, Fuck this. Whether I die or not I don't give a flying fuck no more. I forgot Frankie's advice. I'm not giving this guy the satisfaction.

"I went into a fucking frenzy. I just exploded. I stood up and I was yelling, 'Yes, it's true. This fat scumbag was robbing me. He was robbing the family.' I explained how he was cheating on all the paperwork. He deserved to die. I said, 'Paul, give me the permission and I'll kill him right here and now.'"

There was total silence at the table, as if no one could actually believe their ears. Sammy saw Castellano pale, possibly at the thought of a hit taking place right in front of him. Conte's lips appeared to be moving, but no words were coming out. DiBono stared at Sammy, wide-eyed. The smirk had disappeared.

Sammy knew that Neil Dellacroce was a hoodlum of the old school. But that was about the extent of it. On occasion, he had gone to Dellacroce's club, the Ravenite, on Mulberry Street in Little Italy, to deliver a message from Toddo. Once or twice he had stayed on to play pinochle with the underboss.

Suddenly, his face flushed with anger, Dellacroce pointed toward Sammy and bellowed, "Here's a guy who's designing his death right now. But I want to tell you one thing. I listened and he's speaking the fucking truth. He ain't lying, and he could lie and try and get out of this. Maybe he did wrong, but he's right. This other one is a disgrace to our life."

Finally, Castellano, having recovered from his initial astonishment at Sammy's outburst, spoke up. "All right, let's take it easy." In the face-saving discussion that followed, it was decided that both sides were equally guilty of wrongdoing. It was put down as a misunderstanding all around. Sammy and DiBono were to end their business relationship. They were to shake hands and that would be it.

When Castellano demanded Sammy's promise that he would obey this edict, Sammy said, "Paul, I give you my word that I'm not going to hurt him."

Turning to the shaken DiBono, Castellano said, "I want your word, too." But before DiBono could reply, Sammy broke in. "Paul, I don't think there's any worry about him hurting me."

News of what had occurred spread throughout the family. No one could recall anything remotely like it ever happening before. The word was that Sammy was on the spot and he had the balls to shoot it out. He didn't even try to hide threatening DiBono. Wiseguys laughed at the thought of how Paul Castellano's knees must have been knocking under the table when Sammy wanted to whack out DiBono right in front of him. If there were any lingering doubts that Sammy was both a racketeer *and* a gangster, they vanished.

At the Bergin Hunt and Fish Social Club, an amazed John Gotti heard about it—and how his mentor, Neil Dellacroce, had stood up for Sammy the Bull.

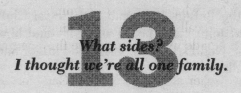

13

What sides?
I thought we're all one family.

BASED LARGELY ON EVIDENCE GATHERED FROM THE microphone in Angelo Ruggiero's dinette, court authorization was obtained for a Title III bug to be placed in Castellano's Todt Hill residence.

It was a daunting prospect. Not only was the mansion in a security-conscious neighborhood of million-dollar-plus homes with no parking allowed on the streets, but it was protected by the most modern alarm system, monitored by a security company minutes away that was run by a private investigator who occasionally replaced Tommy Bilotti as Castellano's driver when Bilotti was otherwise occupied. Beyond this, there were closed-circuit cameras, window sensors, sophisticated locks, watchdogs, and floodlit grounds at night.

When Jim Kallstrom told his two top agents on the special operations team, John Kravec and Jim

Cantamesa, what their next assignment was going to be, he recalls Kravec wisecracking, "A piece of cake. When do we do it? After we finish wiring the Vatican?"

Two other agents on Mouw's Gambino squad, assigned to keep tabs on Castellano, would later publish a book in which they describe participating in a derring-do midnight break-in to place the bug, complete with blackened faces and black clothes, knocking out the watchdogs with drugged meat, and bypassing the alarm system with only seconds to spare before it went off.

In fact, none of this happened. Kallstrom's team spent weeks poring over various scenarios. Blueprints of the mansion were acquired. Informants solved the problem of where to place a bug in a house with seventeen rooms. Big Paul usually conducted his mob business gatherings at a long table at one end of his vast kitchen, presumably comforted, as a former butcher, by the proximity of his cherished meat lockers.

Finally, a decision was reached that the security obstacles were too great for a break-in. In addition, surveillance showed that there was hardly a predictable moment when someone living in the mansion wasn't there. A far more simple, direct approach, just as daring in its own way, was settled on. The bug was installed in broad daylight one afternoon in mid-March 1983, under the very eyes of Tommy Bilotti.

Although many details of precisely how it was done remain classified, the key was Castellano's television sets. According to the memoirs of Jules Bonavolonta, who was then chief of the organized-crime squads in the FBI's New York office, Castellano's home TV reception began to suffer intermittent interruptions. In frustration, he had Bilotti arrange for a service call. On the day of the appointment, Castellano had to leave for a Wall Street lunch with his financial advisers. He instructed Bilotti to shadow the serviceman everywhere he went.

The serviceman was Jim Cantamesa. Down the street, in the guise of a telephone company worker, John Kravec had clamped his way up a pole. The two agents were connected by wireless radio.

Bilotti showed Cantamesa all the sets in the mansion. None of them were working properly. At last they got to one in the kitchen on a shelf by the table. "Uh-uh," Cantamesa said, pointing to the baseboard, "see all those cobwebs there, sir?"

"Yeah?"

"They can screw up an electrical connection like you wouldn't believe."

Bilotti appeared dumbstruck by this revelation. "No shit. So what you gotta do?"

Cantamesa explained that the first thing to do was to clean out the cobwebs and next to examine the wiring in the immediate vicinity to ascertain whether it should be replaced. Producing wires with alligator clips, he said, "I can jump over the bad section here like this." Kravec on the pole immediately eliminated the TV signal interference.

"Unbelievable," Bilotti said. "Fucking cobwebs. Who fucking knew?"

Cantamesa was careful to ask Bilotti if he wanted him to take care of the problem and Bilotti urged, "Yeah, yeah, do what you gotta do."

Once the bug was installed, transmissions from it were relayed by repeaters to a rented room in a warehouse down the hill, where a listening post had been prepared. But all that was being received were broadcasts from an all-news radio station. Two technicians from foreign counterintelligence in Washington were called in. They brought equipment that even Kallstrom's team was not privy to. For about an hour, they fiddled with dials and exotic antennae until suddenly Paul Castellano's voice was heard saying, "There any more of that pie left, Gloria?"

"Gloria" was Gloria Olarte, the Castellanos' live-in Colombian maid. The book subsequently written by the two Gambino squad agents about Castellano had not been authorized by Washington, which may have hastened their departure from the bureau. Among its more sensational revelations was not only that Gloria was Big Paul's mistress, but that the sixty-eight-year-old boss was impotent and had arranged for a penile implant to consummate their affair. Intimate details of

Castellano's explanation to her of the procedure were published. "The rod goes in," he was overheard saying, "and then, *zhup*, it works just like a . . . like a gooseneck lamp."

Sammy knew about Gloria. He had been at the mansion one afternoon with Frank DeCicco when Castellano was angrily complaining that FBI agents had approached her to provide information about him. "I said, 'Paul, do you want me to take her out?' and he gives me this look. 'Take Gloria out?' he said and I said, 'Yeah, if you're worried about her, let's get rid of her.'

"Right away, Frankie started kicking me under the table. My leg was black and blue for a week. So I said, 'Paul, it was just a thought in case you need me.'

"After we left, Frankie says, 'Are you nuts?'

"'Why, what's the matter?'

"'He loves this girl. He's having an affair with her. He's gone berserk over this fucking broad.'

"I said, '*Gloria?*'

"He said, 'Yeah, Gloria. He'll kill me and he'll kill you before he kills her. Are you crazy, or what?'

"I told Frankie, 'How was I supposed to know?' This Gloria was ugly as sin. She was fucking atrocious. She could hardly speak English. I couldn't understand it. I mean, a guy like Paul, who's got a ton of money. So get a gorgeous-looking broad, buy a little place for her, keep her tucked away and do what you want. It don't mean nothing. Who could figure he's going to find the ugliest one in the world and do what he was doing right in front of his own wife under the same roof? *Unbelievable!* And his wife, Nina, was a wonderful woman. Like you would want your mother to be."

Years later, when Sammy learned about the penile implant, he wasn't that surprised. He recalled a time when Castellano had gone to Florida with Tommy Bilotti to avoid a subpoena. Castellano would call in every night to a public phone in a Staten Island pharmacy. One day a son of Castellano's contacted Sammy and told him, "My father wants to speak to you." On the phone, Castellano said that he wanted an update on some construction projects. Could Sammy fly down just for a day? But the day stretched into three days, then four. Castellano rarely ventured out of the hotel suite he and Bilotti—and now Sammy—were sharing, and Sammy was getting stir-crazy.

After Castellano had retired for the night, Sammy said to Bilotti, "Let's go out for a couple of drinks. Not for long."

"No, Sammy, we can't. What if, God forbid, something happens?"

"I think about this for a second," Sammy remembered, "and I said, 'You're right, Tommy. We're like security, I guess. We got to stay here.' So we're fucked. I open up the Yellow Pages and there's all these escort services. I called one of them up and told them to send over two young girls, early twenties, blond, blue eyes. Tommy's a little leery, but I said we're in our part of the suite, how's Paul going to know?

"Sure enough, these two hookers come in, knockouts, really nice, sharp. When we're finished, I start thinking about Paul. 'Listen,' I said to the girl I was with, 'my uncle's in the next room. I want you to knock on the door, don't ask him no questions, don't ask for no money, don't ask him nothing. Just go in there and do whatever he wants you to do.' I think she wanted fifty dollars, so I gave her a hundred to make sure everything goes right. Now Tommy's in a panic. What if Paul takes offense? What if he does this, what if he does that? I said, 'I'll take the weight. If he don't want her, he'll throw her out. He wants to get mad, he'll get mad at me because I did it.'

"This girl knocks on the door. It opens. She's standing there. All of a sudden, I see his hand come out and grab her by the wrist and she goes in. I figured, so far, so good. He didn't throw her out. About thirty minutes passed before she comes out. 'How'd it go?' I asked. 'Did he say anything?'

"'No. He just took my arm and went back in bed and laid down. But he never got it up. I did everything I could. I guess he wasn't too excited. Then he said, "You can leave."'

"I said, 'That's it?'

"'That's it,' she said. Now I'm thinking, my God, I'm in trouble. I'm going to get my ass chewed out

big-time for sending in a hooker. The weird part was
that when we all went down for breakfast in the
morning, Paul never said one fucking word. It was like
it didn't happen. Afterward, Tommy gave me a little
hint that maybe Paul had a problem and to forget it.

"Personally, I thought it was nauseating for the
agents to put all that stuff in their book. Paul was
long gone by then, but it was humiliating to the
man's memory."

Although Paul Castellano had run the most powerful Cosa Nostra family in the nation for seven years,
since 1976 he had remained practically unknown to
the public at large and seemingly immune to prosecution. But now the layers of insulation he had
enjoyed were beginning to fray.

The Gambino squad agents made no attempt
to hide their physical surveillance.

Then, quite apart from the squad, just as Kallstrom's team was looking at various ways to bug
Castellano's house, a combined federal, state, and
city task force was zeroing in on a huge auto theft
ring headed up by a family soldier named Roy
DeMeo. DeMeo's *capo* was Nino Gaggi, in whose
house Castellano had been officially confirmed as
the new family boss while Dellacroce settled for
his old role as underboss.

Sammy knew DeMeo very well. "Roy was a
tremendous earner and he was as dangerous as you

can get," he said. "Paul used him for a lot of hits, on and off the record. I was in a diner with him once talking about stolen cars. There was a whole bunch of senior citizens eating in there, minding their own business. All of a sudden, for no reason at all, right in the middle of our conversation, he says that with a couple of nine millimeters, he could blow them all away before they knew what was happening. I remember thinking, I've killed people myself. But a roomful of senior citizens? What kind of insanity is this?"

During one nine-month period, DeMeo's ring shipped 351 stolen vehicles to the Middle East, principally to Kuwait, at an average profit per car of $5,000. Castellano, of course, knew few of the details of how the ring operated—or about the twenty-five murders associated with it. Stealing cars was beneath him. But he didn't turn his back on the money. DeMeo handed over roughly $20,000 a week to his *capo*, Gaggi, who every Sunday would then deliver an indeterminate amount of cash— "wads of hundred-dollar bills"—to Todt Hill. Although the Gambino squad was after much bigger game, this was just the kind of RICO case that G. Robert Blakey had envisioned—DeMeo a participating member of a criminal enterprise and Castellano the overall head of that enterprise who had reaped illicit proceeds from a pattern of racketeering, whether or not he was personally involved in it.

Castellano was perfectly aware of the pitfalls.

To make matters worse, from his standpoint, DeMeo had also become a heavy dealer *and* user of cocaine. His behavior was increasingly erratic. This made him even more dangerous.

"Then Frankie DeCicco told me that Paul had ordered a hit on Roy. Frankie's crew was given the contract. They couldn't get to him, so Frankie used two guys who were with Roy. He told them that this was what the boss wanted and they did it.

"I understood why Frankie tipped me when I was up seeing Paul a day or two afterward. He had me sit down. That girl, Gloria, got me coffee, and Paul threw down a newspaper in front of me. It was open to a page. 'Here, read this,' he said, walking all around. The story was about Roy DeMeo being found in the trunk of a car.

"'What do you think of that?' he said. He don't know that I know that he gave the order. He's being devious. He wants to see my feelings. Like maybe I would say, 'Hey, Roy was my best friend. I'm going to get even with whoever the fuck did this.' He's trying to gauge my reaction.

"So what I did as soon as I got done reading the article, I looked at him and said, 'Paul, if you're mad, I'm mad. If you ain't mad,' I said, putting the paper aside, 'I don't give a fuck.'

"He looked at me and said, 'Oh, all right. You want something else with the coffee?' Those were his exact words and it was over and done with. I guess he was happy with that answer."

• • •

Far more serious clouds hovered on Castellano's horizon.

In August 1983, about six months after DeMeo's murder, four months after Big Paul's kitchen was bugged, the Gambino squad arrested Angelo Ruggiero, Gene Gotti, John Carneglia, and eight other men associated with the Bergin crew for heroin racketeering. For the first time, it was revealed that much of the evidence was obtained via the bug in Ruggiero's Cedarhurst home.

Since death was the family's official position on drug-dealing, the garrulous, hulking Ruggiero took the only option available to him. Through John Gotti and Neil Dellacroce, he sent messages denying everything. It was a bullshit case, he insisted. The feds didn't really have anything on him. He even went so far as to say that if the FBI had tapes, it wasn't his voice on them. It was all a sham, a frame. He wasn't into drugs. The feds were just trying to tie him in with his late brother, Sal.

Paul Castellano elected to proceed with some caution. This case involved not one or two renegade soldiers but for all practical purposes the entire Bergin crew—one of the family's key work crews—with the notable exception, so far, of its acting *capo,* John Gotti. He could break John down to a soldier on the grounds that he had failed to control the crew and disband what was left of it. But there was Neil Dellacroce to consider.

Dellacroce had not displayed the slightest sign of disloyalty to the precepts of Cosa Nostra. Still, there was a lingering uncertainty in Castellano's head about Dellacroce. As boss and underboss, their relationship was unusual. They had little in common. If Paul was into white-collar organized crime, Neil was his blue-collar hoodlum equivalent. The truth was that Paul had accepted Neil as underboss simply to smooth over a potentially tense confrontation that might have prevented his coronation as boss. He knew that Dellacroce was an immensely popular figure in the family and that not only was John Gotti extremely close to him but Ruggiero was his nephew.

Castellano never hesitated to employ violence when it served his immediate purpose. He was not, however, as Sammy said, an instinctive gangster. To back the Bergin crew into a corner was to invite civil war. Castellano had seen how persistent blood-soaked warfare in the Colombo family, beginning with the assassination of Joe Colombo and continuing on through the lengthy imprisonment of Carmine Persico, was tearing that family apart. At this stage of his life, it was the last thing Castellano desired. He loved the money being boss brought him, but he had begun to detest the job itself. And, of course, he had no idea that the electronic surveillance of Ruggiero had led to the bug in his own residence.

Dellacroce, playing for time on behalf of his nephew as well as Gotti, provided Paul with a face-saving way out. "Look," Neil told him, "sooner or later the government's got to turn over them tapes. Let's see what's on them."

Then the Gambino squad's Bruce Mouw learned that Ruggiero had already started playing another high-stakes card. At the request of the FBI's Colombo squad, Jim Kallstrom's team had bugged a table in a Brooklyn restaurant where the family's acting boss in the absence of Persico, Gennaro (Gerry Lang) Langella, and one of his top captains, Dominick (Donnie Shacks) Montemarano, regularly met.

One memorable night Angelo Ruggiero joined them. Lang and Shacks were furious about $50,000 due them in extortion money on a construction project, which Paul Castellano had convinced the Cosa Nostra commission to nullify. Ruggiero seized the moment. He said his uncle was "disgusted" with Castellano's construction interests. "I can't believe it," he quoted Dellacroce as saying. "That's all he talks about. Money, money, money."

Big trouble was brewing between his uncle and Castellano, said Ruggiero. "I think Paul's looking to whack Neil." He said that he had told Dellacroce, "Why don't you just do it and forget about it? Go in and fucking smoke him!"

Gerry Lang interjected to Donnie Shacks,

"What did I say, Donnie, after the holidays, what would happen?"

"That Neil and Johnny Gotti will die."

"It's getting worse and worse, too," Ruggiero said bitterly. "Paul don't know what it's like to be on the street without a quarter in your pocket."

"He ain't gonna get away with it no more," Lang said. "I tell you, Ange, somebody's gonna . . ."

Before Lang could finish, Ruggiero said, "I know. Believe me, Gerry, I know."

Listening to this, Bruce Mouw remarked to Kallstrom, "I don't think we're the only problem Paul has to worry about."

"I liked Angelo," Sammy said. "He had a lot of balls. Not too much in the brains department. But he seemed then like an up-front guy. He caused a lot of people a lot of heartaches with his mistakes, his actions, everything he was doing. He was crude, but he was funny with his crudeness. He could make you laugh. So I kind of liked him.

"I didn't know till later that the bug on him gave the government the OK, the right legally, to bug Paul's house. It was Angie's big mouth. I mean, he's caught on tape all over the fucking place. His tapes, the tape with Gerry Lang and Donnie Shacks. You name it and Angie's on tape. And always talking about stuff that he ain't supposed to be even mentioning to nobody.

"We find out about the tapes on Angie when he was arrested. And they eventually would become a major fucking problem. Ultimately, people would say these tapes and what was on them probably led to Paul's downfall. But what really led to it was also a lot of things he was doing that people in the family were against, and when the time came, when it came down to the wire, this was why me and Frankie DeCicco and other guys went along with it. Right then, though, Angie's tapes had nothing to do with me whatsoever. I was never at Angie's house. I'm not on any of his tapes in any way, shape or form. That was all Angie's problem. John Gotti's problem. And Paul's."

Meanwhile, the tapes from the bug near Castellano's kitchen table kept rolling, slowly building court-admissible evidence that he was indeed the chairman and chief executive officer of a huge criminal enterprise. Among those in attendance at the table were his *consigliere,* Joe N. Gallo; Tommy Gambino; an aging trusted *capo,* Joe (Joe Piney) Armone; James (Jimmy Brown) Failla; the porno king, Robert (DiB) DiBernardo; as always, Tommy Bilotti; occasionally Frank DeCicco along with a crafty associate in his crew, Joe (Joe the German) Watts, whose father was actually a Welshman; and Joe (Joe Butch) Corrao, a *capo* who used the freezers of a Mulberry Street restaurant he owned to store cash deposits and withdrawals for his loan-sharking.

Corrao was of special interest to both Castellano and the Gambino squad. The mother-in-law of one of Corrao's soldiers was a deputy clerk in the federal court for the Southern District of New York, which included Manhattan. The bug revealed that she was regularly passing on inside information to Corrao on what investigations were under way, what indictments were being presented to grand juries.

This was how Big Paul, to his dismay, learned in early 1984 that despite the murder of Roy DeMeo, he was going to be charged in the Southern District, along with nine surviving members of DeMeo's ring, on seventy-eight counts of car theft, twenty-five killings, cocaine dealing, extortion, prostitution, and racketeering. Castellano's lawyers assured him that the charges he faced were a reach that no jury would buy, an opinion Bruce Mouw's agents privately shared. But as Mouw reminded them, "It's not our call."

Mouw was just happy that the Title III court applications he had made to bug Ruggiero, Castellano, and others were not in Manhattan, but in the Eastern District of New York, which embraced Brooklyn and Queens. And there had been no leaks.

Singularly absent on any of the tapes that recorded the gatherings around Castellano's kitchen table was Neil Dellacroce. And he was never spotted in any of the cars entering and exiting the Todt Hill mansion.

Nor was the voice of Sammy Gravano ever heard.

Although Mouw was unaware of it at the time, Castellano preferred to hash over the construction projects so dear to his heart during one-on-one meetings that did not take place at the kitchen table. Each of these meetings was usually with Robert DiBernardo, who in addition to his porno responsibilities was Paul's emmissary to Local 282 of the Teamsters; with Frank DeCicco; with a sallow little family soldier named Funzi Mosca, who served as Castellano's construction bagman and his expert on union jurisdiction—*and* with Sammy.

Still, the constant physical surveillance finally landed Sammy on Mouw's Gambino family chart. Ever cautious, Sammy had made it a point to go to Todt Hill in a car registered to Gem Steel. Neither Joe Polito, Gem's president, nor Mario Mastromarino, his chief engineer, the assumed occupants of the car, appeared to be mobbed up. Then one afternoon a car with New Jersey plates was noted. A check showed it to be registered to a horse farm. The owner of the farm was a Debra Gravano. A further check showed that she was married to Salvatore Gravano, a made member in Toddo Aurello's crew. Years ago, he had been acquitted in a double homicide case. He was currently embroiled in a tax evasion case that involved the sale of a Brooklyn disco.

That was it. He didn't seem very important.

Whenever the topic of construction came up in Castellano's kitchen, it concerned reported disputes between families, which one was entitled to what on shared projects. Paul would promptly table the discussion for further review in what were called mini-commission meetings outside the mansion, which required the attendance of the bosses involved.

Sammy was present at one of them where he got his first close-up look at Vincent (the Chin) Gigante in action. Although Fat Tony Salerno, almost a caricature of an old-line hoodlum, with his cap and baggy pants, his teeth invariably clenching the stub of a cigar, his undershirt peeking above his unbuttoned collar, was listed on FBI charts and reported in the press as the boss of the Genovese family, Gigante was the real power. Family members were under strict orders never to breathe his name in passing on his wishes. They were simply to point to their own chins when referring to him.

Some three decades earlier, he had gained fame in a bungled attempt to assassinate Frank Costello on the orders of Vito Genovese. Now, residing in his aged mother's Greenwich Village apartment, he had achieved even greater notoriety in the tabloids for wandering around neighborhood streets unwashed and unshaven, attired in pajamas, a tattered robe and worn slippers, muttering incomprehensibly to himself. Time after time, psychiatrists, both his own and court-appointed, had persuaded judges that he was mentally unfit to stand trial. As an ex–prize-fighter, they said, he had taken too many punches to the head.

"They called them mini-commission meetings," Sammy said, "because they weren't really to talk about Cosa Nostra. It was to talk about the construction business. Paul loved them because in his heart he was a businessman. There was a million bullshit problems in construction all the time. What contractor should get the bid on the concrete? Your guy got it last time out, we should get it now. How big were the teamsters in this one, the laborers in that one? Where's the jurisdiction? Who got in on the ground floor? Paul ate that up. He loved that shit.

"Paul was smart as they come. The Chin was more of a gangster, but I would say he was right up there with Paul. And he was pissed. He said that commission meetings should be just about family business, not the construction business or any other business. These things should be handled by captains and never even reach the commission level and have to be straightened out by bosses.

"The Chin said, 'What are we doing at these

fucking meetings, sitting around talking about bullshit. Talking about construction. Does that require
this? What if we were taking a surveillance? We're
going to end up paying the piper for these meetings.'

"He said that a commission meeting is meant
to take a life or to save a life. To prevent a war
between one family and another. To set overall policy. It wasn't to resolve whether you should pay this
guy five thousand because he belongs to that
union. That was for the captains to decide. Not the
bosses.

"The Chin made some good points. I had to
agree. He didn't sound so crazy to me."

After his indictment in connection with
DeMeo's murderous auto theft ring, Paul Castellano grew visibly more tense and withdrawn. "It
didn't seem like he was guilty," Sammy said, "but
that doesn't mean nothing. That don't mean you're
going to win the case, because you're not guilty.
They've got him hornswoggled into a lot of things
that he didn't know about, but he's got a problem.
He did take the money. And he was using Roy for
hits all over the place."

For Sammy, Castellano's efforts to find out
what was on the Ruggiero tapes remained a matter
that did not concern him.

Still, other incidents were causing him to take a
second look at the family boss. "There's this Eddie
Garofalo," Sammy said. "He's in demolition work

and also construction. He gets a major job and he wants it nonunion. So he comes to me and I hook him up with Louie Giardino and Local 23, which is the mason tenders. Now Garofalo is going to make a couple of hundred thousand out of this. I told him that he has to kick back one-twenty. He agrees. When the first forty comes in, I told Giardino, 'Paul gets the whole forty. He's the boss. Let him get paid first.' And that's what we do. The next forty comes in and I think, What the hell, we use the union, it's our union, and Louie is a friend of ours. Let him do what he's got to do with the union. I don't take a penny. I can wait. That whole forty goes to Louie and the union.

"Before I know it, the job's almost done. I still don't have the last payment. *My* forty. One day, I went to Eddie and said, 'When are you coming up with the fucking forty?' He said, 'I came up with it last week, Sammy. I gave it to Louie Giardino.' I was taken aback, but I don't show any reaction.

"I sent for Giardino and I said, 'Eddie gave you forty thousand last week?' and he said, 'Yeah, that's right.'

"'Well, what did you do with it? That's my fucking forty.'

"He said, 'I gave it to Paul.'

"'You gave it to Paul? Oh, all right. No problem. I'll get it off Paul.'

"So I go up to Paul's house. Frankie DeCicco's there. I'll never forget this. I went in and it's, 'Hey,

Paul, hi Frankie, how's it going, buddy?' Then I said, 'Paul, I believe Louie Giardino gave you forty last week. That was mine. You were paid and the union was paid.'

"All of a sudden, he whispers, 'Shhh!' And he looked up at the ceiling like there were a hundred bugs in it. He said, 'Don't bring it up to me anymore. I'll bring it up to you.'

"There wasn't anything more I could say. There was some talk about this and that. When I leave the house, Frankie's with me. He's laughing. 'Gee, Sammy,' he said, 'you're so fucking dumb.'

"'What the fuck you talking about, dumb?' I said.

"He said, 'This guy gets his hands on money, he never gives it back. He's never bringing up that forty again.'

"I said, 'Are you nuts, Frankie? He's got a trillion dollars. I gave him his end first. I paid the union second. I waited for my end. You mean to tell me he's keeping my end?'

"Frankie said, 'I tell you what. A steak dinner he never brings it up.' We shook hands. It's a bet.

"Well, I bought Frankie the steak dinner. I couldn't believe it. That bum kept the forty thousand. Never brought it up. Never said nothing."

It was as if Castellano, beset by the unrest brewing in his own family, was seeking allies in other families. "We had this captain up in Connecticut," Sammy said. "I think his name was Frank

Piccolo. The Genovese people hated him because he was their competition. They—Chin—come up with some concocted story about how he was a thorn in their side, a real pain in the ass. That's all I heard. They want permission from Paul to kill him and he gives it and they do kill him. For being a thorn in their side and a pain in the ass? He was doing his job for our family. He was doing what he was supposed to do. And Paul gave him up, a captain in our family, in two seconds, against every Cosa Nostra rule.

"It was a big disgrace for the family. A real black eye. You give him up in five minutes to the Genovese family? Would you want your father giving you up like that? That was a bad, bad move Paul made. A real bad move. You want to know your boss is going to fight for you tooth and nail. But now you're not so sure anymore. Probably, he thought it was a good move business-wise or racketeering-wise, but gangsters don't think like that.

"The Chin would never do that. Nobody fucked with him. He ran a tight ship. And he ain't interested in the money. He already had a ton of money. His biggest problem was where to hide it. He didn't take money from most of his captains. I guess he didn't want some captain to flip and say, 'I been giving him money.' But it was clear as a bell that he was the boss. So why was he doing his nut act? Sometimes I would think that he really was crazy and took medication when he had to be sane.

People told me he could have dirt on him that got so dirty, it wasn't like dirt, but turned kind of crusty white. Maybe our life was the only life he had. Maybe he enjoyed driving the feds nuts, which he was."

Worse yet, it became apparent to Sammy, DeCicco and others that Big Paul was lining his pockets with proceeds that should have been shared with members of the Gambino family. "He gave away the bread association, which was ours, to the Colombo family," Sammy said. "I don't know what he got on that. And he started being real greedy with the concrete. What he did was to hook up with Vinnie DiNapoli of the Genovese family—Vinnie's a tremendously smart guy and a good mover in construction—and he lets Vinnie have Biff Halloran to handle. Halloran's got Transit-Mix and Certified Industries, two of the biggest concrete suppliers in the city. We used to control Halloran. And we hear Vinnie is bringing suitcases of money to Paul.

"I remember one day Frankie DeCicco saying to me, 'Hey, Sammy, what's this? Why don't he stick somebody in our family in the middle of this thing?' We got soldiers who are broke. And he got his son-in-law to go partners with Nick Auletta of S and A, who's also with Vinnie. So when we're dictating to the Concrete Club, a lot of the jobs, most of them, went to S and A. Now I ain't a captain yet, but I was a made guy. I own a business. I'm getting small jobs, but these guys Paul made deals with are getting the bulk of everything. So that's another big mistake Paul is making. We can see he's not doing this for our family, he's doing it for his *personal* family, for his personal pocket.

"This is when the grumbling, so to speak, really starts with us and we're talking to one another. I don't know why Paul thought that we would never talk to each other. John Gotti, who's got his own thing with Paul about Angie's tapes, picks this up, of course."

At a pre-Christmas gathering at Todt Hill in 1984, Sammy arrived with the requisite envelope of money. He stayed for a short while and then said he had to leave.

Paul asked him where he was going.

"I want to stop by the Ravenite and pay my respects to Neil."

"What are you going down there for? You're on my side."

Sammy looked at Castellano and said, "What sides? I thought we're all one family. Neil's our underboss."

14

We talked about sending a crew right into Paul's house.

ACROSS AMERICA, 1985 WAS NOT A VINTAGE YEAR for Cosa Nostra.

Family bosses in Cleveland, Chicago, Milwaukee, and Kansas City were convicted and received lengthy sentences for conspiring to skim vast sums of cash from the Las Vegas casinos that they controlled through the use of Teamster pension funds. For all practical purposes, the mob was through in the city of dreams.

The hierarchy of the Patriarca family, which operated out of Boston and Providence, was convicted on multiple RICO counts ranging from loan-sharking to murder.

An all-out federal assault was launched against the Philadelphia family, which would lead to life in prison for its violent boss, Nicky Scarfo.

In New Orleans, the family had never recovered

from the conviction, for trying to bribe a federal judge, of the previously untouchable Carlos Marcello, who was often rumored to have been involved in an assassination plot against President John F. Kennedy.

In Tampa, Buffalo, Los Angeles, and San Francisco/San Jose, the families were wobbling on their last legs.

And in New York, the Manhattan U.S. attorney, Rudolph Giuliani, announced the ultimate RICO racketeering case against Cosa Nostra, charging that the commission itself was a criminal enterprise. All five local bosses or acting bosses would be indicted, among them the Colombo acting boss, Gerry Langella; Anthony (Tony Ducks) Corallo, the Lucchese boss; Phil (Rusty) Rastelli, the Bonanno boss; the Genovese boss, Anthony (Fat Tony) Salerno; the Colombo boss, Carmine Persico—and Paul Castellano.

Only Chin Gigante escaped unscathed. While he was the true power in his family, Salerno was the ostensible boss. Gigante had never been caught on tape, no one in the family had incriminated him by name on tape, and the reality was that prosecutors also faced the uninviting prospect of trying to prove that he possessed the mental competence to stand trial.

The bail set for Castellano, who was described as the de facto head of the commission, was the highest for any of the defendants—$4 million.

After a night in jail, he had no trouble meeting it. Now Paul learned for the first time that his home had been bugged. And that the Ruggiero tapes were the legal basis for it.

"Give me those tapes," Big Paul demanded of Dellacroce in June 1985. Transcripts weren't good enough. It was an article of faith among wiseguys that at worst the government doctored them and at best made transcribing errors.

But the dynamics of the play had dramatically changed. Dellacroce was terminally ill with inoperable cancer. His scheduled hospital stays for treatment allowed Kallstrom's team to place a bug in his Staten Island home that recorded the conversations.

Dellacroce tried to placate Big Paul, saying that there were many personally embarrassing moments on the tapes that Angie did not want anyone to hear. "Tell him," Castellano snapped back, "not to worry about that. All right? Don't worry. I don't want these tapes in order to get the proof I need to kill him. . . . I want these tapes because it's part of my case." He said his lawyers were trying to suppress the introduction of his own tapes in the commission trial. That was why he had to have them.

"Let me talk to him," Dellacroce said. His voice sounded weary.

In ensuing sessions between Ruggiero, Gotti, and Dellacroce, Ruggiero remained adamant about not giving up the tapes. He accused his uncle of betrayal for even entertaining the thought. He told his lawyers he would kill them if they gave up the tapes.

Listening to this, Bruce Mouw could appreciate Ruggiero's dilemma. He was truly between a rock and a hard place. Besides narcotics trafficking, Ruggiero had prattled on about commission meetings to one of his heroin dealers, who was not then a made member. If that ever got out, nothing could save him.

"You don't understand Cosa Nostra," Dellacroce said, as though addressing a recalcitrant child.

Gotti, anxious to maintain his standing with Neil, chimed in, "Ange, what does Cosa Nostra mean?"

Before Ruggiero could reply, Dellacroce said, "Cosa Nostra means that the boss is your boss." If Ruggiero didn't give up the tapes, he warned, the likely outcome would be "war" in the family. Both Gotti and Ruggiero protested that was the last thing they wanted.

The tone was quite different afterward at Gotti's club, which the FBI had finally decided to bug. "Fuck Paul," John Gotti told Angelo.

"We heard about this," Sammy said. "How Angie, never face-to-face, always through Neil, was telling Paul to go fuck himself. I don't think Neil had any great love for Paul. But first of all, Paul was the boss. You can't kill the boss. That's the rule. And Neil was for our life. I don't think if he lived, he would've let Angelo get killed. He would've probably put him on a shelf somewhere and appease Paul that way. If he let Paul kill him, there would've been a war. I think he felt, Paul's the boss, so let's 'fess up, this is the truth, this is what happened, here are the tapes. Then, if Paul followed up and said, 'Well, I want him dead,' Neil would have fought tooth and nail to save him. And if he couldn't, who knows what the fuck would've happened? But that's all hypothetical. I'm just guessing.

"I don't think John really gave a fuck about Angelo—or the tapes. I think he was looking to create a situation to capitalize on our other grievances about Paul. I think John did give a fuck when Neil died, which we all knew would happen sooner or later. He's looking ahead, and he sees trouble. Even if he isn't killed himself, all of John's sights on being Mr. Big Shot are crippled. Paul is already talking about when Neil dies, he's going to close down the Ravenite. He's going to break John down to a soldier, stick him somewhere in a crew, maybe under Joe Butch, and treat him like a fucking hard-on. Without even being dead, he's finished.

"Then there is the possibility they would move

on John and kill him. I mean, if tapes come out about drugs, even though it's a bullshit rule, what are you gonna say? I lied. That I was kidding on the fucking tapes. Hey, it's your voices. Maybe not John's, but all of his guys, including his brother, Angie and everybody. So he could be finished all around, no question about it. A lot of people would jump on the bandwagon with this stuff. Plenty of guys really disliked John. It was common knowledge that Tony Ducks hated him. On the other hand, he did have a large crew, a work crew, and you know you couldn't just disregard that. Only one thing was certain. John wasn't going nowhere without Frankie DeCicco and me."

While this imbroglio raged on, Sammy, that summer of 1985, had more immediate concerns. He was in the middle of the Plaza Suite tax evasion case and was bracing himself for a long sentence. Everyone, including his own lawyer, thought he was going to be convicted.

By then, he had a new headquarters for his construction consulting company, S & G, a two-story building on Stillwell Avenue between Bensonhurst and Coney Island. It was in his wife's name. In fact, she had bought it, and he bore the expense of remodeling it.

Debra had been successfully dabbling in real estate, and she banked everything she made. And she boasted a winning ticket in the New York State weekly lottery.

Sammy had seen her penciling in the numbers on a lottery slip and couldn't resist needling her about it. "That's only for suckers," he said. "What are the odds? Thirteen million to one?"

The next night, when he arrived home, she waved the ticket at him. "Say hello to a sucker," she said. It was worth $800,000.

Sammy held twenty-five percent of the stock in S & G. The other seventy-five percent was in Debra's name for her and the children.

She also purchased the home where they now resided, in a middle-class neighborhood in mid–Staten Island, convenient to the expressway that led to the Verrazano Bridge and Brooklyn. Once again, Sammy was responsible for the renovations, which turned out to be a massive reconstruction. On a corner plot, it was a rundown wooden-frame house. By the time Sammy was finished, it was brick, with marble floors, the original 2,300 square feet nearly doubled, with an in-ground pool in the backyard, all surrounded by a 16-foot-high wall. The union construction crews were quite cooperative.

One day in late September 1985, Robert DiBernardo brought a message to Sammy. Could he go to Queens? Angelo and John would like to see him.

"So I went," Sammy said. "But only Angie was there. He said, 'Sammy, we're gonna make a move. I'm making a move on Paul. Are you with me?' I remember him hitting himself on the chest and saying, 'I'm gonna blow this fucking mother-fucker away.'

"I'm listening, not saying anything. Then I said, 'Ange, let me ask you a couple of questions. Where's John?'

"'He's with me, Sammy. But he thought it was best for me and you to talk first.' So already John was playing the big shot.

"I said, 'Where's Frank DeCicco on this?'

"'We're gonna get to Frankie. And Frankie's gonna be with us, you'll see.'

"'So right this minute, Frankie don't know what you're telling me?'

"'No.'

"I said, 'Angie, I'm not going to tell you what my position is. But I'll tell you what I'm going to do. I'm getting in my car and I'm going to see Frankie myself and tell him about this meeting we're having now. You got any problem with that?'

"'No, no. Go ahead and tell him. Come on, Sammy, I love you and Frankie. I need you. You know I'm dead without you.'

"I went over to Frankie's house and rang the bell. For me, Frankie's an awesome guy. His crew is double mine, Toddo's. And everybody loves him. He's about six foot. Big, tough, muscular. Nose a little smashed over to one side. His father's a made guy. His uncle George right now is a captain. Another uncle's not made, but a street guy nonetheless.

"I said, 'Frankie, come on out. Let's take a walk. I got to have a long talk with you.' And I tell him what's going on, what Angie said.

"'All right, Sammy, what do you think?' he said.

"I said, 'Frankie, what do *I* think? That's why I'm here. What do *you* think? What do *we* think, together? I mean, as boss, Paul's selling the family out.'

Both Sammy and DeCicco were acutely aware that what was being suggested was practically unheard-of. There hadn't been an unsanctioned hit on a family boss in New York since Vito Genovese's botched murder attempt against Frank Costello nearly thirty years ago.

"I said, 'I guess the point is should we let John and Angie fight it out with Paul? Should we stay on the sidelines? Just sit back. Or should we join in?' We bounced everything off each other for two, three hours, whatever it was, and we concluded that we're not laid-back guys. We were really going to oppose this, or we're going to approve it. And if we approve it, we would join in.

"Then Frankie said, 'Neil's not long for this world, and Paul may go up on these cases he has. If he does, the word is he's making Tommy Gambino the acting boss and Tommy Bilotti the underboss.'

"I had heard some of this already, and it made me sick. Tommy Gambino was a fucking dressmaker. I went one time to the garment district to see him about something, and there he was, on his knees, pinning the hem on some model. 'How does that look to you, Sammy?' he said. 'Isn't it beautiful?' And Tommy Bilotti is a fucking abusive gorilla. We're going to have to answer to them? *They're* going to run our family?

"We keep talking, and finally we decide we'll back the move, be part of it. Then I told Frankie, 'The only thing I want is that you become the boss after this is over.'

"That's when Frankie said, 'John's fucking ego is too big. I could be his underboss, but he couldn't be mine. Look, he's got balls, he's got brains, he's got charisma. If we can control him to stop the gambling and all his flamboyant bullshit, he could be a good boss. Sammy, I'll tell you what. We'll give him a shot. Let him be the boss. If it don't work out within a year, me and you, we'll kill him. I'll become the boss, and you'll be my underboss, and we'll run the family right. Let's give him the shot.'

"I said, 'Frankie, if that's the way you feel, that's good enough for me,' and we shook hands on it.

"The next day, we sent for Angie, both of us, to come to Frankie's club. We told him, 'We're with you. We need a series of meetings. And when you come down again, come with John. He's no big shot here. If John don't come down for the next meeting, we retract this. We won't be with you. We'll be against you if you go ahead and make the hit.'

"John is at the next meeting. Angelo's there. I'm there. Frankie. DiB is there, too. No phones are being used. DiB is our messenger back and forth, the in-between guy. He's giving us information about Paul. Besides the porno stuff, DiB is Paul's main guy with the Teamsters, Local 282. He's involved in some of these conversations in the beginning stages. Then we exclude him 'cause he's not a hit guy. He's an earner, but he's got no crew, no strength and power.

"We ask John what about the old-timers? And John says he spoke with Joe Piney—Joe Armone— a captain who's very respected in the family. He handles the restaurant unions for Paul, the entertainment business, stuff like that. John says he's on the bandwagon. And he says Joe Piney has talked to Joe Gallo, Paul's *consigliere*. Joe Gallo is not on the bandwagon. He don't oppose it. If we do it, he'll go along. But he's not going to be part of it. In case it backfires, he's in the clear. OK, he wants to be a fox. Let him.

"Me and Frankie want to make sure that Joe Piney said what John said he said about Joe Gallo. We make an appointment with him to meet us in the basement setup Joe Watts had in his house. We want to hear this out of his mouth. Not John's mouth. Not Angie's mouth. John and Angie are there. We send Joe Watts outside and Frankie says to Joe Piney, 'You know what you're here for?'

"'Of course.'

"Frankie starts to ask Piney about Gallo, when John jumps in and Frankie said, 'Please, John. Let me do the talking now.' Then he says, 'We understand you have Joe Gallo.' 'Yeah, I spoke to him. He won't be part of the move. His name can't be mentioned. But he will go along if we take over.'"

Sammy remembered how DeCicco stared at Joe Piney Armone and asked how sure he was that Gallo wouldn't tip off Paul. The sixty-seven-year-old soft-spoken *capo* with his horn-rim glasses replied, "If he betrays us, or he backs up one inch, I'll kill him."

"Well, that was good enough for us. Frankie told him, 'We don't need you up front. We need you, after the fact, to appease some of the old-timers in the family.'"

The next consideration was the reaction of the other families.

Ruggiero reported his meeting at the Casa Storta restaurant with Gerry Lang and Donnie Shacks of the Colombos. Even more recently, they had said, "What's John waiting for? To go to his own funeral?"

Gotti boasted that he had Joe Messino, the underboss of the Bonanno family, in his hip pocket. The family was still denied a seat on the commission because of its drug-trafficking. Chances of reclaiming it would be greatly improved with Castellano out of the way.

As for the Lucchese family, Tony Ducks Corallo not only hated Castellano but was immersed in preparing his defense in the forthcoming commission trial. He had suffered a particular humiliation. The New York State Organized Crime Task Force had successfully placed a bug in the Jaguar of Corallo's driver. Corallo had not only chatted in the car about commission meetings but also made sneering comments about his fellow bosses, including Castellano.

One member of the Lucchese family, however, was a force to be reckoned with: Anthony (Gas Pipe) Casso. "Gas Pipe was tough," Sammy said. "But, like with everybody, Frankie got along good with Gas Pipe, and he sounded him out in a roundabout way how he felt about Paul and suppose he wasn't the boss no more. Frankie said Gas Pipe told him he didn't give a fuck about Paul. So we figured we had tacit approval there. If he ever tried to do anything later, we could throw that in his face."

The plotters concluded that the Genovese family was the only one that would not be approached. Big Paul and the Chin went back too far. "They were too tight," Sammy said. "They had all their big money arrangements. So we decided, 'Fuck Chin.' If it comes down to it, we'll go to war with them. And we decided when we take down Paul, we got to take out Tommy Bilotti. They must go together. Everybody agrees to that, one hundred percent."

That autumn Castellano's lawyer, James LaRossa, at last obtained the Ruggiero tapes on behalf of his client.

Upon learning this, Bruce Mouw couldn't help thinking that, with Dellacroce on the verge of death, it was kill or be killed for John Gotti.

There were more meetings.

"We had to think ahead," Sammy said. "OK, after Paul and Tommy go down, what happens? We could have to hit the mattresses. We could be in the midst of a fucking war. Let's make a list and see who else we have to take out, who we think is a potential threat, who's going to be a problem. Maybe there's some Gambino family members who ain't going to be too happy. There's Paul's personal family and Tommy Bilotti's brother, Joe. Greaseball hit guys from Sicily could be brought over. We believe there's a real good chance the Chin and the Genovese family will come at us. I mean, this is some massive guy we're taking out, with massive connections. And we're breaking the

Golden Rule. We could be looking at a war that could take eight, ten years."

On December 2, Neil Dellacroce died.

And the plotters received an unexpected bonus. Paul Castellano did not attend either his wake or his funeral. Shock reverberated through the Gambino family at this stunning breach of respect. Because of the DeMeo racketeering case, Castellano explained, he couldn't afford the bad publicity that his presence might engender. No one bought this. Holed up in his mansion every night, consumed by his own judicial problems, he appeared to have no conception of the contempt he was being held in.

"Even before this, we decided we had to split up and go underground," Sammy said. "If there was a leak, somebody had to survive and keep playing. Frankie said him and me would move into Joe Watts's basement. Joe and his wife and kids would stay upstairs. John and Angie could do what they wanted. I told Debbie I had to leave for a while, maybe for weeks, maybe months, years. Don't ask. I don't know how long. Nobody in my crew knows anything, except Old Man Paruta.

"We stayed in contact with John and Angie using certain phone numbers. But all we said was 'We'll meet at three at our friend's house,' or 'I'll see you by the park,' whatever.

"One idea was to have Joe Watts tell his wife that he wanted his house painted, and we would put up plastic on the walls and everything. Early in the morning, Joe Watts would reach out for Tommy Bilotti and have him come to the house. Joe would open the door for Tommy and walk him into this corridor. I would be by the first archway, where they would pass me. Frankie would be at the other archway. As Tommy went by me, I would step out and shoot Tommy in the head. Frankie would go up to Paul's and tell him Tommy had called. He was sick, so Frankie would be Paul's driver that day and then take him out. We kicked that around. What if Paul don't want to come out? What if this, what if that? It was too haphazard.

"We talked about sending a crew right into Paul's house. We don't mind killing the maid, if she was there, after all the heartache she caused Paul's wife. But what if his family was there? We would never kill his wife, his daughter, any of the kids around.

"We're ripping our hair out on how to put this together properly. Now the Roy DeMeo thing has started and we know that Tommy Bilotti picks up Paul, and they go to this diner in Brooklyn. They eat breakfast, they sit at the same table, near the back, near the men's room, every single day and then go to court in Manhattan.

"We conclude that Old Man Paruta, who

Frankie knows, and I vouch for with my life, could go into the diner. Paul don't know him. Tommy don't know him. Paruta could walk right past them to the men's room. In there, he would put on a ski mask and come out with two guns. They'd be sitting there, and Paruta would just blaze away. The rest of us would be outside, inside, surrounding the place—backing up Paruta."

But DeCicco reported that Castellano had sent him a message to be at a meeting. Among others who would be present, according to DeCicco, were Tommy Bilotti, the *capos* Tommy Gambino and Jimmy Brown, and a Gambino soldier named Danny Marino, who was Castellano's contact man with the Westies, the Irish gang of killers operating out of Hell's Kitchen in Manhattan. DeCicco did not know what the meeting was about.

"Frankie said it was set for around five o'clock. December sixteenth. At a steak joint down in the city called Sparks."

15

It was, like they say,
"Elementary, my dear Watson."

"THE MORE WE THOUGHT ABOUT IT, THE BETTER IT looked," Sammy said. "We concluded that nine days before Christmas, around five to six o'clock at night, in the middle of Manhattan, in the middle of the rush hour, in the middle of the crush of all them shoppers buying presents, there would be literally thousands of people on the street, hurrying this way and that. The hit would only take a few seconds, and the confusion would be in our favor. Nobody would be expecting anything like this, least of all Paul. And being able to disappear afterward in the crowds would be in our favor. So we decide this is when and where it's going to happen.

"The day before, we have a meeting in the basement of my office on Stillwell Avenue. John comes down with Angelo and the entire hit team.

John is supplying them, because it's basically his problem. If everything gets fucked-up and the team is killed, whatever it may be, why should we take down our own guys, put them at risk?

"Frankie DeCicco comes down with Joe Watts. Altogether, there are eleven of us. There are the four shooters, all from John's crew. Only one of them, John Carneglia, is a made guy. They'll be waiting for Paul at the front door to Sparks. Another guy with John, Tony Roach Rampino, will be a backup right across the street from Sparks. Sparks is on East 46th Street between Third and Second Avenue, closer to Third. Up the street towards Second as backups will be Angie, Joe Watts, and another associate with John, Iggy Alogna. John and me will be in a car on the other side of Third Avenue. If it comes down to it, I'll be the backup at that end. So we had Sparks Steak House sandwiched in.

"John, Angie, me, Frankie, and Joe Watts know who's going to be hit. John just says to everybody else that there's gonna be two guys killed. He says he ain't saying who they are yet, but it's a huge hit. John tells them that no matter what, don't run, even if there are cops around. These two guys have got to go. 'Don't worry about the cops,' he says, 'because if you run and these guys ain't dead, we'll kill you.'"

The following afternoon everyone except DeCicco gathered in a park on Manhattan's Lower

East Side. "Frankie will be inside Sparks making sure that Jimmy Brown and Danny Marino—all the people there for the meeting with Paul—don't do anything.

"Joe Watts drove me to the park. The shooters were there. The four of them wore long white trench coats and black fur Russian hats. You couldn't tell one guy from the other. I don't know whose idea that was. I guess John's. But I thought it was brilliant. Nobody would pay any attention to them. I mean, in New York you could practically walk down the street naked and nobody would notice. Besides, Sparks was only a couple of blocks from the United Nations. You saw all kinds of different clothes. But the big thing would be confusing the witnesses. 'Well, what was their weight, their height?' 'I dunno.' 'What did they look like?' 'I dunno, they all looked alike.' And these would be people who don't even know what was going on, who weren't prepared for it. All they would remember were the outfits.

"Walkie-talkies were handed out so we could communicate with one another. Then John told everybody that it was Paul and Tommy Bilotti who were going. We went over real quick what everybody's position would be. I left the park with John in a Lincoln. He owned a Lincoln, but I don't think this one was his personal car. Frankie had told us that after court, Paul was first going to go to the office of his lawyer, Jimmy LaRossa, so we figured he wouldn't get to Sparks before five o'clock.

"I don't think we said hardly anything on the way uptown. Our minds were on what was going to happen. John pulled the Lincoln in on the northwest corner of Third Avenue and 46th Street. People were swarming all around, just like we thought. I could see the canopy that said Sparks. The shooters in their white coats were already waiting by it. I could see Tony Roach across the street. The other guys up toward Second I couldn't see. The problem was our parking spot on the corner wasn't too good. We were sticking out into the crosswalk. So John said he was driving around the block again. There was the chance that Paul would arrive while we were doing this, but a cop might come over to ticket us the way we were parked and might recognize John. Besides, if it went the way we wanted, we were just observers.

"John circled the block. When we came back, the spot was a little better, and we pulled in again. A couple of minutes later, another Lincoln came up next to us and stopped for the light. The dome light was on in the Lincoln and when I looked into it, I saw Tommy Bilotti and Paul. They were talking to each other. Tommy wasn't three feet away from me. I turned and told John. I got on the walkie-talkie and warned the guys outside Sparks that Paul would be there any second. I reached for my gun. I said to John if Tommy turns toward me, I would start shooting.

"'No, no,' he said. 'We got our people in place.'

"'Yeah,' I said, 'but if Tommy sees us, maybe they won't go there.'

"Just then the light changed, and Tommy pulled up in front of Sparks. I didn't see Paul getting out, only the white coats moving toward the Lincoln. But I saw Tommy get out from the driver's side. All of a sudden, he was squatting down, like he was seeing something, which was Paul getting shot. And then I saw a white coat come up behind Tommy, and Tommy went down. The white coat was bending over him. I looked to see if any of the people on the street was doing anything. They weren't.

"John slowly drove across Third Avenue into the block where Sparks was. I looked down at Tommy Bilotti laying in a huge puddle of blood in the street and I said to John, 'He's gone.' I couldn't see Paul. John picked up speed, and we took a right down Second Avenue and headed back to Brooklyn, to Stillwell Avenue. I didn't see any of the shooters or the backup guys.

"We had the radio on, 1010 News, I think. On the way, we heard the report that there was a shooting in midtown Manhattan. And next that one of the victims was the reputed mob boss Paul Castellano. But I was in such a haze that I don't remember anything else about that ride. If you offered me two million dollars, I couldn't tell you.

"Frankie DeCicco came to my office to meet me and John. He said one of the waiters at Sparks came over to him and Jimmy Brown—Jimmy Failla—and said Paul had been shot. He said Jimmy turned white and told him he could have been in the car with Paul, and Frankie said, 'Don't worry, you wouldn't have been hurt.' And Frankie said when they left the restaurant, they ran into Tommy Gambino. Frankie told him that his uncle just got shot and to go back to his car and get the fuck out of there.

"I don't know who shot who. You don't ask. I only heard later from John that one of the shooters, Vinnie Artuso, didn't get a shot off. His gun jammed. Everything else went according to plan. It was, like they say, 'Elementary, my dear Watson.'

"We made an agreement that nobody involved in this from here on out would ever speak to each other about it at any time under any circumstances and wouldn't admit anything to anybody else in our family or in any of the other families."

The manner and place of Castellano's death catapulted him from relatively minor media interest to the sort of coverage reserved for the assassination of a head of state. Not only did the tabloids go all out— "Big Paul, Chauffeur, Take Their Last Ride"—but the *New York Times* featured it on the front page above the fold two days running.

Castellano and Bilotti were each reported to have been shot six times, each also the recipient of a coup de grâce to the head.

The city's police commissioner said that according to witnesses it was uncertain whether two or three men had carried out the gangland executions. No one remembered seeing four. What eye-witnesses most recalled was that the assassins were wearing identical Russian fur caps and long coats, variously described as either dark- or light-colored. They were then seen fleeing on foot toward Second Avenue. A witness said that one of the gunmen had been holding a walkie-talkie immediately prior to the shootings.

The head of the state's organized crime task force declared that Castellano's violent death would have required the formal approval of the bosses of the other four families in the city.

Bruce Mouw knew better, but he wasn't available for interviews.

Sammy owned a quarter interest in Caesar's East, a restaurant on 58th Street off Third Avenue, twelve blocks due north of Sparks.

"We had to have a meeting of the captains in the family," Sammy said. "Frankie DeCicco spoke to me about doing it in Caesar's East. We rushed the meeting. It was a couple of days after Paul went down. After the regular customers cleared out, all the captains met downstairs at a long table. Except Tommy Gambino, who I don't believe we called. The drivers and anybody else that was brought stayed upstairs. The only ones down there who wasn't a captain was Angelo and me. We stayed behind everybody at each side of the table. We had guns. You could say we were there for intimidating purposes. Joe Gallo was at the head of the table. Frankie and John were on each side of him. He was our *consigliere*. With Paul gone and Neil being dead, he was now in official control of the family.

"He was an old-timer, and he's playing this game with the captains. He knew what to say. He knew the ins and outs of Cosa Nostra. He told them that we had no idea who killed Paul. He said he was going to use Frankie and John to help him run the family and to investigate what happened. He told them not to discuss anything with anybody outside our family about the hit and not have any members carry guns or overreact to anything. Anything they heard or found out, they were to report it back through John Gotti or Frankie DeCicco. I think they were all shook-up. They knew we probably did it, but they didn't know for sure. And they could see Joe Gallo was not saying, 'Arm yourselves and get ready for war.' He was communicating that they would be all right.

Nobody was in trouble. Nobody was going to get hurt. We're going to have an investigation.

"Officially, this is how we went to the other families. We told them we didn't know what happened with Paul, but our family was intact. We weren't in a position that a war would break out. We had no internal trouble. And we didn't want anybody to get involved in our problems.

"A couple of weeks later, all the captains were called in again. The meeting was held in the recreation room of some big housing project in downtown Manhattan. Somebody knew somebody who gave us access to that room. Joe Gallo reiterates that we still don't know what was going on, we're still investigating. But the time had come to put our family together and vote for a new boss. Everybody has got the drift by now. It's all over the newspapers that John Gotti did the hit. And they can see the closeness of Frankie DeCicco, Sammy the Bull, Joe Piney, Joe Gallo.

"Between themselves, before Paul was hit, Frankie and John have agreed that John will be the boss and Frankie the underboss. At the meeting, Frankie gets up and votes for John Gotti. It zips right around the room. Nobody opposes. It's unanimous. At that point, John announces that Frankie will be his underboss and that Joe Gallo will stay on as *consigliere* of the family. He says he's making Angie Ruggiero the captain of his old crew. Frankie's uncle, Georgie, will replace Frankie.

"Now I'm going to be made an official captain, too. But I don't want it announced there and then. Toddo Aurello was at the meeting, and he knew I was part of this whole move. I want to give respect to Toddo and not have anything like that done while he's sitting there. I went to him afterward and I told him that if he wanted to stay on as captain of the crew, I would start up a new crew. I said, 'It's completely up to you. Whatever you want,' and he said, 'Sammy, I'm tired. I been using you as acting captain. I'd like to step down.'

"I said, 'OK. You have been like a father to me. I'll take the crew, and you'll be directly with the administration of the family.' 'That'll be great,' he said. He shakes my hand and gives me a kiss and says, 'Be careful.' I set up an appointment with John, Frankie, and Toddo, where Toddo asks official permission to step down. They give it, and that same night they make me a *capo*.

"John makes some other moves. He appoints his brother Genie a captain. And he breaks Tony Scotto down from being a captain to a soldier. Scotto had been away for payoffs and tax evasion. I happened to be at Paul's when Tony had recommended Sonny Ciccone to be acting captain to run the dockworkers in his absence. Tony had mixed in with a lot of celebrities—politicians, like that guy running for president, Eugene McCarthy, entertainers, whatever—and John wasn't too fond of him. So he replaced him officially with Sonny.

"Now was the point to see if we were gonna get retaliation from any of the other families. If there would be a war. So we sent out committees to notify them that we had elected a new boss, who our new boss and underboss was, who our new captains were. We said, 'This is our new administration. We're still investigating the Paul situation. There are no problems in our family. We don't want no sanctions against us. And we want our commission seat.'

"We got recognition from every family, including the Genovese family. Except the Genovese people said that there was a rule broken, that this situation with Paul had to be put to rest, and someday somebody would have to answer for that, if and when the commission ever got together again. We said, 'Don't worry. As soon as we find out, we will retaliate. Until then, we're just going to run our family.'

"We had our commission seat, and from what we thought, it didn't seem like there was going to be any war. There wasn't going to be anything. It had gone up as high as the commission level and there wasn't any opposition in any way, shape or form. Frankie and me had still been hiding out with guns in a safe house set up by Joe Watts. We were still tight, but after about a month, we started to loosen up somewhat. And then, about three months after this, it happened."

•   •   •

On Sunday, April 13, 1986, like politicians rallying loyal supporters, Gotti and DeCicco planned to visit the Veterans and Friends Club in Bensonhurst, the headquarters of the family's private trash collecting *capo*, Jimmy Brown Failla. Sammy also would be on hand.

"We're doing our little stops," Sammy said, "gathering power and strength, building momentum. Me and Frankie get there. We have coffee, see the boys, do a little 'Hey, how you doing? Good to see you.' And then John gives a call. He can't make it. He'll meet us in the city. Frankie tells me this. So we plan to go to the city in Frankie's Buick Electra, but we stay for a while doing our thing, talking to the boys.

"Then this made guy in the Lucchese family, Frankie Hearts—Frank Bellino—comes over and asks Frankie DeCicco, 'Hey, do you have a card for that lawyer, Alaroni?' And Frankie says, 'Yeah, I think I got it.' He looks through his wallet, all the other cards he's got in his pocket. But he doesn't have it. He says, 'You know what? It's probably in the fucking car, in the glove compartment.'

"I said, 'Frank, you want me to get it?' And he says, 'No, you'll never find it. There's a lot of shit in there. Come on,' he says to Frankie Hearts, 'I'm sure it's there,' and they both walk out of the club.

"I'm still inside the club. From what I heard later, as they walk across the street, they could see a bag under the car. A paper bag. Frankie De-Cicco joked with Frankie Hearts. 'Look at that bag. There's probably a bomb under my car.' He don't think anymore about it. It's an absolute rule in Cosa Nostra that you don't use bombs.

"Frankie DeCicco opens up the door and slides in on the passenger side and he's looking through the glove compartment while Frankie Hearts is standing there. That's when the bomb went off. Frankie Hearts goes flying backward. The blast blew his shoes off. And his toes.

"When I heard the explosion, I didn't think of a car. It was so fucking powerful, it sounded like a whole building blew up, a boiler or something. I came out of the club, and Frankie's car is in fucking flames. And there's Frankie Hearts with the blood shooting out of his feet.

"I go flying across the street. I saw Frankie DeCicco laying on the ground beside the car. With the fire, it could blow again. I tried to pull him away. I grabbed a leg, but he ain't coming with it. The leg is off. One of his arms is off. His uncle Georgie came running over with another guy, Butterass, and a guy named Oscar. They're trying to help me. I got my hand under him and my hand went right through his body to his stomach. There's no ass. His ass, his balls, *everything,* is completely blown off.

"Just then a police van comes by on patrol. It backs in and they lower the tailgate and we pick

Frankie up, holding whatever we can of him together, and put him in the van. Then they got Frankie Hearts and put him in the van and they shoot off for Victory Memorial Hospital.

"I was wearing a white shirt. I looked at my shirt, amazed. There wasn't a drop of blood on it. The force of the blast, the concussion, blew most of the fluids right out of Frankie's body. He had no blood left in him, nothing, not an ounce. I told my brother-in-law, Eddie Garafola, who had tried to help me with Frankie, to get going right away and go to John's club. I said, 'He's supposed to meet us in the city, but he's in Queens still. Tell him what happened.' Then I told him to get all my guys to meet at my place, Tali's, and to come heavy.

"Everybody who was in the club is out on the street. I looked over and I thought Danny Marino had the strangest expression on his face. He's with Jimmy Brown's crew and him and Jimmy were waiting at Sparks for Paul. But I thought then that he was just scared. I'm telling them all to go to Tali's. Jimmy Brown said he'd be at home if I needed him. Danny Marino said the same thing. A guy named Paulie, a made guy in the family, comes near me and says, 'What the fuck good are they at home?' That remark never left me. In my head, I was thinking it was true, who needed them at home? But I didn't even answer. I was too busy.

"My brother-in-law had come back and said, 'John wants to see you right now, immediately.' I got in the car and go to this restaurant in Queens, where John is. He says, 'Well, we got problems.'

"'I know,' I said. 'I don't know what the fuck is going on, but we definitely have problems.' For four months, since Sparks, we figured it was over. No problems. And here's Frankie, all at once, blown to bits. I'm still at the restaurant when one of John's people walked in and said, 'John, Frankie's dead. They said he died on the way to the hospital.' He was already dead on the street, I thought. He had nothing left in him.

"John said the only thing was to stay on full alert and see what comes next, what we could find out. It looked like there could be a war after all. Our first thought was the Genovese family. But the Chin was a real stickler for the rules of our life, and one of the rules was you don't use bombs. Nobody had pulled off a bombing in New York since the beginning of Cosa Nostra. Would Chin break this kind of rule? Was Frankie fucking some guy's wife that we didn't know about? Maybe greaseballs from Sicily did it. Paul had a lot of connections over there, and in Sicily they bomb all the time.

"When I went back to Tali's, I told everybody to keep their eyes and ears open. Report anything they picked up. But there wasn't anything. Not a peep. Everything stayed quiet. It seemed like whoever was behind this was willing to settle for the satisfaction of taking down Frankie.

"It was only a long, long time afterward that I found out what happened and that it was Frankie *and* John they were really after. The 'they' being Gas Pipe Casso from the Lucchese family and Chin Gigante. I was shocked. It goes to show how Cosa Nostra was just one double-cross after another. We had reached out and got Gas Pipe's tacit approval about Paul. Maybe Chin don't know this. But after Paul goes down, Chin grabs Gas Pipe—they had a relationship—and says, 'Well, Paul's out of the picture, let's take out John Gotti and Frankie DeCicco. It'll be a real hit parade.'

"They tell Jimmy Brown and Danny Marino what they're gonna do and that Jimmy and Danny will be appointed by the commission as a committee to run the Gambino family for Chin. Let me tell you what a stand-up guy Jimmy Brown is. If some b!ack guy walked in and said he just killed Paul Castellano and was the new boss, Jimmy would say, 'Gee, great. What do you want me to do, boss?' So basically the Genovese and Lucchese families would control our family.

"Gas Pipe was a couple of blocks away when the bomb went off. The mistake was using a couple of West Side guys, meaning they were associated with the Genovese people. I still don't know who they were or even if they're alive. One of them put the bomb under Frankie's car. The other one was on the remote control. When he sees Frankie come out of the club with Frankie Hearts, he thinks Frankie Hearts was John. Frankie Hearts has kind of the same build as John and the same grayish hair. And he presses the button. *Boom!*

"I got along good with Gas Pipe. I still like him. For him, it was business, a master Cosa Nostra double-cross scheme, nothing personal. The only thing I didn't like was the bomb. I would have more respect for him if he used a gun, according to the rules. I think the bomb was probably a devious Chin idea to make us think the Sicilians done it. I heard when my name came up, Gas Pipe said, 'Forget it. We're not gonna kill Sammy.' That would've been another mistake. If John had been in the car and they put in Jimmy Brown and Marino, I would have killed them both. They were the true betrayers. They knew what was going to happen. And then I would've gone after Gas Pipe and Chin. I don't think I could've won, but I would've fought until my death.

"Besides his toes, Frankie Hearts got mangled up a little. But he survived. That was how I found out what was going on just before the blast. I decided one thing. I used to drive myself. I was getting a driver. Not to say that joke line like in the movies, where the old boss tells his wife, 'Go start the car.' But to never leave my car alone anymore, so nobody can fuck with it."

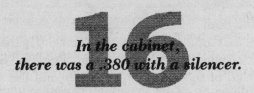

16

In the cabinet,
there was a .380 with a silencer.

THE DAY AFTER PAUL CASTELLANO AND TOMMY
Bilotti were shot, Bruce Mouw dispatched agents
on the Gambino squad to check on high-profile
family members.

Two agents, Frank Spero and Matty Tricorico,
were assigned to Frank DeCicco. Spero and Tricorico, who were born, grew up and lived in
Staten Island, had been on the squad since its
inception. Their responsibility was to keep tabs on
Staten Island residents in the family, which
included DeCicco.

They headed for DeCicco's social club on Bath
Avenue in Bensonhurst. On a street corner near
the club, they spotted DeCicco and were not surprised to observe him in animated conversation
with Jimmy Brown, Robert (DiB) DiBernardo,
and Angelo Ruggiero. What did surprise them

was the presence of Sammy Gravano. And clearly, Sammy was not merely an acolyte. From his body language, it was almost as if he were chairing the conference. While they knew Sammy by sight, he had attracted no particular investigative interest. Now, suddenly, he appeared to be a major player. For the first time, Sammy made Mouw's A-list.

But for the public at large, he was as anonymous as ever.

Not so, John Gotti.

As recently as 1984, Gotti, the would-be mob boss, retained many of the characteristics of a street thug. That year, near a bar in Queens, Romual Piecyk, a refrigerator repairman, returned from cashing his weekly paycheck and found his car blocked by Gotti's double-parked Lincoln. Furious, Piecyk started blowing his horn. A man, later identified as Frank Colletta, came out of the bar, punched him and seized the $325 sticking out of his shirt pocket. In the altercation that followed, Colletta was joined by Gotti himself, who also emerged from the bar and slapped Piecyk so hard in the face that his nose bled profusely. Gotti told him to get lost.

Piecyk found two cops and said that he had just been beaten and robbed. He led them back to the bar and pointed out Gotti and Colletta as his assailants. As Gotti was being handcuffed by one of the cops, he demanded, "Don't you know who I am?" To his evident displeasure, the cop replied, "No, and I don't care."

After being booked, Gotti and Colletta were released on bail and subsequently indicted for felony assault and theft.

After the Castellano hit, Gotti dramatically refined his act.

Hollywood churns out our myths. And for a decade, *The Godfather* epics—and the Mafia— had eclipsed westerns in popular culture to fulfill America's mythic needs. Life wasn't so simple anymore. A shoot-out at the O.K. Corral didn't seem so relevant. At the first sign of sagebrush, audiences began nodding off.

Enter the Mafia to embody and reflect our deepest anxieties, yearnings, wonderment, our imagination. What better mirrored fierce free enterprise with everyone's (shiver) life on the line, the resourcefulness of a nation ever on the move, constantly plunging into innovative and profitable technologies (say, casino gambling)? What was the difference between someone out to control private garbage collection with the judicious use of baseball bats on kneecaps and a cabal of ostensibly upright, churchgoing savings and loan officials bilking taxpayers out of billions of dollars? Who among us, having been wronged, had not fantasized about calling upon brothers in blood to wreak suitable vengeance—an ice-picked body, perhaps, trussed like a turkey, bobbing up somewhere?

The fictional *Godfather* was myth-making at its most compelling. It took an intricately structured "other" world that was in fact without the slightest hint of social redemption and reinvented it, populated not with good guys and bad guys, but with people you could root for and against. Its protagonists were flawed, not superhuman projections of good and evil, caught in destinies not of their own making. Never mind that loyalty and honor played no part in the actual Cosa Nostra. Perceived reality was what mattered. The *Godfather* saga contained everything that concerned and excited us: family, romance, betrayal, power, lust, greed, legitimacy, even salvation. And all played out on a grand stage, with death, inevitable and often violent, waiting in the wings.

The problem was that there were no nonfiction equivalents. All the media had left to contend with was the gray corporate executive image of a Paul Castellano, the visage of a dour Tony Ducks Corallo or a cigar-chomping Fat Tony Salerno, the nutty Chin Gigante, the unappetizing Carmine (Snake) Persico.

John Gotti fixed all that.

Because of the sensational nature of Castellano's execution, he became the immediate object of intense press attention when federal, state and local law enforcement let it be known that he was the prime suspect behind the murder, the new, real-life Godfather.

He rose to the occasion—and dressed for it. He looked the way Americans wanted a gangster to look. It was as if he had studied every gangster movie ever made and absorbed the lessons learned in his own persona. With his diamond pinkie ring, meticulously styled silvery hair, a healthy tan from regular sunlamp treatments, his wardrobe of $2,000 custom-made Brioni double-breasted suits and $200 handpainted ties, the tabloids were soon labeling him the Dapper Don.

Instead of skulking in the shadows, he reveled in his new celebrity. Always flashing a smile, he embraced TV cameras. He was ready with quotable quips, "Sure, I'm the boss of the family—my wife and kids." He projected a courtly manner. Making way for a female reporter, he told her, "I was brought up to hold doors open for ladies." There were breathless reports of how mobsters had lined up at a Christmas party at the Ravenite club to kiss him and pay homage. He appeared, at every opportunity, to be saying, "Yeah, I'm a gangster, but can you prove it?"

All but unknown prior to Castellano's demise, his past was dredged up. He'd been the avenger in the kidnapping death of an innocent youngster, albeit Carlo Gambino's nephew, and had taken the rap for it in manly fashion. The mysterious disappearance of the neighbor who had run over Gotti's own son evoked delicious chills. His regular solitary vigils at the boy's crypt were somberly described. Who could not sympathize with a father's pain and anguish?

There were more awed shivers when the Romual Piecyk assault case finally went to trial on March 24, 1986, some three months after Castellano was gunned down. Piecyk read the papers and by now was well aware of whom he was dealing with. On the stand, he declared in a shaken voice that he was unable to recognize anyone in the courtroom who had "punched and smacked" him. "To be perfectly honest," he insisted, "it was so long ago I don't remember." The judge had no choice but to dismiss the charges. Afterward, Piecyk offered reporters a more reasonable explanation for his memory loss. He had an extreme interest in living the rest of his life without fear.

Before the year was out, *Time* magazine had featured Gotti on its cover, accompanied by the stark line "Crime Boss" in a painting by the pop artist Andy Warhol. Till then, the only other gangster to have graced a *Time* cover, a half-century before, was Al Capone.

The Piecyk case, however, would have some unpleasant repercussions for Gotti.

Lost in the avalanche of big-league federal attacks against Cosa Nostra the year before—among them the commission case, the Bonanno family's "pizza connection" heroin trial, the Colombo family's criminal enterprise case—Gotti himself had been indicted on RICO charges.

The case had been developed by a young assistant U.S. attorney in Brooklyn named Diane Giacalone, who had grown up in Ozone Park and often walked by the Bergin Hunt and Fish Social Club, observing the unsavory characters hanging out there, on her way to and from Our Lady of Wisdom parochial school. She had won a conviction against a gang of local armored car hijackers, who she learned had tried to curry favor with the Bergin crew by passing on part of the proceeds. When she believed she had gathered enough evidence to substantiate these tributes, she proceeded against Gotti and others.

The Gambino squad was not happy. The case was too tenuous. Confident that Gotti's high-wire celebrity turn would do him in, it was looking forward to nailing him in a major—and foolproof—case. Then Mouw learned that Giacalone was threatening to reveal that one of Gotti's codefendants, Willie Boy Johnson, was a prized Gambino squad informant. She intended to use this as a club to force him to testify for her prosecution. She had learned about Willie Boy from the New York Police Department. When narcotics detectives had nabbed Willie Boy in a drug deal, in an effort to extricate himself, he said he had been an FBI source and offered to perform the same services for the cops.

The FBI attempted to dissuade Giacalone, but she remained obstinate. Finally, the Bureau stepped out of the case completely, citing "administrative and procedural differences." Johnson pleaded with Giacalone to reconsider. "I will be killed," he said. "My family will be slaughtered." At a pretrial court hearing, despite vehemently denying he had been an informer, he was held without bail and against his will placed in protective custody in a federal detention facility in New York, the Metropolitan Correctional Center.

Giacalone then made a second move that garnered big headlines. Citing clear intimidation on Gotti's part in the dismissal of the Piecyk assault case, she requested that he be denied bail and jailed so that he couldn't tamper with her witnesses. The judge agreed, and on May 19, Gotti wound up in the Metropolitan Correctional Center with Johnson.

"It was up on the ninth floor," Sammy said. "John told Willie Boy, 'You did a bad thing for all them years. But I'll forgive you. It's not the first time it happened. You can never be with us after this case. But nothing will happen to you.' Willie Boy asked John to swear on his dead son's head, and John did. And Willie Boy never did testify.

"John totally conned Willie Boy. I don't know how he fell for this, but he did. Lock, stock and barrel."

About two weeks after Gotti was taken into custody, Sammy received his first order from him to execute a hit.

"Since Frankie DeCicco's gone, John had appointed myself, Angelo the blabbermouth Ruggiero, and Joe Piney Armone to run the family. We're captains and we were all in the move against Paul. Basically, Joe Piney is half out of it. He's basically there to placate the old-timers. I go over to his house in the morning, and he's got all kinds of racetrack forms and stuff. The old man is a good man. He loves the horses. He completely adores his wife and children. But he really isn't equipped to run the family.

"One time he told me, 'I got a plan to get the press off of John's back, a diversion to get the heat off.'

"I said, 'Yeah, what?'

"He says, 'We can kill Oliver North.'

"'Who the fuck is Oliver North?'

"'You know, that soldier that caused all that trouble down in Washington.'

"'Oh, right.'

"'If we kill him,' Joe Piney says, 'there'll be so much attention over that, the public, the news media, won't pay no attention to John anymore.'

"I want to pay him respect, I don't want to embarrass the old guy. I bob and weave a little and say, 'Let me think about it for a while and we'll see.'

"That gives you an example of the thinking power he had at that time. Thank God, he never brought this up again.

"Anyway, John has limited visitation. Only his lawyers, his immediate family and his closest friend, Angie, can see him. So Angie is the messenger to communicate what John wants done. In early June, Angie came to me and said John has sent out an order to kill DiB—Robert DiBernardo. He said DiB was talking behind his back, and there were other reasons, which Angie didn't say.

"Now I have been seeing DiB a couple of times a week. We share responsibility for dealing with Bobby Sasso, who's running the Teamsters. DiB's a brilliant, wealthy guy. Paul used him directly with the unions and other business and he's in with these Jewish guys as the largest distributor of X-rated films and stuff in the country. He was one of the owners of Great Bear auto repair and tire service. But DiB is no threat. He's got no crew, no strength.

"I already have a sense of what this is about. Angelo wants to be underboss. Joe Piney had told me DiB said to Angie he had the balls to be underboss, but not the brains. If anyone should be underboss, DiB said, it should be Sammy. That didn't mean anything to me. I don't even want to discuss it with Joe Piney. I loved Frankie like a brother, and I'm sick that he's dead. I had lost the one guy whose advice I could trust. Right then, I'm not interested in the position, or even talking about it.

"I said to Angie that if DiB was saying anything, it didn't mean nothing. Just talk. DiB wasn't dangerous. I asked Angie to reach John and see if we couldn't hold up on this, and when John came out, we would discuss it. It was something we could hold up on.

"But Angie immediately responded that it had to be done. John was steaming. John's brother Genie and Genie's crew would do the hit at this house of the mother of one of the soldiers. I was to get DiB there for a meeting, and whoever was sitting behind DiB would shoot him. But the house wasn't available.

"Angie came back to me. He said John was really hot. He wanted it done right now, he wanted it done right, and he wanted me to do it. I didn't know what Angie was telling John about my reservations. I knew Angie was into DiB for two hundred and fifty thousand. I would imagine that this could've played a part in everything. But I don't know if John knew that. Maybe John had some other motives, some hidden resentment from the past. Frankie and me had a tough time even getting John to elevate DiB to captain after Paul got hit. But I never questioned that he gave the order. Obviously, sooner or later, I'm going to be talking to John myself and Angie can't get caught in fucking lies. What was I going to do? What can I do? It's an order from the boss. This was the life I chose, and the boss was the boss.

"I told Angie that DiB would be coming by my office for a construction meeting at five-thirty. He said he would be at the Burger King in Coney Island from six on. If I succeeded, I should meet him there.

"I sent the girl in my office home at five. Me, my brother-in-law, Eddie, and Old Man Paruta were there. DiB came in and said hello. I told Paruta to get him a cup of coffee. In the cabinet, there was a .380 with a silencer. Paruta took it out, walked over to DiB and shot him twice in the back of the head.

"We picked up DiB and put him in a body bag we got from the Scarpaci funeral parlor. We locked it in the back room. We cleaned up the office and Eddie drove me to meet Angie at the Burger King. I told Angie it was done. I told him I had the keys to DiB's Mercedes. He said he would meet me later at Tali's, around nine, and would arrange to get rid of the body and the car.

"Angie was at Tali's with Genie Gotti and John Carneglia, who were tight with him in junk. Frank Locascio, a captain from the Bronx, was there, too. We went back to my office. DiB was put in the trunk of Locascio's Cadillac. Some kids with Carneglia took DiB's Mercedes. I don't know what they did with the Mercedes, but Carneglia owned a car salvage yard. I have no idea what was done with DiB.

"Now Angie is also a defendant with John in the case this Giacalone is bringing. And sometime after this, Angie is in court for a hearing, and his son says something to him from where the spectators sit. The judge tells the kid to be quiet, and Angie turns around to the judge and says, 'What the fuck is this, Russia? Who the fuck are you to tell me I can't talk to my son?' The judge is in a frenzy. They go at it, and the judge remands Angie. His bail is revoked, and he's in jail with John.

"John is steaming. Blabbermouth Angie can forget being the underboss, if he ever had a chance. Through Genie Gotti, who has visitation rights, we get the word that John has settled on Joe Piney as underboss. But Genie said he told John that while Joe was a beautiful guy, a good choice to smooth things over, he can't really run the family. So John said to tell me that it's in my hands to do it, but to include Joe in everything and treat him with respect. And I do follow the proper protocol. That was when Joe Piney came up with that Oliver North thing. But basically I'm running the family for John.

•   •   •

After jury selection, Diane Giacalone's prosecution began in the middle of September 1986. Because of Gotti, a trial that normally would have been ignored by the media until a verdict had come in—and even then been worth no more than two or three paragraphs—took on a carnival atmosphere. Spectators packed the courtroom every day. So did reporters. Television crews were a constant presence.

Gotti's sartorial splendor received daily press attention. He was said to have instructed his codefendants to appear in jackets and ties. He was heard to chastise one of them for unacceptable color coordination. His apparent coolness under fire, his brash confidence in being acquitted, was most commented on. "I'm not worried," he was quoted as jauntily saying. "They got no case. It's a frame. You'll see. I'll be walking out of here."

Bruce Cutler, a hitherto minor figure in the criminal defense community, basked in Gotti's glory. He had represented Gotti in the Piecyk case, and Gotti had elected to keep him on. He appeared to fawn over his client, aping his dress. If he had a son, he told reporters, he could think of no finer role model for him than John Gotti. Bellicose, a former college wrestler, he attacked from the beginning. Brandishing the indictment in front of the jury, he bellowed that it was "rancid" and "rotten." "It makes you want to retch and vomit," he cried. He carried the sheaf of papers to a trash can and hurled it in. "This is where it belongs!"

Partway through the trial, all the bosses in the Cosa Nostra commission case being tried in federal court in Manhattan were convicted. Paul Castellano would have been one of them. They would receive sentences of a hundred years each. Asked by a reporter if this wasn't disheartening, Gotti continued to display a remarkable sangfroid. Waving a dismissive hand, he said, "That's got nothing to do with me. I'll be home soon."

The trial dragged on for nearly seven months. The verdict—not guilty—was rendered after a week's deliberation on March 13, 1987. Gotti's supporters and hangers-on cheered. Cutler hugged Gotti and kissed him.

Cutler was hailed as a defense genius.

And in the headlines the next morning, Gotti had a new trademark sobriquet: the Teflon Don.

Gotti had every reason to be nonchalant throughout the trial. And Bruce Cutler wasn't quite the genius he was cracked up to be.

Sammy had fixed a juror, and not just any juror, but one who turned out to be the jury foreman. The head of the Westies had come to Sammy and told him that he knew someone on the jury who was available for a price. "How much of a price?" Sammy asked. The answer was $120,000. Ever the negotiator, Sammy whittled it down to $60,000, payable in installments. You never knew, he figured. The guy could get sick or something.

Certain that there would be at least a hung jury, with little likelihood of a retrial, Sammy's mind was elsewhere. The news was traumatic. He was about to lose his second, and last, Luca Brasi.

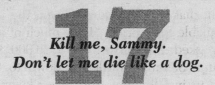

**Kill me, Sammy.
Don't let me die like a dog.**

"I LOVED THE OLD MAN, JOE PARUTA," SAMMY said. "My feeling for him went beyond any blood oath of Cosa Nostra. He was the only one during all the plotting for the Castellano hit—all the what if this, what if that—that I confided in, was able to walk with, talk with, relax with. In one second, he agreed to take down Paul and Tommy Bilotti in that diner like I asked him to before we changed the plan. He never asked me any questions if I wanted him to do something. He would take any risk. After Stymie got shot, he practically never left my side. I think about him a lot, and I never know whether to laugh or cry.

"I remember once when he brought his wife and kids to Tali's for dinner. She'd been complaining that he was always with me and never had any time for her and the children. So this was a night he was going to make up for it.

"We had a pretty decent kitchen at Tali's and one of the chef's specialities was an ice cream tart that was really delicious. So the night Joe was having his Paruta family dinner, he had left word with the chef to be sure to have plenty of them tarts available. Everything was going good until it came time for dessert and Joe asked for the tarts he'd been touting. He was told that there wasn't no tarts left. He couldn't believe it. He knew the chef was told about this dinner and the tarts he wanted. Where were the fucking tarts? The chef said he was sorry, but another guy with me, Huck—Tommy Carbonaro—a mountain of a man, had eaten all of Joe's tarts.

"Paruta was fuming, steaming. He waited till his family left Tali's, and he approached me and asked my permission to clip Huck.

"I could see he wasn't fooling. 'Why would you want to hit Huck?' I said. 'What's going on?' And he told me the story. He said, 'That fat fuck eats everything in sight. He ate all my tarts.'

"I said, 'You want to kill Huck because of some ice cream tarts?'

"'Yeah.'

"I couldn't help myself. I started laughing. 'Well,' I said, 'I ain't giving you permission.' I said, 'Come on. Ice cream tarts?'

"Finally, even Joe had to start smiling. I called

Huck over and told him he owed me his life. And we all had a drink together.

"To me, Joe never seemed to change. He always looked the same, old and decrepit, always chain-smoking. But then, after the DiB hit, his smoker's cough got worse and worse. Whatever doctor he was going to told him he should see a specialist, it could be serious. I made arrangements through doctors I knew and took him to Sloan-Kettering, the big cancer hospital in Manhattan, for tests.

"The prognosis was bad. We were all stunned. He had lung cancer, and the cancer had spread in his body. He had only a year left. The chief attending doctor pulled me aside. After acknowledging his awareness of my reputation, he admitted that he had told a lie to Paruta and his family. The old man didn't have a year to live. It was more like three months.

"The old man had his little gambling and shylock operations and he had a piece of Tali's. He was satisfied. He never asked for anything more. But I felt I had to honor him. John Gotti was still incarcerated. I sent word to him through Genie Gotti for permission to make Paruta a made guy in the family, and John approved right away.

"I personally carried his name to the other families, so there was no question who was sponsoring him. We arranged for Joe's wife and everybody to be out of his house one afternoon. I got a bunch of captains together. We assembled around Joe's bed in the smoke-filled room. He wasn't going to stop smoking now. From what the doctor said, there was now only a month or two left for him.

"I closed the bedroom door, and the ceremony started. I was giving the oath. When it came time to ask the question that was the test of the candidate's loyalty—'Would you kill for this family?'—I almost said, 'I know you did kill for this family!' And when it came time for me to prick Joe's finger for blood to mingle with burning the holy card, I realized how bad off he was. I could barely get a drop. It was a solemn ceremony. Maybe it wasn't as lavish as others I was at, but I can't remember one with more meaning of what Cosa Nostra was supposed to be. Now Joe was not only a friend of mine, but a friend of ours.

"I felt real good the next day when his wife—who was more of a sister to me than my own sisters—called and said that all of a sudden, Joe was full of new life.

"But who was kidding who? No fucking oath was stopping them cancer cells. Every time I went to visit him, I could see him getting weaker. He was like a living skeleton. He called me to his bedside. Tears were streaming down his face. He asked me to give him the dignity he was losing. He wanted to die like a man, not like this. He asked me to kill him.

"I stood there, my mouth open. How could he ask me such a thing? I couldn't even answer. 'Kill me, Sammy,' he said. 'Don't let me die like a dog.'

"Every visit, it was the same. He wouldn't let it go. 'Kill me, Sammy. Kill me, *please.*' He tried to get me to understand that a swift bullet was the best gift a true friend could give him. He couldn't stand the pain no more.

"Like every hit—even a mercy killing of a made member, which this probably was the first—you got to get permission. I sent a message with Gene Gotti to John. I prepped Genie. I tried to explain the situation the best I could. I don't know for sure what Genie told John when they discussed Joe Paruta, but John's reply was no. There was no way he would authorize a hit on a made guy under these circumstances. It was like if Paruta wasn't made, it would be all right. Wasn't that ironic?

"I brought John's decision to Joe. He did not accept it. He said, 'Fuck John, Sammy. I'm asking *you.*' He prevailed on me that our friendship was above everything. The only way I could prove I was his friend was to kill him.

"So I went against John Gotti's wishes—and it wouldn't be the last time—as to what was right. I ordered my brother-in-law, Eddie, to get a gun with a silencer. I was going to give Joe one day's notice to have his family away from the house when our friendship would be tested. Huck would be outside the house in a car. Eddie and myself would go through a back door that would be left open. We would go up to the bedroom. Eddie would help me sit the old man in a comfortable position and then join Huck in the car. I would kill my friend and stop his terrible pain and allow him dignity in death.

"It was all set. I was home waiting to be picked up by Huck and Eddie. My wife was there. The night before I had been real irritable. When Debbie mentioned this, I put her off. I said I had things on my mind. Now I stepped outside for a second, and when I came back, she said she had sad news. Eddie had just called. He said that Old Man Paruta suddenly took a turn for the worst. He was rushed to the hospital by ambulance, but died on the way. He was only fifty-nine. My man of loyalty, of heart and soul, a man of honor, was gone.

"Debbie looked at me kind of funny. She couldn't understand the smile on my face. She didn't know that the happiness I felt came from a piece of work I didn't have to do."

"I took care of his wife, Dottie, financially, like I done with Stymie's wife.

"A couple of days after the funeral, I was in my office. I was devastated, completely destroyed. In the space of a year and a half I lost Stymie, then Frankie DeCicco and now Paruta.

"Big Lou Vallario came in. He had five, six years on me. He was a big guy, about six foot two, two thirty. He was already with Toddo Aurello when I went with Toddo. So there was a long-term relationship here. After I was a captain, I got him made in the crew. He was super loyal and solid. He handled my appointments and kept me straight about what had to be done.

"He said, 'I know what you're feeling. I can't fill Stymie's shoes, or Paruta's. I wouldn't even try. But I promise I'll be there for you.'

"I said, 'I appreciate that very much.'

"Well, I thought to myself, you can't put back what happened. You got to just keep going, no matter what."

18

*I wanted my son to be legitimate,
to have nothing to do with what I did.*

FBI AGENTS FRANK SPERO AND MATTY TRICORICO
quickly established that Sammy was not the usual
wiseguy.

Members and associates of the various Gambino crews—twenty-one in all—would usually be
found lounging around on the street outside their
social clubs in apparently endless gabfests.

But whenever Spero and Tricorico stationed
themselves in the afternoon near Sammy's office on
Stillwell Avenue, they invariably saw him playing
fast-paced handball for an hour or so in a nearby
park with neighborhood teenagers. And more than
holding his own with them.

His handball partners tipped off Sammy that
he was under observation. So did the teachers at
an elementary school a couple of blocks down
from his office.

Sammy had set up his daughter, Karen, in a florist shop on Stillwell. "There was some kind of a holiday coming up," Sammy said. "Mother's Day or something. And this little kid came in and asked my daughter how much a rose was. When Karen told her, the kid started to cry and was walking out of the shop. Karen asked what was wrong, and the little girl said she didn't have that kind of money. So Karen, instead of giving her a rose, which was expensive, got a carnation and wrapped it in green tissue paper and put it in a small box with a card. For nothing.

"The kid, like kids are, told all the other kids at the school. And the next thing, Karen has grabbed me. 'Dad, there must be fifty or a hundred kids coming into the shop for carnations.' Then she told me the story. She can't give out that many. She's got a partner. I said, 'That was a nice thing you did. Tell you what. Give every one of them kids a carnation. And give me the bill. I'll pay for the kids.' Of course, this got around at the school. I think one of the teachers went and thanked Karen, and she said, 'No, it was my dad.'

"Anyways, a couple of the teachers came to me and said, 'Mr. Gravano, can we talk to you?' 'Sure, what can I do for you?' and they said, 'Nothing. We just want you to know there are people watching you. With binoculars and cameras. Is everything all right?'

"I smiled and said, 'Don't worry. I must be getting

a little on the famous side. You're not going to ask for my autograph?' They laughed and said no and started to leave. I grabbed one of them and said, 'Why are you telling me this?' She said, 'You're good for the community. You were so good to the kids. We'll never forget it.'

"I felt real good about that. After all those years, Bensonhurst was still a community. I didn't just like that, I loved it."

Spero and Tricorico immediately noticed something else about Sammy. Wiseguys were not renowned early risers. But Sammy was out of his new walled-in home on Lambert's Lane on Staten Island at 6 A.M. His driver, Louis Saccente, would pick him up. He would usually breakfast about a mile away at a diner called Dakota. He would then cross over the Verrazano Bridge and work out at a gym off the Belt Parkway in Brooklyn before arriving at his Stillwell Avenue office around ten.

To Spero and Tricorico, the office seemed to double as a social club for Sammy's crew, which enabled them through photographs and license plates to put together a fairly accurate rundown of who was in the crew. It was also obvious how much respect he was being paid, just in the way he was accompanied at lunchtime to a small Italian deli down the avenue featuring hero sandwiches.

"A lot of the scores I made, I cut up with my whole crew," Sammy said. "No other guys like me did that. As a matter of fact, John Gotti called me in one time, and he said, 'Sammy, what are you doing? All of your guys are making money, too much money.'

"I said, 'Hey, John, they've wrapped up their lives around me, twenty-four hours a day. When I'm sleeping, they're making sure I get picked up, who's gonna drop me off, where I'm supposed to be, what meetings I have to be at. They don't have a life of their own. They can't really, a lot of them, go out and earn money.'

"He said, 'No, no, Sammy. You got to keep them down. Bobby Boriello'—who's his driver and bodyguard—'I give him six hundred a week.'

"I looked at him and said, 'Six hundred a week? He picks up one tab, he's broke for the week. How can he support a family? How can he live? How can he do anything?'

"'Listen to me,' he says. 'Keep them broke. Keep them hungry. Don't make them too fat.'

"I can play Machiavellian like John—John was always quoting Machiavelli, I guess he did read him—so I just said, 'All right, yeah, that's good thinking.' But I went to Tali's that night and I think we cut up fifty thousand. I put it on the table out back. Big Louie, Huck, Eddie, this one, that one, everybody cut it up. I always took the bigger end, because I'm the boss and that was right. I'm their boss. But to leave them broke? That ain't right.

"I mean, John was caught on tape about Big Louie Vallario, who opened a club called Illusions, where the Plaza Suite used to be. John dropped in with some of his guys to make a show, and he told Louie, 'Good luck, this is what we need, places like this. Makes us look good.'

"And then on the tape, John is saying, 'This fucking bum, Louie, was nothing more than a coffee boy. He didn't have two cents to rub together. And all of a sudden now, he's opened up a million-dollar disco. This Sammy's crazy.'

"That's how John thought. Hold them down."

Spero and Tricorico saw more evidence of Sammy's stature in the Tuesday night gatherings at his bar and restaurant, Tali's, on Bensonhurst's main thoroughfare, 18th Avenue, and 62nd Street. During their surveillance, on any given Tuesday they would spot scores of men crowding in there, members of Sammy's crew and others in the Gambino family, some of them captains, as well as captains and soldiers from the Colombo and Lucchese families.

By then, Sammy had become, as they say in the mob, a shylock's shylock, and Tuesday was settle-up night on either the weekly interest or the principal due from such customers as other loan sharks or bookmakers who had been caught short. Gambino squad intelligence sources had already identified Sammy as a rising force in the construction industry, and at Tali's on Tuesday night, Spero and Tricorico could see it for themselves—concrete company executives, building contractors and subcontractors, shop stewards in the construction unions, and the Teamsters all flocking in to eat and drink, to touch base with Sammy.

Spero and Tricorico would have been delighted to mix in with the crowd. But there wasn't a chance. Someone with Sammy was always out front, and while there wasn't a closed-door policy, you had to be a recognizable regular from the neighborhood to gain entrance. Spero and Tricorico would try to get an early parking space to observe the goings-on. Tricorico remembered, "There'd be guys on the street, guys coming in and out. It was hard to hide. We used to be out there, two guys in a car, smoking cigars, watching Tali's, making notes. And in a sense, we got a lot of information because we saw who came with who, from what companies, what unions."

Sometimes they would see Sammy himself emerge from Tali's and stroll down 18th Avenue with a visitor. Once they saw him in deep conversation with Mario Mastromarino, chief engineer of the Gem steel erection company. That was especially frustrating. There was no record of Mastromarino being mobbed up. What were the two of them talking about?

Stymie's eighteen-year-old son, Joey D'Angelo, whom Sammy thought of almost as a son, would cover two or three blocks in each direction, "bird-dogging." "He'd come by," Spero recalled, "and probably saw us and was back to Sammy reporting, 'They're down the street.' But we were gathering general intelligence. We weren't trying to be discreet. On that block, you couldn't be."

The two agents considered renting an apartment with a view of Tali's. However, that wasn't a viable option. "Over there, in Bensonhurst," Spero said, "the word would spread right away. 'Hey, guess what? The FBI's on the second floor next to the dentist.'"

There was consideration, as well, of bugging Tali's. But a survey by Jim Kallstrom's special operations team reported that it wasn't worth the effort. The jukebox during these get-togethers was on full blast, and there was the clatter of dishes and a deafening clamor of voices, making it impossible to differentiate one speaker from another.

For the Gambino squad's Bruce Mouw, Sammy's Tuesday nights at Tali's had another significance. To command such gatherings, Sammy had to be important to the family. Otherwise, John Gotti's vanity was such that he would never have allowed them to take place. For Spero and Tricorico, there was at least one blessing to their vigils. Sammy was no all-night carouser. By 11 P.M., he was headed home.

Meanwhile, consideration was also given to bugging his Stillwell office. It was rejected. The feeling was that Sammy was too cagey. And as it turned out, when the state's organized crime task force eventually did decide to bug the office, thousands of hours of recorded conversations produced nothing of evidentiary value.

On Stillwell, Sammy didn't need the teachers or the kids he was playing handball with to tell him he was under surveillance. He became aware of it himself almost at once. In fact, Spero and Tricorico did not go out of their way to disguise their presence. One of the objects of the surveillance was to let Sammy know he had been targeted, to see how he would react and at least disrupt his normal routine. And to that degree, some success was achieved.

After DiBernardo's murder, Sammy became the Gambino family's link to Local 282 of the Teamsters. "I had control of the whole thing," Sammy said. "The president, who was Bobby Sasso, the vice president, the secretary/treasurer, delegates, foremen. If I wanted a foreman in there, I'd tell Bobby, 'Put this guy to work.'

"I told Bobby that DiB was missing. We were trying to find out what happened to him. I said to report directly to me if he heard anything. From here on in he was to answer to me on the construction jobs. He wasn't to meet with anybody from any other family unless it was strictly union business. Anything else, any schemes they had, was to go through me or John Gotti. It was for his advantage, too. That way he was protected from anybody leaning on him.

"I said we shouldn't be seen in public together. There was getting to be too much heat. He wasn't to go to any family weddings and funerals and social functions. We would set up meetings at two, three o'clock in the morning at hotels and motels, like the Golden Gate off the Belt Parkway.

"John called me and said he was changing the structure that pertained to the construction industry. Under Paul, Paul got seventy-five percent of what was coming in and DiB and myself split the other twenty-five. 'Sammy,' he says, 'you were getting twelve and half percent. Now you're getting twenty. And I'm taking another five percent.'

"'John,' I said, 'you're the boss. Whatever you want is good with me. What comes out of the unions and that stuff, I have no problems with, because I'm handling it for you.'

"And that's what we did. Other deals were different. Like if I have a legitimate business deal—drywall work, steel erection—that was mine, I'd pass along maybe twenty or thirty percent, whatever I decided. I would give my crew some, give him some, and take some.

"Even though I was doing all the work—John didn't know anything about construction—I didn't feel uncomfortable giving John his eighty percent. Hey, that's the structure—it belongs to the family boss. The money, in that capacity, meant nothing to me. The money was coming in. But in these deals, setting them up, I enjoyed the negotiations, giving people a rough time. To tell the truth, I enjoyed the whole process more than the dollar value that was in it. I'm not stupid, and I don't want to be screwed. I'm going after the buck, there's no question about that. But in the give and take, just the money wasn't my ultimate goal. It never was. The deal was the thing."

Before it was over, Sammy's wheeling and dealing with the Teamsters alone would bring John Gotti about $2 million annually.

"I don't believe he ever shared a penny of it with anybody," Sammy said. "So what did he do with it? I remember one time that Joe Watts came to me and said, 'Sammy, I'm giving you a tip. When you go down to New York today, he's probably gonna look to borrow off you. He's desperate. He's looking for cash.'

"I said, 'Borrow off me? For what?' And Joe Watts says, 'I'll tell you this much. I know for a fact that he lost over three hundred thousand this week in gambling.'

"I know John would never 'fess that up to me. So I don't think anything more of it. But when I go down that night, sure enough, he asked me how I was sitting, how much I was holding. What he was talking about was the money from Bobby Sasso, which I would turn in every five, six weeks, whatever, to his brother Pete Gotti.

"I said, 'Well, it ain't time yet, but I am holding some money. About a hundred. Maybe a little less. If you need it, let Pete come over, and I'll give it to him.'

"'Yeah,' he said, 'I could use it now. I'm gonna give out a big shylock loan, and I'm short. I want to give this one out.'

"Which was bullshit because I know he's not a shylock. Now I knew Joe Watts was telling the truth. Another captain, Good-Looking Jackie—John Giordano—told me the same number a couple of days later. 'Wow,' he said, 'this fucking John is out of his mind. This guy's betting with two fucking hands. He can't earn enough money.'

"So I had heard it from two people, plus he made his little bullshit request that he wanted to push out money that week. God knows what he lost the week before, or the next week. Here's a guy losing three hundred thousand in one week that we know of! And that has nothing to do with his other spending—clothes, broads, wining and dining, Cristal champagne in the discos, weddings, funerals. He went through a ton of money, just to keep that persona of Big John Gotti."

•   •   •

Sammy's biggest legitimate business venture was with the Gem steel erection firm—now called Atlas Gem. For years he had been arranging jobs for it in return for relatively modest kickbacks and had seen it grow into the dominant company in its field in New York.

He wasn't interested in kickbacks anymore.

"Take the Concrete Club that the families set up. It always made me laugh. The victim, the so-called poor contractor who we supposedly victimized, did this and that to—it was a total bunch of bullshit. He was more greedy than we were—and a lot smarter. We rig the bid on, say, a twelve-million-dollar job and before he's through, once he knows he's got it, he's jacked it up another four million. We still get our two percent, but what's he getting? He's taking a third more, thirty-three percent. Paul Castellano would say, 'Let me be the poor victim. Let him be the gangster.'

"So that's what I decided to do when I formed S & G consulting over on Stillwell. I don't want no kickbacks no more. I'll do my own thing. I'd rather give the kickback. And we never twisted arms. You know, maybe to get on the first job, I'll intimidate a little bit. But I never intimidated again.

"My brother-in-law, Eddie, would get a call. 'Tell Sammy we have another job and we're sending the blueprints down.' Why? Number one, I wasn't like the normal gangster. We went in and did the job almost to perfection. That's me, my personality. I did it for my own pride and at a fair price. Number two, this general contractor or subcontractor says to himself that when Sammy's on the job, he has no problem with the minority worker coalitions because Sammy knows who to take care of. He has no problem with the unions. He has no problems with nothing.

"Maybe he needs a favor. Another subcontractor could be bullying him. Or a guy from another family might be breaking his chops. So I visit whoever it is and say, 'I'm doing the work here, what the fuck are you trying?' 'Well, Sammy, I got a legitimate beef.' End result, I resolve the beef one way or another. It could cost my contractor some money. But like what maybe was a two-hundred-thousand-dollar problem is down to ten or twenty thousand. So he knows being with Sammy actually brings him a lot of benefits.

"I had a good reputation, and I valued it. Some jobs in construction are just a bastard. They go sour, and there ain't nothing you can do about it. There would come a time that happened with this fourteen-story building in Brooklyn by the Gowanus Expressway, where I had a piece of the general contracting work. It looks like we're going to take a major loss. The lawyers say, 'Sammy, at your end, you're going to lose two hundred thousand.' My scheming brother-in-law is with me at the meeting, and he takes me aside and advises,

'Let's pull out now. And lose nothing. Fuck the job. What the fuck can they do to you?'

"I look at Eddie and say, 'You're right, they can't do nothing, but you know what will happen with that? Everybody in the world will hear about it. For everybody in the world we do work with, it'll be Sammy does work and makes money, all well and good. If he loses money, he'll abandon you. How do you think that'll sit with people, Eddie? This will be the best two hundred thousand I'll ever spend because people will say not only is Sammy qualified to do the job, but he'll stay with you, win or lose.'

"'That's important to businesspeople, Eddie,' I said. 'That's why you were never successful in business. Because you scheme too fucking much.' So I went back to the meeting and told them, 'When the time comes, tell me what my end is, what my check should be.' Right afterward, some other big contractor calls me, 'Jeez, I hear that Gowanus job is going bad.'

"'Yeah, it is.'

"'You're gonna stay with it, huh?'

"'What do you want me to do, walk away?'

"'No, you're doing the right thing. Listen, I got a couple of jobs coming up. I'll send you the specifications, and you give me your numbers.'

"I turned to Eddie and said, 'See, already more work's coming our way. And this is just the first example.'

"Now with Atlas Gem, for years after Mario Mastromarino asked me to give its president, Joe Polito, a hand, I had been helping this little company to grow, and now it's about the biggest in the city. I don't want the kickbacks no more. What I did was I called in Mario and told him I'm going to open up my own legitimate steel erection company. Nobody is more respected or has more know-how in steel erection than Mario, and I want him with me. I asked how many men could he take and he says, 'Forty or fifty, the key guys. They'll follow me.'

"'All right, good,' I said. 'But Joe Polito is a decent guy, a cool guy, and I want you to tell him what we're doing.' So he does, and Joe Polito obviously has a heart attack. He wants to see me right away.

"We have a meeting, and I go over again what I'm intending. And he says, 'Sammy, could we work out a deal? You have your consulting company, S & G. We'll work out a contract. There won't be any more cash payments under the table.'

"I said, 'You know what we can do. Our lawyers should get together to work this out.' I told him I wanted a quarter of a million up front. S & G would get seventy-five hundred a week, out of which I would pay Mario the five thousand he was getting from Joe. And every month S & G would receive three percent of every job Atlas Gem got, not from the profit, but the gross.'

"He said, 'In return, you won't go into the business yourself. All the men will stay at Atlas Gem. You'll be paying Mario, but he will work strictly for me. And you, too.'

"I said, 'Absolutely.' So the lawyers wrote up the agreement. There's no need for sneaking around with the unions, because Joe is now a hundred percent union. The only thing he asked was for the quarter of a million to be broken up into two payments, and I said, 'No problem.' That was put in the contract, like everything else, all legal and aboveboard. I'm going to be paying my taxes. I don't want to be like a lot of made guys who end up in front of a jury and can't explain their sources of income.

"It was a beautiful relationship. Joe don't have any union problems, but I pulled weight with the general contractors and could still help him get jobs like I did before. And he touted me for drywall, painting, and concrete. Remember, I got Marathon concrete. I set up the same consulting deal there, not as big, but the same.

"I'm in a position to guarantee a contractor that he will get a priority from Atlas Gem. A lot of these contractors borrow big money, and time is money to them. Speed is money to them. I would say, 'Don't worry, it'll be done. You want fifty guys, you'll have fifty guys. Now how about the concrete work?' 'Well, I got somebody.' 'No, no,' I say, 'it don't work like that. It's a two-way street, pal. Give it to Marathon.' 'Well, is Marathon capable?' 'Hey, they'll get the job done. I stand responsible.'"

In the months after John Gotti's acquittal in the Giacalone prosecution, the Bergin club in remote Ozone Park was not quite what he had in mind to go with his new celebrity status. He wanted the sizzle of Manhattan, so he decided to hold court at Neil Dellacroce's old club, the Ravenite, in Little Italy. He would arrive around five o'clock each evening in a gleaming, chauffeured Mercedes in suitable pomp and circumstance. Made members and associates would be lined up outside to greet him with hugs and kisses. Gawkers crowded the opposite side of Mulberry Street to catch a glimpse of the great man, who would flash a smile and respond with a thumbs-up wave. About all that was missing was to list him in guidebooks as one of the city's major tourist attractions.

Then Agents Spero and Tricorico, in their periodic monitoring of Sammy, saw that he was now going to the Ravenite every night. Although they didn't know this at first, Sammy had been appointed acting *consigliere*. He was now part of the Gambino family administration.

From time to time, Spero and Tricorico drew surveillance duty at the Ravenite. They would be concealed in the back of a black van driven by another agent. He would park on Mulberry Street. "When we were finished," Tricorico said, "we'd radio him, and he'd come back and take us out of the area, and we'd get in our own car and go home."

Matty Tricorico would handle the binoculars. Frank Spero would be on his knees with a flashlight, pen and pad, noting the identity and license plates of those who came and went as Tricorico called them out. Tricorico would often see the brawny figure of Gotti's attorney, Bruce Cutler. "Cutler would come up and he'd be kissing all the guys, too, like he wanted to be a made guy so bad," he remembered. "I told Frank, you know, if we were standing out front, Cutler'd kiss us."

Sammy's arrival was different. "He'd usually be in a T-shirt, a windbreaker and jeans. All these other fellows, being that it's John Gotti, would dress up," Tricorico said. "Sammy dressed down. He didn't go for the protocol with the hugging and kisses. He wasn't that kind of a guy. You could tell the respect he was getting, but he'd just nod, maybe shake one or two hands. Lots of times, there'd be reporters and TV crews hanging around. From what we saw, it was like the last place Sammy wanted to be. You could just hear him saying, 'Let me out of here.'"

"Sammy would be driven to the Ravenite by one of his made guys, Big Louie Vallario," Spero said. "Afterward, he would go to one of his

favorite restaurants in Brooklyn—for instance, La
Tavola, off Fort Hamilton Parkway—and meet his
wife for dinner. She'd be taken by Sammy's regular driver, Louie Saccente, and then they'd go
straight home. Sammy was a no-nonsense guy.
When he got done with his business, that was it.
He wasn't John Gotti, heading uptown to some
fancy restaurant with a whole retinue and winding
up at Regine's, the Park Avenue disco, until three
or four in the morning."

"It was ridiculous how the guys, made guys, out
front of the Ravenite were acting," Sammy said.
"It was like they thought they were in some movie
or something. That was what John was doing to
them. Well, I wasn't in movies. Any kissing, that
kind of stuff, I had to do, I did inside the club.

"One night I did go with him to Regine's. We
were at a wedding, and he grabbed me and said,
'Come on, let's go over to Regine's.' He knew better
than to make an appointment with me to go out
drinking. I wouldn't go, and he knew it. He wouldn't
even ask. But it was spur-of-the-moment at the
wedding, so I went. He had his regular eight, ten
guys with him—Joe Watts, Good-Looking Jackie,
Bobby Boriello, whoever. It had to be the best
champagne. Not Dom Perignon. The other one.
Cristal. Cristal Rosé. The more expensive, the
better.

"A couple of girls were looking at him, and he
sent Bobby over to talk to them. 'Would you like

to have a drink with John Gotti?' Fuck that shit! I mean, I did that when I was eighteen, nineteen years old. And there was 'Oh, look, there's so-and-so, the big movie star, and so-and-so, the big TV personality.' Who gave a fuck about them? That wasn't me, to go somewhere just to be seen. We're not actors, we're not actresses. We're gangsters and racketeers. We're not supposed to be known to the public. What happened to that prick in the finger, when Paul said, 'We're a secret society'? What kind of secret is this?

"Another time, I had dinner with him in one of the uptown restaurants. He sent for me. It was about business, so I had to go. Big Louie drove me. I forget what the business was about. What I remember is sitting alone with John at the table, and he leans over and says, 'You see that guy and that woman over there?'

"So I peeked out of the corner of my eye and said, 'Yeah.'

"He says, 'They're looking at me like a bastard, huh?'

"And they were. Louie and Bobby are out by the bar, and I tell him, 'You want me to have them go see what they want, these people?'

"'No, no!' he says. 'This is my public, Sammy. They love me.'

"*My public*? What the fuck is this guy talking about? I thought. I was stunned. I didn't even know how to answer that."

•   •   •

"John appointed me acting *consigliere* after he comes out of the can. Joe Gallo is retired. He's called to a meeting I set up for John in the basement of the house of the brother of Big Louie Vallario. John told Gallo, 'We're leaving you out. You're not helping the family.' John came close to saying he was retarded. 'You can stay as *consigliere* in name, but as of now you're inactive.' 'I understand, John,' Gallo says. He's pushing seventy-seven. Besides, he's got his own problems. Him and Joe Piney have been indicted on RICO charges.

"To keep the old-timers happy, John leaves Joe Piney as underboss. But John and myself are basically running the family. At that point I recommend that if and when I ever become the official *consigliere*, Big Louie would become the official captain of my crew and I'm going to start using him in that capacity now.

"Around Christmastime that year, which is 1987, I was having my Christmas party at Tali's. Everybody comes—John, Frank Locascio, the captain who's running the Bronx for the family— and that's when we get the news that Gallo and Piney have been convicted.

"Because of his advanced age and bad health, the judge lets Joe Gallo go home for Christmas pending sentence. But he don't do it for Joe

Piney. If Joe wants to go home for the holidays, he has to renounce his life of crime and being part of the Gambino family, and the judge might be a little lenient on his sentence as well. Joe Piney stood up in court and refused. And the papers all had it that he represented the old Mafia, so tough, so this and that.

"But that was bullshit. Joe Piney would have done it in a hot minute. He's sickly. He feels he's not going to live through his sentence. All he wants is one last time with his personal family. Joe wants to do it. He sent the message through Good-Looking Jackie.

"John asked me what did I think? I said, 'Fuck it. Let him go home to his wife, his kids and everything. You know how he feels about them. Let him do it. And then let him go in and take him down as underboss. Let him just do his time.'

"John says, 'No, we can't do that. It would send out a bad message. It's no good.' He sends back word to Joe Piney that he's to tell the judge to go fuck himself. The administration has denied his request. And simultaneously, John sends a message to Joe Gallo that he's out totally as *consigliere*. I now officially have that position. With Joe Piney gone, he elevates Frank Locascio to acting underboss and Big Louie is captain of my crew."

About then, the Brooklyn U.S. attorney was also prosecuting Angelo Ruggiero, John Gotti's brother Gene and John Carneglia, among others, for heroin trafficking, a case that had its genesis in that first bug placed in Ruggiero's dinette by Jim Kallstrom's special operations team.

But not long after the case began in court, evidence of jury tampering was unearthed. The government asked for and received a mistrial ruling from the bench "without prejudice," which meant that the defendants could be retried. When the defense appealed, all the judges in New York's Eastern District were convened en banc and upheld the decision.

"I'll say one thing for John. With his big ego, he did believe in himself. All over the country, Cosa Nostra families are on the run. And here in New York, there was the commission case, the pizza connection, on and on. All the old bosses have been put away for a hundred years. There's Joe Gallo and Joe Piney. There's Angie and Genie Gotti.

"And the feds aren't hammering just on our family. It's the other families, too. The DeCalvacante family over in Jersey. A lot of people are saying the whole thing is falling apart. It was unbelievable. Unbelievable what that law professor Blakey did coming up with RICO. And you got to give Rudy Giuliani credit when he was the U.S. attorney in Manhattan. He showed them how to work this fucking RICO. The witness protection program became stronger and more guys were going in. These things that the government implemented years before were starting to hit us in the ass now.

"Then the other thing was that the FBI, when you go back to J. Edgar Hoover, would not recognize there was a mob. He wouldn't let agents go after the mob when they wanted to. But with Hoover gone, the FBI is all over us. This all catches up with our era.

"But John wasn't fazed. He told me he's going to change the face of Cosa Nostra. Show everybody how to win cases. He's going to show them how to do it, how to beat the government. How to put your head up, your chest out. He's going to show everybody the light, show them the road, show them the way."

Toward this end, in 1988, Gotti desired a formal meeting of the Cosa Nostra commission. It was the first—and last—one that Sammy would attend. He helped set it up with the underboss of the Genovese family, Benny Eggs Mangano, and the Lucchese *consigliere*, Gas Pipe Casso.

The morning meeting would be held in lower Manhattan in an apartment of the brother of a Gambino family captain. "We were surprised that Chin Gigante went along with this," Sammy said. "We only learned later that he had a relative living in that same building. He knew all its ins and outs and spent the night there ahead of time in case a hit was being planned."

One of the key items to be addressed—*the* key item, as far as Gotti was concerned—was two family vacancies on the commission. Because of its heroin trafficking, the Bonanno family still did not have a seat. And because of the unsettled state of the Colombo family, Junior Persico, in prison, could not decide who he wanted as acting boss.

"On the street, John and myself met Vic Amuso, who was running the Lucchese family now that Tony Ducks was away, and Gas Pipe. Our captain came out to take us to his brother's apartment. He led us through an underground garage to the elevators. As we were walking, Gas Pipe turns to me and said, 'What a great place for a hit.'

"Chin comes into the apartment with Benny Eggs. He's in his bathrobe and pajamas. He has a four- or five-day growth of beard. He looked real grubby.

"We resolved certain issues, and then John announces that we have reached out to Junior. That he had to make up his mind about his acting boss. Junior Persico has finally approved one of his top guys, Vic Orena, and he's agreed that only the commission can remove him. John backs Orena, and Orena is accepted. He will be seated at the next commission meeting. By backing Orena, John figured he had a puppet. He would be able to control the Colombo vote.

"Now John wanted the Bonanno family to have its seat back. John owns Joe Messino, who's running the family. With Orena and Messino, John could count on controlling the commission, three votes out of five. But Chin said that decision should be put off to the next commission meeting, and the Lucchese people backed him.

"Then John made another play. He said that Cosa Nostra had to replenish our ranks. He brought up the fact that the Genovese family had forty replacements to make and hadn't made any new members for a very, very long time. John figured if he could get Chin to agree to make these forty guys, he would leak it that he was behind them being made and they would ultimately look to John.

"Chin stared straight at John and said, 'When the time comes, I'll make those moves inside my family. I appreciate your concern, but I'll do it when I'm ready.'

"One thing I'll never forget from that meeting was John telling Chin in sort of a proud way that his son, John Junior, had just been made. Instead of congratulating him, Chin said, 'Jeez, I'm sorry to hear that.'

"We were a little shocked by this, but Chin was right. Paul Castellano didn't want his kids in the life. None of Chin's sons were made. I myself would be dead set against it. I wanted my son to be legitimate, to have nothing to do with what I did.

"So here was Chin, who's supposed to be crazy, saying who in their right mind wanted their son to be made? And there was John boasting about it. Who was really crazy?"

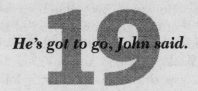

19

He's got to go, John said.

"LOUIE MILITO WAS A FRIEND OF MINE, 'A FRIEND of ours,' but there came a time when Louie, who had helped me in a few hits, had to be hit himself.

"He was a good-looking guy," Sammy said. "A little taller than me. Stockier. Nobody went back more in the mob with me than Louie. In the beginning, we were true street partners. Instead of talking about Sammy or Louie, people would say Sammy *and* Louie in the same breath. In those early days, Louie was much more successful than me with his car theft ring. He was well-off financially. I was a brokester. That didn't mean nothing to me. Good for him!

"In the family, we did a lot of work together. Louie had put the .357 magnum against the head of Johnny Keys in that hit we did for Paul

Castellano. He stood over the body of Frank Fiala and shot out his eyes in front of the Plaza Suite. Louie's kids called me Uncle Sammy.

"I got made, in Toddo Aurello's crew, before he did. Louie was still an associate with John Rizzo, the old-time soldier, who was also in Toddo's crew. Afterward, Toddo told me Paul was looking to enlarge the family. I immediately suggested Louie as a candidate and asked him to talk to Rizzo.

"Toddo took me with him to see Rizzo. We figured it was a sure thing. We both expected him to promote his own son as well as Louie. But when Toddo said the boss was looking for new candidates to be made, Rizzo said he had nothing but garbage around him. He wasn't interested in advancing anybody, not even his son.

"I told Louie I would try to do something. Even though I was made, I couldn't propose Louie myself because he was with Rizzo. I went to Toddo and explained that since Johnny Rizzo was a soldier under him, so, in reality, Louie was under him, too. Toddo said he thought I had a good point, and despite the chances of a beef from Rizzo, Toddo sponsored Louie directly to Paul.

"After the induction ceremony, I took Louie right over to John Rizzo's club. You should've seen the look on Johnny's face when I introduced Louie to him as a friend of ours. He calmly shook Louie's hand and kissed him on the cheek. There was nothing else he could do. Louie was a made guy, just like him. And he knew me and Louie both had reputations of being stone killers. I didn't really enjoy going around Rizzo, but he left me no choice. Louie deserved to be made.

"Now Louie and me were closer than ever. Besides the work we did together, I took him in on the partnership I had with Eddie Garafola in the painting company I set up, and Louie and I developed Gem steel.

"The only problem was Eddie and Louie didn't like each other. Eddie was complaining that Louie never shared his financial success with me, so why should I do it for him? And Louie was saying Eddie was a schemer and a liar, who didn't belong in Cosa Nostra. I knew about Eddie's faults, but he was married to my sister and I had to think about her and my nieces and nephews. Instinct told me Louie was right about Eddie. I didn't realize it was like the pot calling the kettle black.

"It was after Fiala's murder, after I had been in all that trouble with Paul Castellano because the hit wasn't sanctioned, that Louie met me in the lounge of the Golden Gate in Brooklyn. He announced that he was breaking up our partnerships.

"I was stunned. 'Let me ask you a question,' I said. 'Why?' And he said, 'Sammy, I just got my reasons.' Then he starts ranting that my brother-in-law is a swindler and a lying piece of shit. 'I advised you five times to kill him,' he said, 'and you don't want to do it.'

"So I assume the problem is Eddie. Fine, we'll break up. But I told him I'm not giving up Gem. At that time, I didn't have the legitimate consulting relationship with Joe Polito. We still have the kick-back arrangement with him, but I was already thinking ahead.

"What I didn't know is Louie had this business opportunity that he took to Tommy Bilotti, who in turn took him to Paul. At this meeting, Paul mouths off that he should have had Sammy killed over the Fiala situation. This was classic Paul—divide and conquer. Paul saw and seized an opportunity to drive a wedge between us. The Fiala business was history. But Louie figured that it wasn't resolved in Paul's mind and panicked. He thought if Sammy's going to be killed, he'll be killed as well. He took Paul's word at face value. He don't know Paul well enough to know that Paul was just talking. Everybody in close contact with Paul knew his bark was worse than his bite. Sure, Paul was mad at me about the Fiala hit, but he wasn't going to kill me, then or ever.

"Then Louie went back to Paul again and told him he was completely separating himself from me. Louie wanted Paul to stop thinking of him and me as one person. Milito was no longer part of Gravano. And to prove it, he went secretly into partnership with Tommy Bilotti in Tommy's shy-locking business.

"I found all this out from Frankie DeCicco.

DiB—Robert DiBernardo—told him. DiB was present at both meetings. Louie figured none of this would ever get out, because DiB was supposed to be so tight with Paul. He didn't dream DiB would be our messenger on the Castellano hit.

"Louie had got pinched for something and was away for a short time when we made our move against Paul and Tommy Bilotti. Frankie was steaming. Louie could have betrayed us if he wasn't in jail. He was playing both sides. As soon as Louie got out of jail, Frankie said he had to be killed. A guy like that was too devious.

"I argued for Louie's life. I asked Frankie, who was now our underboss, to let Louie come under me. After all, we had spared people before. I would tell Louie what we discovered. I would put him on the shelf. I tried to convince Frankie that we didn't have to kill him. But Frankie was adamant. Louie had to die. He had slapped us all in the face with his double-dealing. Even if Paul's threat to kill me wasn't real, Louie didn't know it and he never tried to warn me. Then Frankie got blown up.

"When Louie was back on the street, John Gotti called me in. What about the hit? It had already been sanctioned. I talked again for Louie, and John said I was the one Louie had double-crossed. If I wanted to spare him, he'd go along with it. But he cautioned me to keep a sharp eye on my so-called friend.

"I read Louie the riot act and told him all that

we knew. He never tried to deny anything. I said he was going to get a pass. But he didn't buy it. I was acting out of friendship, but Louie was looking for the angle. He would question all the people around me. He wanted to know everything and anything I might have said about him. Paranoia became his middle name.

"He went to Tommy Bilotti's brother, Joe. After the Castellano hit, Joe Watts argued that we should kill Joe Bilotti because he was a danger to us. I had argued to John Gotti that I didn't think this was necessary. Joe Bilotti knew the life. I thought he would accept what had happened and become a good, loyal soldier, which he did. John said that if I met with him, and he decided to strike back, I could be the first to go. Did I still feel the same way? I said yes. Then Frankie DiCicco jumped in and told John that he felt like I did, and he would go along to the first meeting with Joe Bilotti.

"So the meeting was arranged in a Brooklyn diner. Joe was obviously nervous. I told him that our move was primarily against Paul, but that given his brother's relationship with Paul, his brother had to go, too, and I knew he would understand that. I pulled back my jacket and showed him the cannon I was carrying. I told Joe, 'You know me a lot of years. If we wanted you dead, do you think you'd be dead already?' He looked at me and nodded his head. I said, 'Joe, I give you my word that you got a pass. I'm gonna be your captain. Don't worry when I send for you. You're a friend of ours in good standing. If you need me to sit down for you, I will. You got a tough job. You have nine kids. Tommy had nine kids. You have eighteen kids to take care of.' And Joe's still alive today.

"Anyway, now Louie goes to Joe and tells him they're in the same position, something has to be up. Joe said, 'No, no, we're not in any position. I'm still alive. I'm the proof. Sammy gives his word, you can bank on it.'

"Then Louie made his big mistake. He must have been all fucked-up in his head. When I became *consigliere*, I appointed Big Lou Vallario captain of my crew. And now Louie Milito was going around bad-mouthing Big Lou and saying *he* should be captain. Unbelievable for him to even think I would consider it after his betrayals.

"This is a serious matter when a soldier is backbiting his captain. And John Gotti hears about it. We both discussed Milito. He's got to go, John said. John was concerned that Louie could snap anytime. He reminded me that he spared Louie's life once under certain conditions, which Louie wasn't abiding by. You couldn't predict what he'd do next. He was tough and dangerous. I was sick, but I had to agree with John. This time my mind and my gut won over my heart.

"John decided that he wanted to avoid any appearance of a grudge hit. I wouldn't be given the contract, but I would be present. The hit officially went to John's brother Genie and his crew. Vallario would set up Louie. Joe Watts would get rid of the body."

The date was a Tuesday, March 8, 1988. "Big Lou called Milito to tell him John Gotti finally decided to kill 'Johnny G,' a guy everybody knew John hated. So Louie had no reason to doubt his captain's call. Big Lou said his crew was handling the hit, but Gene Gotti and myself would be there.

"Louie Milito showed up at Big Louie's club in Bensonhurst close to seven P.M. When he came in, Big Louie was standing behind the service counter. Gene Gotti, one of his guys, Arnold Squitieri, and myself were at a round table playing cards. John Carneglia was sitting on a leather couch watching TV. After saying hello, Milito went to the service counter for a cup of espresso. As he was telling Big Lou how much sugar to add to it, Carneglia got up from the couch and came up behind Milito with a .380 with a silencer. He put a quick shot into the back of Louie Milito's head. Louie fell faceup on the floor. Carneglia bent over him and shot him once under his chin. He was quite dead.

"We put him in a body bag. Arnold and Carneglia went out to get their car. I had placed Eddie Garafola and Huck along two streets away from the club as lookouts. Everything was clear. Arnold and Carneglia drove off with the body bag in the trunk to bring it to Joe Watts. Big Lou, Eddie, and Huck cleaned up while I took a walk/talk with Genie. Then Genie went home.

"Tuesday was when all my guys came to Tali's, every Tuesday night at eight P.M. Everybody knew it. The FBI knew it. They were always there. So I had the FBI for an alibi. But Milito's body was never found.

"I made sure his wife had enough cash. I felt bad for her and the kids. They were why I had fought to keep him alive, even though her and Louie were getting close to a divorce. It cost me another twenty thousand to finish all the construction he was doing on his house. I told her that if she had any problems with anybody over anything, she should come immediately to me. Because sometimes there are assholes who will get their little brave pills because a guy is dead.

"Even though the hit had to happen, I was really bothered by it. I liked Louie, and I loved his kids. John Gotti sensed that I was fucked-up over this hit. But he said, 'This guy wasn't our friend. This was best for the family.'

"Louie wasn't no innocent. He was a made guy and a killer. He knew the rules, and he went against them. He had played a very dangerous game—and he lost."

20

John just fell in love with himself.

"PERSONALLY," SAMMY SAID, "I THOUGHT ALL THAT stuff Paul and some of the other bosses said about no drugs was bullshit—stay out of it because drug-dealing gave Cosa Nostra a bad name and brought too much heat. Even Paul was taking drug money. He just pretended he didn't know where it was coming from. Drug-dealing was about greed. The bosses have got theirs, and you got guys on the street with nothing. There's too much money in drugs. People want to buy drugs. Other people sell it. Supply and demand. How can you stop it?

"The real problem was guys in the family doing drugs. When a guy's dealing drugs, you can talk to him. Reprimand him. You don't have to kill him. In my crew, when I was captain, there was no drug-dealing. But drugs were everywhere you looked.

One of the guys with me, Nicky Cowboy—Nick Mormando—got hooked on crack cocaine. He became like a renegade. He went berserk. He didn't want to be in the crew no more. He was going to start his own little gang. I couldn't take a chance on him running around. He knew too much. So I got permission from John to kill him.

"We finally got Nicky to come by Tali's, and he went with Huck to pick up the Old Man, Paruta, who was still alive then. Joe got in the backseat and shot Nicky twice in the back of the head. Me and Eddie were trailing in a car behind. We dumped the body in a vacant lot. It was found the next day.

"The same thing happened with Mike DeBatt. I think Nicky got him hooked on crack. He went crazy. He didn't come down for days. And when he does, he's sweating, he's all jumpy. His wife came to me, crying. 'I don't know what happened to him,' she said. 'He sits in the house behind a window with the blinds down, and he's got a rifle.' She said he's saying, 'If they come, I'm gonna battle it out.'

"I've lost control of him. I tried to talk to him, but he's too far gone. He ain't listening. And he's done work with us and our family. He was a good man, Mike, until this. Not only did I like him, I went back with his father, who was originally with me. Remember, when the father died, I took the kid under my wing. I know the mother, the wife. These people came to my farm in Jersey. They came to my house. They came to my parties. This just tore my fucking insides out. Afterward, I stayed with them, helped them. But there's nothing I can do about Mike. This was the life.

"I got John's permission. Mike worked the bar at Tali's. I decided he would be killed in Tali's and to leave him there to make it seem to the cops that the murder was because of a robbery. So nobody would think that it was related to Cosa Nostra or any mob matter.

"Huck shot Mike while he was behind the bar. My brother-in-law and Big Louie were there. I was waiting at this joint in Brooklyn, the Brown Derby, with John when Eddie came and advised us it was done."

In addition, a series of hits was ordered by Gotti, which Sammy either supervised or set up, that received scant, if any, press attention. One was "this greaseball," as Gotti put it, who had beaten to death a Gambino soldier. Another was a Gambino soldier who, Gotti learned, had decided "to tell the truth" to a grand jury about the family's role in private trash collection. Still another was a face-saving hit on a family-connected demolition and excavation contractor whose swindling ways had become such an embarrassment that the Colombo family had sought permission from Gotti to kill him.

Sammy had a marginal role in two other murders. One, which understandably did receive considerable press, was the execution of Willie Boy Johnson for informing. His time had finally come, despite Gotti's oath on his dead son that Johnson had nothing to worry about.

"John discussed how it should go, using me to bounce off ideas about the best way to do it. That was my only involvement. John is concerned that if it's fucked-up, Willie Boy will go all the way with the government on stuff he hasn't told them yet. I agreed with John that Willie Boy's gotten a little lax by now. He surely thinks he's got a pass. He still lives in his neighborhood. John gives the contract to Eddie Lino, who was one of the shooters in the Castellano hit. Willie Boy has a construction job, plus he's dealing drugs. We caught him with thirteen bullets in the head after he came out of his house early one morning. When I say 'we,' it's because, legally, I guess I was part of the 'we.'"

A second contract was one Sammy would have been happy to fulfill—Louie DiBono, whom he once threatened to kill in front of Paul Castellano. "He was still robbing the family," Sammy said, "and I asked John for permission to take him out. But John had a meeting with DiBono, and DiBono told John that he had a billion dollars of drywall work that was coming out of the World Trade Center. John bit, hook, line, and sinker, and refused my request. John said he would handle DiBono personally and become his partner. But DiBono was up to his old tricks—double-dealing. He had obviously been bullshitting John. So when John called Louie in for meetings to discuss their new partnership, DiBono didn't show up. John was humiliated."

This meant an automatic death penalty. Gotti gave the contract to DiBono's captain, Pat Conte. Conte botched an ideal opportunity to kill DiBono. Then, as Gotti grew increasingly impatient, Conte explained that the problem now was trying to corner DiBono again. Whenever a meeting with him was arranged, DiBono never appeared.

"It was a joke, what was going on," Sammy said. "I couldn't help laughing to myself. I told John why didn't Pat simplify everything. Just call Louie up and tell him to hang himself. Ten months went by. John looks like an asshole. He was too embarrassed even to ask me for help.

"Then, completely out of the blue, this drywall subcontractor asked me if I could get him some work from Louie DiBono, that Louie was doling out work for the Port Authority at the World Trade Center. He gave me DiBono's business card. Then I found out where the construction site was and where DiBono parked his car.

"I went by the Ravenite and asked John how he was making out with the DiBono situation. John tells me, 'That guy never does the same thing twice. We're having a hard time.' I took out the card and told him where DiBono parked at the World Trade

Center every single day. You should have seen John's face. A couple of days later, Louie's body was found in his car in the World Trade Center parking lot.

"As *consigliere* and then underboss, I wasn't supposed to be doing these hits or getting into the details of them. All over the country, there were restrictions in all the Cosa Nostra families not to get the administration members involved, even captains, on hits. Captains in our family were saying when was John going to stop sending me out. 'Hey, Bo,' I told them, 'he wants me on one of these fucking things, I don't want to hear another word about it.' This is what I want to teach my men, my guys. He's the boss. That's it.

"The only thing that bothered me was while I'm exposing myself, I'm also jeopardizing him. We're too close. I'm not only doing work with my old crew, but I'm exposing myself doing work with twenty-five, thirty other guys, and one of them could end up testifying.

"Every time you go on the street, no matter how tough or how good you think you are, there is thirty thousand NYPD cops out there, not counting FBI agents and who the fuck knows who else is around, plus potential witnesses.

"But the truth was that if I was him, I would have picked me. I was efficient at what I did. He knew it, and I knew it. I was probably the best hit man in the family.

"When John Gotti wanted you dead, he wanted you dead yesterday. That way, he could walk around and look like he's so fucking ferocious."

By the end of 1989, Gotti, in his meteoric rise to stardom, had eclipsed the fame of any Cosa Nostra figure in history, with the possible exception of Al Capone.

Besides his appearance on the cover of *Time* magazine, he had been on the cover of the *New York Times* Sunday magazine, *People,* and *New York.* The men's fashion magazine *GQ* featured him in its pages. Newspaper stories about him were a common occurrence locally and nationally. Television crews followed him constantly, many of them from overseas. Newspapers and periodicals throughout Europe, Asia, and Latin America continually updated his activities.

During all of this, although Sammy the Bull Gravano was generationally part of a new, younger breed of show-off mobsters, he remained bound to traditional Cosa Nostra values, hugging the shadows and avoiding the limelight at all costs, never calling undue attention to himself.

In a perceptive 1987 article by Nicholas Pileggi, the writer and mob expert, Pileggi observed that while Gotti was being held in jail for Diane Giacalone's RICO prosecution, Sammy was "keeping things in line" for the Gambino family. Even

this brief aside upset Sammy greatly and he redou-
bled his efforts to remain inconspicuous.

"John used to get up at his house in Howard
Beach about eleven A.M., whatever," Sammy said.
"He'd put on one of his designer jogging outfits,
and he'd get by the Bergin Hunt and Fish Club
around noon or so, especially when he starts getting into this media thing.

"Actually, there was two little clubs side by
side. The bigger one was where all the guys hung
out. The other one, smaller, was his private club. In
there, he had a desk and a couch. Like an office.
On the wall, he had a blown-up and framed picture
of himself, the one that had been on the cover of
Time magazine. And in the back room, he had what
was almost like a beauty parlor. All the regulation
stuff. Big mirrors all over. He had a professional
barber's chair. He had that sink with a curve in it
where you can lay your head back for a shampoo.

"The barber, the stylist, would come every single day. Shampoo his hair, cut it, blow-dry it, comb
it out, and shape it. I used to tell him, 'Bo, why do
you get a haircut every day? Your hair can't grow
that fast.' And he'd say, 'Well, he finds little things.
He snips the hair in my nose and ears, he snips this
and that.'

"He had already showered. He would take off
his jogging outfit and this guy Fat Bobby, who

picked out his clothes, would have everything all lined up. John probably had a shitload of clothes at home, but there, in the club, there had to be a couple of dozen suits. Sports jackets. All kinds of shirts and turtlenecks. Ties. Shoes, all shined up. Socks. He'd have his own underwear and jewelry, but Fat Bobby had laid out everything else for that day. The suit, shirt, tie, socks, shoes, the hankie for his coat pocket.

"Then Bobby Boriello or Jackie Nose—John D'Amico—would go and have the car washed and cleaned out. Not even a speck can be on the car or in the car in any way, shape, or form.

"The whole thing was like a show. By the time four-thirty or five came, washed, dressed, shaved, hair cut and combed, with a custom-tailored overcoat on if it was that season of the year, he'd say, 'Let's go,' and he'd head down to the Ravenite. On Mulberry Street, there would be all them people waiting and watching. Mr. Gotti's here! He'd bump into the news media, which he knew. There'd be that reporter from Channel 4, NBC, John Miller, a sharp guy, who'd be trying to get him to say a few words, which he sometimes did.

"And then he'd come inside and Joe Watts would be saying, 'Gee, John, you know, you looked really good on television last night.' 'Yeah, what a beautiful suit!' one of these blow jobs would be telling him. We'd be sitting around in the club and somebody would say, 'Shhh! John's gonna be on the TV in a minute.'

"John loved this. He'd stay in the Ravenite for about two, two and a half hours, and conclude our day. Then from there, he'd go down Mulberry, maybe to Taormina, to eat, or uptown, like to Da Noi, before he did his thing at Regine's, or whatever.

"I paid him homage, too. But I'm not a jerk-off about it. When he was walking, he didn't like anybody in front of him, so I walked a slight step behind him. When it was raining, I held the umbrella. When he goes to a car, I open the door for him. I was showing guys how to conduct yourself around the boss. It was about respect.

"John just fell in love with himself. We couldn't control these magazines and newspapers and the stuff they're running with, that's for sure. John's a handsome man. He's got charisma. I understood that. I've seen a lot of smart people do stupid things because of an ego. John was no different. After a while you get power-struck. He started believing these newspaper and magazine articles, what they were saying about him on television. He went past having a big ego. You're talking now about an egomaniac. He don't want to hear the truth. He's not looking for it. He's looking for people to say what he wants to hear. Not only was the media having a love affair with him, he was having it with himself. He was always talking about his 'public.' He was completely and totally in love with himself.

"One thing I got to admit. He never took a bad picture. Cameras just sort of loved him. Of course, he started out looking good, but if you get anybody and you have professional people polishing you up all the time and if it's in your brain that you're going to carry yourself a certain way, walk a certain way, talk a certain way, if that's what you live for, you're going to look good. Like actors and actresses, some of them, look real good because they work at it. John worked at it real hard, that whole image of himself. Being the boss, the God-father. The Don. The Dapper Don. The Teflon Don. He loved them terms. If that news guy would have went to John first and told him, 'I'm gonna call you the Dapper Don,' I think John would have given him a couple of hundred thousand right on the spot.

"That's why all the old foxes in Cosa Nostra hated him. And a lot of the bosses. It wasn't the life. Just like when we said Paul Castellano was being selfish about money, this was equally selfish. Because it was for me, me, me. It wasn't for Cosa Nostra. Cosa Nostra was supposed to be family. Not me, me, me.

"John didn't realize this was going to blow up in his face. Yeah, all right, you won a battle. You look great on television. Fuck the battle. You learned that from the Russians. Yeah, they were dogs, they

kept backing up. They let them Germans come
right into their country. They made them freeze
their asses off, run out of supplies, and then they
destroyed them. So it's not the battle, it's the war.
That was obvious to me all my life.

"John wins a battle or two. He's the Teflon
Don. He gives these huge Fourth of July parties
with free hot dogs and hamburgers and the fireworks that the cops can't do nothing about. The
signs are up all over the place: 'We Love You,
John!' I'm watching these moms and dads eating
those hot dogs and hamburgers and calling out
how they love John. I always wondered how fast
those people would have spit out the dogs and
burgers if they had known they were being paid for
from drug-dealing to their own children in that
neighborhood.

"But you can't win a war against the government the way he was doing it. For Chrissake, if I
didn't learn nothing, I learned that walking and
marching on that FBI building with Joe Colombo
was a total horror for the Colombo family and the
whole mob. That was years and years ago, but I
never forgot it. A lot of those guys on those picket
lines didn't want to be there. They were ordered
to it. And there's a million agents all around us,
taking notes, taking pictures.

"John is giving the FBI the same kind of finger.
Maybe he thought he was some sort of Robin
Hood with the people cheering him. Hey, what is

this? All of a sudden, the government is the bad guys, and we're really the good guys? I don't think I'm Robin Hood. I think I'm a gangster. I think I'm somebody with a very, very limited education, and I fought and kicked and punched and did the best I could to get ahead. I dealt with the reality that someday I will probably be killed or go to fucking jail, and I lived with that reality all my life. That's the life I chose. That's the road I took.

"I mean, do you need a psychiatrist or psychologist to tell you what goes on in the head of a degenerate gambler, like John was? I've heard degenerate gamblers deep down want to lose. He loved to come in and say, 'Oh, man, I lost that fucking race by three inches, a fucking nose.' Or he'd say, 'Them fucking Jets, they missed covering by half a point. I dropped ten dimes.' He wanted to talk about that. He must have had winners. But I never heard him talking about one winner. All I ever heard was about a million losers. Maybe he truly didn't want to win this. Maybe he wanted to go down as a legend. I don't know what the fuck ran through his mind. Maybe he thought he was invincible.

"I told him once maybe it wasn't such a good idea flaunting our life. 'No, no, Sammy,' he said. 'Don't worry about it. You'll see, this will be OK. We're going to change the face of Cosa Nostra. We're going to show everybody how to do it.' He started belittling the bosses in the commission case.

'Look,' he was saying, 'look at Tony Ducks wearing a sweater, those fucking bums, all of them trying to act like old men to get the jury to feel sorry for them. And what happened? They all lost. You got to go in there with your suits, your jewelry. Put it in their face. When people go to the circus, they don't want to see clowns. They want to see fucking lions and tigers, and that's what we are.'

"That was his theory or thinking or excuse on how he conducted himself. And the thing was that other families reached out to him, like he did have all the answers. Chicago reached out. Could he OK Bruce Cutler coming out to defend one of their people? Matter of fact, Cutler lost that case for the Chicago underboss. The New Orleans boss came up with a problem. I could hardly understand his accent, Creole, whatever the fuck it was. The Patriarca family came to him to settle a dispute. Philadelphia reached out. But Philadelphia would only do it through me, which ticked him off.

"And always there is his tremendous ego. One time he gets on Big Louie Vallario to dress nice. So Louie gets a gift certificate for this place where John buys his hand-painted two-, three-hundred-dollar ties. Louie buys a tie and he's wearing it with his suit, and John tells him, 'Hey, that's the same fucking tie I got.' We all laugh. But now I take a walk with John and he's actually mad that Louie has the same tie. I said, 'How could he know? His mother got him a gift certificate. You got a couple of hundred ties.' Later, when I got in the car with Louie, I said, 'Take that tie off, cut it up and throw it away. I don't care how much it cost. And don't go near that shop again.' Louie threw the tie out the window."

Gotti required the acting underboss, Frank (Frankie Loc) Locascio, and Sammy to be at the Ravenite five evenings a week. The crew captains had to come in at least once weekly.

"Some of the old foxes in the family," Sammy said, "would come to me and say, 'Sammy, go talk to him. You're the only one who can get through to him. We got to stop this.'

"They don't have to tell me. The government has bugs, zoom lenses, video stuff. They didn't have to go anywhere to find us. They didn't have to do anything. Just focus on the club. John's bringing every captain and every made guy in the family down there. They'll see who kisses who, who talks to who, who gets the handshakes. John gave the government the entire family and then some—other people in other families—on a silver platter.

"I would sit in the Ravenite and think there's got to be bugs all over the place. And they're probably listening to everything we say in the walk/talks. I mean, you could be watching a football game on television and, if they want to, they can pick up the players talking on the field. The FBI can't do that?

"I told him, 'John, why are we meeting in the club? They're all outside. Cops, state guys, federal guys. What are we doing here? Why?'

"'Listen to me, Sammy,' he would say. 'Everything will be good. I know what I'm doing. Fuck the government. They're nothing. Don't worry about it.'

"'OK,' I'd say. 'Fuck the government.' The boss is the boss. The boss's word is the final word. Right, wrong or indifferent, he's the boss. I told the guys, 'He won't do it. He won't change. This is where he wants to meet. And that's it. I don't want to hear any more about it.'

"One day we go out of the club on a walk/talk. We go around the block and walk down two blocks. We turn, make a left and go for two more blocks. We turn right along another block. Now we're six or seven blocks away from the Ravenite.

"We're getting to a corner, me, John, and Frankie Loc. Behind us was Bobby Boriello and another guy. His bodyguards always walked behind us. We pass a van that's parked, and as we were talking, I looked into the van. A guy is sitting in the front seat. Next to him there's a television screen and on it I saw John Gotti, me, and Frankie walking. I have spotted a live picture of ourselves. I walked another couple of feet before I said, 'John, I can't believe what I just saw.'

"'What?'

"'We're live on television.'

"'What do you mean?' he says.

"'The guy in that van. He's got a television in there with him, and we're on it.'

"'How could that be? We're six blocks away from the club. Where the fuck could them cameras be?' He yells at Bobby behind us, who's just passing the van, 'Bobby, the van!'

"Bobby rushes over, but the guy has closed down the TV. Now we're all over the guy, 'Hey, pal, who the fuck are you?' and he says, 'You know who I am.' And, of course, we do. He's law enforcement.

"Before he pulls out, to goad him, I said, 'Hey, you big-nosed cocksucker. Were we on TV, or what did I see?'

"He says, 'All I can tell you is we have very sophisticated equipment,' and off he goes.

"I could understand this if we were standing outside the club and they had zoom lenses in a building a couple of blocks away. But you walk five, six blocks and they're still on us? Maybe they figured out the walk/talks and set up stations to monitor us. I never found out how they did it. I don't know if our voices were on it, but they were filming us live.

"At that point I'm telling John—I mean I was always telling him—but at that point I told him, 'Bo, we're committing suicide here. We're feeding right into them. We're doing what they want.' That day he wasn't so cocky. When we went back to the Ravenite, he's saying, 'From here on in, what we're gonna do is, we're gonna get in the car and drive twenty blocks away. Then we'll just get out and start walking and go to different spots every day.' Which we did, but only about two or three times. And that was the end of that. He wouldn't do it. He just wouldn't do it no more."

Then Sammy unexpectedly saw a side to John Gotti so mean-spirited, so removed from the normal cruelties of family business that even he was left searching for answers.

After the first heroin-trafficking case against Angelo Ruggiero, Gene Gotti, and John Carneglia ended in a mistrial because of jury tampering, Ruggiero remained in federal detention, his bail still revoked, for the second trial. This also resulted in a mistrial, again for suspected jury tampering. For the third trial, in 1989, Ruggiero was finally released on bail and severed from the case. He had terminal lung cancer. Gene Gotti and John Carneglia were both convicted and sentenced to fifty years. The earliest they could realistically expect parole was twenty years.

"Then I heard John wants to whack out Angie. 'For what?' I asked. 'For his fucking big mouth on them fucking tapes,' he says. 'Look at the trouble he caused.'

"I said, 'John, he's dying of cancer. Let him die that way. We'll look like fucking animals here.'

"Finally, he says, 'OK, OK. I'm not gonna do nothing. Don't worry about it.'

"So John breaks Angie as captain and put him on a fucking shelf so bad that he didn't even go to the hospital to visit him. Everybody was begging him to go, his own brothers. He wouldn't. I literally had to drag him to the funeral. 'John,' I told him, 'whatever your feelings are, other families are going to be totally confused by this. I don't think we're sending a good message.'

"If I didn't say a word and he don't go the funeral, none of us would have gone. That's how John really wanted to send Angie out. With nobody. With no respect. Nothing. And I'm talking about a lifelong thing, like from when they were five, six years old."

Toward the end of 1989, Gotti was indicted again, this time by the Manhattan D.A.'s office. The case dated back four years and was not especially earthshaking. But because it involved Gotti, a press conference announcing his indictment was packed with reporters. And it posed a problem for him. He had two felony convictions on his rap sheet and a third one would make him a "predicate felon," carrying a twenty-five-year sentence.

John O'Connor, business agent for Local 608

of the carpenters' union, had come upon a restaurant being extensively renovated in the Wall Street area with nonunion workers. Apparently unaware that the Gambino family had a large stake in the restaurant, O'Connor brought in union goons to wreck the place.

"Bust him up. Put a rocket in his pocket," Gotti was overheard saying through a bug placed in the Bergin club by the state's organized crime task force. Since the local was Irish dominated, the assignment had been given to the Irish gang of killers, the Westies, that Paul Castellano first used for off-the-record hits. "They were just supposed to give this O'Connor a serious beating," Sammy said. "But a lot of the Westies were all fucked-up, drug addicts and drunks. And they end up shooting O'Connor in his legs and ass for whatever reason. So now when the D.A. eventually gets into this, it's a major thing."

"Three to one, I beat this case," Gotti declared as he swaggered into court. And for once he was betting on a sure thing, thanks to Sammy. Sammy had sent a message to O'Connor through the Westies that, all things considered, it wasn't such a good idea "to testify against John." O'Connor obliged. On the witness stand he swore that he didn't have the slightest idea who would want to harm him.

After his acquittal, Gotti returned to a tumultuous reception on Mulberry Street, complete with celebratory fireworks, his reputation as the Teflon

Don swelling to monumental proportions. He even invited a horde of reporters into the Ravenite. By then they had discovered that the Brooklyn U.S. attorney's office had originally declined the O'Connor assault case on the grounds that it was too shaky.

A reporter asked Gotti if he felt that he was the object of a law enforcement vendetta. Without the help of the media, he replied, "setting the record straight and all, who knows what they would've done to me."

The aura of invincibility Gotti had cloaked himself in, however, would be short-lived.

"John wanted Angie whacked because of his big mouth," Sammy said. "Instead, it was John's big mouth that would wreck the family."

21

*As underboss, I was to go on the lam
and run the family for him, John said.*

FOR MORE THAN A YEAR AND A HALF NOW, A BUG
had been operating inside the Ravenite club.
Bruce Mouw and his lead assistant on the Gambino squad, George Gabriel, had listened to some
six hundred hours of tapes. There had not been a
single useful conversation. Wiseguys had learned
never to talk about any subject of importance in
their social clubs.

But the initial bugging of the Ravenite, seemingly so unproductive, finally paid off in dramatically unexpected fashion. Out of stubbornness
more than anything else, Mouw and Gabriel kept
listening to the tapes over and over again and
finally discerned something on the more recent
ones that previously had escaped their notice. It
was what was not being heard. On occasion, John
Gotti's voice would be unaccountably missing for

as long as an hour. Where was he? Logs of Ravenite comings and goings did not show him exiting
the club.

The Ravenite was on the ground level of a
Mulberry Street tenement. It had its own entrance.
There was a second entrance for the rest of the
building. Inside the tenement, another door connected the club to the adjoining hallway. Was Gotti
conducting meetings in the hallway? It seemed
unlikely that he'd be spending that much time in
such uncomfortable surroundings with residents
passing by.

Then Gabriel developed an informant who confided that when Gotti had something important to
discuss, he retreated to "the apartment upstairs."
But there were several apartments.

Mouw delved into past investigative records
concerning the Ravenite club. He discovered that
a now-deceased Gambino family soldier named
Michael Cirelli had lived in a third-floor apartment, and that back in the Neil Dellacroce era it
had occasionally been used for private meetings.
The apartment was currently occupied by Cirelli's
aging widow, Nettie.

Prosecutors in the Brooklyn U.S. attorney's
office obtained court authorization to place bugs in
the hallway and the apartment itself. When the
widow Cirelli left on a Thanksgiving vacation trip
to visit relatives in Florida, Jim Kallstrom's special
operations team gained entry through the rear of

the tenement and installed the tiny transmitters.

The results of the Cirelli apartment bugs were beyond anything Mouw could have hoped for. After ten relentlessly frustrating years of trying to cut off the head of the dominant Cosa Nostra crime family in America, success was at hand.

There were five recorded sessions in the apartment, dating from November 30, 1989, to January 24, 1990, when the bug stopped functioning. But it didn't matter.

On the tapes, in his own words, Gotti had clearly identified himself as the head of a racketeering criminal enterprise, the Gambino family.

He was heard announcing his intention to promote Sammy to official underboss of the family. Locascio would be shifted to acting *consigliere*.

And on the most crucial tape, recorded on December 12, 1989, he acknowledged that he had ordered the murders of Robert DiBernardo, Louie Milito, and Louie DiBono.

If there was a disappointment on these tapes, it was a Gotti reference to the Castellano hit. With Frank Locascio present, he said to Sammy, "Every time I went there [to Castellano's mansion] on a Saturday or Sunday, I hated it . . . probably the cops done it to this fuckin' guy. Whoever killed this cocksucker—probably the cops killed this Paul. But whoever killed him, he deserved it."

Amazingly enough, all those directly involved in murdering Castellano, who did not include

Locascio, had honored their vow never to admit it, even among themselves.

"I remember the wink, the little smirk John had when he was saying that," Sammy said. "Our little joke with Frankie."

After Gotti's acquittal in the O'Connor assault case, on February 9, 1990, a turf battle broke out over the issue of who would next prosecute him. The main combatants were Andy Maloney, the U.S. attorney for the Eastern District, which embraced Brooklyn and Queens, and the Manhattan district attorney, Robert Morgenthau. Regardless of who won this jurisdictional dispute, it was understood that Gotti had to be charged with the Castellano hit. The case was too high-profile.

Morgenthau enlisted the support of the U.S. attorney for the Southern District, which included Manhattan. The two offices had joined forces in investigating the murder. The Southern District had come up with the nephew of the Philadephia family boss, Nicky Scarfo, who would testify that in the presence of his uncle, he had heard Gotti say he had received official approval from the New York Cosa Nostra commission to kill Castellano.

The New York police, meanwhile, had reported to Morgenthau that an eyewitness had been unearthed, a respectable businessman, who would attest that he saw Gotti standing on the sidewalk near Sparks Steak House as Castellano was being gunned down.

Morgenthau was a legendary law enforcement figure who had once been the U.S. attorney for the Southern District. Indeed, Andy Maloney had served under him as an assistant U.S. attorney there. Widely respected, even revered, Morgenthau would without question be elected D.A. as long as he cared to run. And stung by Gotti's acquittal in the O'Connor case, he was determined to prosecute the Castellano murder. He reminded everyone that traditionally in a murder case, the local D.A. had priority in prosecuting it.

The one thing Morgenthau and the Southern District did not have were Gotti's damning admissions on the Cirelli apartment tapes, which Maloney intended to use as the basis for a massive RICO racketeering indictment.

A compromise was proposed: Morgenthau would get Castellano, and Maloney could keep the RICO charges. But Maloney and his chief of the organized crime section, John Gleeson, fought back. Gleeson, thirty-eight, with an Irish street urchin's face that made him look even younger, argued that the Castellano hit, if tried by itself, was no sure winner. If it were lost, it would only buttress Gotti's aura of invincibility and heighten the public perception that the government was engaged in a mindless vendetta against him. On the other hand,

if Castellano's murder were lumped in with the
other murders Gotti had admitted sanctioning, the
Castellano predicate would be greatly strength-
ened.

By the end of July, the warring parties had
agreed to consolidate the cases. The question still
remained, however, of where it would be prose-
cuted.

Morgenthau, along with the Southern District,
took one last shot. The Eastern District was
famous for jury tampering. Gleeson seized the
moment. If that were so, he said, the chances of
getting a sequestered jury were that much better.

The impasse would be resolved at the Justice
Department in Washington. After another lengthy
round of fierce wrangling, a decision was finally
made. The case would go to the Eastern District—
to Maloney and Gleeson. A grand jury was secretly
convened. Sealed indictments were returned
against Gotti, Sammy, and Frank Locascio. But
before they could be arrested and the indictments
announced, Sammy the Bull Gravano suddenly
disappeared.

Gotti had a paid source, a detective assigned
to the police department's intelligence division,
who was privy to the Morgenthau/Southern District investigation. He reported that Gotti's indictment in the Southern District for the Castellano
murder was imminent. The bug in the tenement
hallway adjoining the Ravenite club recorded a

brief conversation between Gotti and a defense attorney, Gerry Shargel, about the implications of this. Shargel explained that pertinent federal law for a single murder in the aid of racketeering had a five-year statute of limitations. This meant that if he were arrested, it would have to be before December 16, 1990. Gotti's corrupt cop, however, had no knowledge of the Cirelli apartment tapes, which had been kept tightly under wraps in the Eastern District, or the multiple RICO counts he would actually be facing there.

Gotti was confident he could beat any rap based solely on Castellano. At worst, he told Sammy, bail would be denied and he'd end up spending a year, a year and a half, in detention. But it was conceivable that Sammy might also be pinched.

"As underboss, I was to go on the lam and run the family for him, John said."

22

The king insisted that the meeting
be held in the throne room of his castle!

"I TOOK OFF IN LATE OCTOBER," SAMMY SAID. "IT
was the night of a confirmation party for my niece
Gina.

"I had become aware that the surveillance on
me had increased. It used to be a sometime thing.
I got to know the two agents, Frank Spero and
Matty Tricorico. One time they had parked out in
front of my office. It was a cold day, and when I got
there, one of my guys said them two agents have
been sitting there for a couple of hours. I walked
out to see where they were. They said they had a
subpoena, some bullshit civil thing for records. I
asked them why didn't they come to my house?
Why were they sitting in the cold like this? 'We
didn't want to hassle you in front of your wife and
kids,' they said. I took the subpoena, and although I
didn't show it, inwardly I thought that was a pretty

decent thing they did, not to bother my family at home.

"Now the surveillance was more than them, more agents, more cars. At the party, I tried to keep up appearances. I mingled with my relatives. I knew I was making a tremendous sacrifice going into hiding. By being pinched and not having to hide, John was taking the easy road. All he had to do was sit back and wait for his arrest, give a big smile to the media crowd who would be there, and do all his fighting from his jail cell. On the other hand, I would be a wanted fugitive. Law enforcement would have me listed as 'armed and extremely dangerous.' Life in jail isn't easy, but life on the run is a lot harder, especially since you could be confronted by some trigger-happy cop who wanted a piece of Sammy the Bull. John's family would be able to visit him. My family was not going to have any contact with me at all.

"I was dancing with my wife. Suddenly she told me that she felt something was wrong, something was bothering me. I said there were serious problems, which I couldn't explain. I held her tighter and told her that I was going to have to go away for a while. I wouldn't be able to telephone her or be in touch with her. She might hear rumors that I was dead. She was to disregard them. I asked her to have the courage and responsibility to hold the kids, to hold the Gravano family together while I was gone.

"Debbie's eyes filled with tears. She just told me she understood. She was smart enough not to ask any questions. But she was obviously completely and totally brokenhearted. As I looked at her, I understood how much she loved and trusted me. And I understood how much I loved and trusted her.

"Although my faith in John Gotti's Cosa Nostra was deteriorating, my basic loyalty to the true Cosa Nostra still came before loyalty to my own family. But I was now aware that this fact was bothering me more and more.

"My law enforcement tails always left when I returned to my house in the evening. Hundreds of hours of surveillance showed that once I was home, I stayed home. The kids went up to their bedrooms. Debbie made a pot of coffee in the kitchen. That's when I told her I was leaving that night. I went on to tell her I didn't want to jeopardize her with agents, cops, who came around looking for me. I told her that I thought it would be better if she truthfully didn't know where I was, or what was going on. That way she could answer any questions without lying.

"I had already called my driver, Louie Saccente. I went up to kiss the kids. They were half asleep. I went back down and kissed Debbie. The good-byes were over.

"I had arranged with my father-in-law to borrow the keys to a vacation home he had in the

Pocono Mountains in Pennsylvania. He agreed not to ask any questions and to keep this strictly between me and him. When we got there the ground was all snow-covered. It was biting cold. This house was among others that primarily were for summer vacations. Not a soul was around. Louie and me built a big fire. In the morning we found the only local store that was open where we could buy groceries. The siege was on.

"The plan was for me to stay in touch with Big Louie, Huck, and my brother-in-law, Eddie. I would contact them for messages and news. We set up codes. We used beepers. We only used public phones away from our usual haunts.

"After a couple of days, the reality of my situation finally sunk in. I was looking outside the house's sliding glass doors, watching the snow fall, watching the icicles form on the trees, hearing the fire crackling behind me, when I spotted a deer coming through the woods. The fucking serenity of the moment brought home the chaos of the situation I was in. I had asked my father-in-law to trust me while I lived with the emotional horror of the pain I had caused him, even though at that time he was unaware of any involvement I had in his son's death. I questioned in my soul how I could have hurt him like that. Now he could be accused of harboring a fugitive.

"I turned from the window and told Louie, 'Pack it up. We're leaving.' I wasn't going to involve my in-laws in my troubles. I remembered Louie had a condo in Florida and a brother down there, who was a powerboat builder with connections. We couldn't stay at the condo. That would be one of the first spots they'd be looking for us. Louie called his brother and asked him to make reservations for us.

"Louie got the plane tickets. He had me traveling as Frank James, Jesse's brother. Very appropriate.

"We took off from Newark Airport. We were in a plush hotel in Miami. But one night I'm at dinner in a restaurant and I noticed a good-looking woman with an elderly guy. I immediately realized I knew her from Bensonhurst, and I turned my back. Another time, me and Louie were coming off the elevator into the hotel lobby. The lobby was packed. It turned out my hideout was the temporary home of the Los Angeles Raiders. Some hideout! I started to think that Florida was a totally ridiculous place to hide in.

"So now I'm staying in my room. Louie sees how preoccupied I am and suggested that we meet his brother, Bobby, for a drink. To tell the truth, I was looking forward to a night out. Bobby takes us to this club. He saw a girl he knows with some other girls and they all come over and join us. Bobby starts dancing with his girl, and this other girl asked me if I wanted to dance. It was a slow dance and I got my arm around her waist. I suddenly realized that she was petite like my wife. I couldn't get the image of my wife out of my brain. I remembered holding

Debbie and watching her eyes well up with tears the night I left.

"I walked off the dance floor. I told Louie I wasn't feeling well and he should stay and have a good time. But he followed me, asking me, 'What's wrong?' I only told him the scene wasn't my scene. What I was thinking was my wife and kids were home suffering, not knowing if I were dead or alive, not knowing anything. And I'm hiding out in a lounge with drinks and girls? No way! This isn't what Cosa Nostra was supposed to be.

"I told Louie we're leaving Florida. Through the contact arrangement I set up, I knew there weren't any arrests yet. We made a quick trip to New York, where I met with Big Louie, Huck, and my brother-in-law. Then we moved to Atlantic City, to a fancy apartment that one of the soldiers in Big Lou's crew owned. It was on the boardwalk. I would spend my days jogging a little on the beach and working out at a gym to stay in shape. I felt comfortable there. Maybe because it was real close to home.

"I stopped shaving the night I had left for the Poconos and by now I had a full beard. One night Louie and me attended a prize fight. I was wearing a hat and sunglasses and with my beard, I must say it was hard to recognize me. Matter of fact, I saw a number of people at the fight who should have picked me out right away, but didn't. My so-called disguise was working perfectly.

"On my way out of the convention center after the fight, I walked past Renaldo Snipes, the fighter. I loved boxing and I had sparred once with Renaldo at the gym where he trained. I couldn't help myself. I called out his name. There was no recognition in his eyes. As we faced each other, I threw a mock combination of punches at him. I raised my arms over my head in a 'Rocky' style victory salute. Still nothing. As I walked away, I turned back toward him and took off the sunglasses. This time the Gentle Giant finally recognized me, and his face lit up in a big smile.

"As I continued walking out, I was tapped on the shoulder. I turned and was stunned to see a lifelong friend, Diane, with her husband. Diane told me she'd know me anywhere. Then she called to another woman in the crowd. It was my ex-fiancée, Louise. We all met later for drinks. They, and everyone else from my neighborhood, knew of the circumstances surrounding my disappearance. The newspapers had speculated that I had been rubbed out in some sort of power play. Louise said how relieved she was that this wasn't true. As we said good-bye, I could see her smile was forced. She told me that if Debbie and the kids needed anything, I could depend upon her to help. That was a tough good-bye. We'd been saying good-bye for thirty years, and we both knew that this time could be a real good-bye.

"I realized that hiding like this wasn't going to

be easy. I had started the process through mob lawyers to arrange phony IDs and investigate countries without extradition agreements with the United States. I told my brother-in-law to coordinate these leads. But I was torn from a combination of thoughts. I couldn't run the family from a foreign country. I couldn't be a father to my children and a husband to Debbie from there. Should I run away and abandon my wife and kids? Should I battle it out with the law? If I went to prison, at least I would be able to visit with my personal family. I still could be a father to my children. If I stayed on the lam, there was a real good chance I would go out in a final confrontation with law enforcement.

"In Atlantic City, I told Louie no matter what I decided to do, he would become a target by the simple fact that he was with me. I told him he should go. But he told me no, even if it meant leaving the country.

"Things started happening real fast now. All of a sudden, the government issued a subpoena for me to come in to provide new photographs and fingerprints for their records. This may have seemed like a routine request, but by not going in, I became officially a fugitive. I knew there was an increased law enforcement presence around my office, Tali's, my house. My attorney of record was contacted to get me to comply with the subpoena. He didn't know where I was. Or even if I was alive.

It was obvious the government wanted to know, needed to know, what had happened to Sammy the Bull.

"I could see this might be a long, long siege. I was torn by my loyalty to Cosa Nostra because, again, John Gotti's Cosa Nostra wasn't the true Cosa Nostra I believed in. But it was hard for me to forget my blood oath. It was easier to hope that John's Cosa Nostra somehow would turn back into the *true* Cosa Nostra.

"I gathered my old crew around me. I came up with the idea to convert a Brooklyn warehouse into the perfect hideout. Inside the warehouse there would be a safe, totally secure apartment, which could have a bedroom, kitchen, living room. If I had to meet with somebody, it would be only a select few family captains and other very high-ranking members of other families and only for the most serious business. One of my crew would pick up the person and transport him in a van that was modified to have no windows and with a self-contained passenger cubicle. Walkie-talkies would be used to maintain contact with the van. Once the driver determined nobody was following the van, he would be instructed to drive in. There also would be surveillance cameras mounted on the warehouse roof. The person who had the appointment would have no idea as to where he was traveling. After the meeting, he would be driven back on a purposely confusing route. There would be a supply of weapons in the warehouse. I would have a guard dog, a pit bull, for added protection. I was ready for a confrontation with the law.

"Messages began going back and forth with John about the warehouse plan. He called me in for one more meeting to firm up everything. I drove to New York. I got rid of my beard. I could always grow it back. Why allow the agents to see what I looked like with a beard?

"The meeting was set for the Ravenite. Once again John refused to listen to reason. Instead of scheduling it at a secret place in the early morning hours, it had to be out in public with surveillance certain. The king insisted that the meeting be held in the throne room of his castle!

"They must have seen me right away. They didn't waste any time. I was only inside the club about fifteen minutes before the door blew up and a slew of FBI agents came in. They announced they had arrest warrants for John, Frank Locascio, and me. The other guys sitting in the club were told they were free to leave after they gave their names.

"John was very calm, like he was expecting this. I wasn't so happy. After weeks of hiding out, I was now caught just because this meeting *had* to be held at the Ravenite. John said to the agents, he wasn't going nowhere until he had a final cup of espresso. Before they could answer, he turned to the club's counterman and told him, 'Norman, give

me, Sammy, Frankie some coffee.' The agents
didn't say nothing. So John had his little moment.
The three of us, the administration of the Gambino
family, sat in the rear of the Ravenite and finished
drinking our coffee with anisette."

The arrests took place on December 11, 1990.

Handcuffed, Sammy and the others were
taken in separate cars to the FBI's New York headquarters a short distance away. Frank Spero and
Matty Tricorico drove Sammy. They adopted a
laid-back manner. They didn't exhibit a triumphant
"gotcha" attitude. They removed his handcuffs.
Tricorico joked, "We thought we had your routine
down pat. You fooled us pretty good."

"Is that what you were waiting for?" Sammy
asked. "For me to show up?"

"I guess you could say that," Tricorico replied.

At the FBI, they asked Sammy if he wanted
some coffee. They introduced him to Jim Fox, then
an assistant director, who headed the New York
office. Fox, whose back was to Sammy, turned and
automatically shook his hand. Fox recalled that he
was instantly appalled at unwittingly shaking hands
with Sammy Gravano. A year later, he would pose
for a photograph in which he was kissing Sammy
on the cheek, a photograph he has on display in
the office where he is now an insurance company
executive.

When a prisoner was held in detention, all his personal effects, except for a minimal amount of cash, were taken from him and not returned until he was released. For Sammy, that could be quite some time, and the two agents offered to bring his valuables to his wife. He accepted. He gave them the wad of hundred-dollar bills he was carrying, keeping only $30 to open a jailhouse account, along with his watch and jewelry.

Then he and the others were driven to the Metropolitan Correctional Center, again separately. Spero and Tricorico decided to take Sammy in a back way to spare him the onslaught of still photographers and television cameramen flocking around the MCC to record Gotti's arrival. They almost made it to an interior garage. But a crunch of cars forced them to walk the last few yards. That was when a video picture of Sammy, flanked by the two agents, was taken. The cameraman, pointing at Sammy, had yelled, "Is he one of the guys who was arrested?"

Spero would always remember Sammy answering, "No, I got these two guys under arrest. I got everything under control."

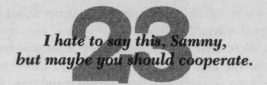

I hate to say this, Sammy, but maybe you should cooperate.

THE INDICTMENTS WERE ANNOUNCED THE FOL-
lowing day. The multiple RICO racketeering
counts included illegal gambling, loan-sharking,
obstruction of justice, conspiracy to murder, and
murder. Only Gotti was charged in the murders of
Paul Castellano and Tommy Bilotti.

All three defendants were placed in the harsh-
est part of the Metropolitan Correctional Center, a
ninth-floor area designated "total sep."

"The whole ninth floor is maximum security,
but total sep is the maximum of the maximum.
They say the toughest federal prison in the country
is Marion, but it couldn't be any tougher than this.
At least Marion was clean. In total sep, there were
roaches, rats, whatever, running all over. Everybody's alone in a cell with a steel door and a little
slot in it that opens up. They allow you an hour to

come out to take a shower and walk up and down the hall, if you feel like it.

"They shake you down every time you come out of the cell. They strip-search you every time you have a visitor. When Debbie and my kids come, I'm taken to this big visiting room, and I said to the guard, 'Where are the other prisoners, all the other visitors?' He tells me, 'You're in total sep. You get a separate, completely isolated visit.'

"'All right,' I said, 'but why don't you go to the other end of the room? Let me talk to my wife and kids.' He actually apologized and said, 'Sammy, I can't. I have to sit here and monitor the visit.'

"So this visit is really nothing. I just tell my wife to hang in there, be strong. Don't worry about nothing. Continue the holidays, continue Christmas, like I was there. We'll talk on the phone. She's shocked. Distraught is the word."

At the request of the defense, a bail hearing on December 21 was closed to the public and the press by the trial judge, U.S. Eastern District Judge I. Leo Glasser.

"John told Frankie Locascio and myself that we all should intimidate the judge, glare at him to show how tough we are, be real aggressive in our attitude. I told John I know the judge. He was the judge in my tax case with the Plaza Suite disco. I said to John he's a tough-minded judge, but he's fair. Why antagonize him? But John don't listen. He gives the judge his look, and Judge Glasser stares right back, like he's doing the same thing almost in reverse. He wasn't intimidated. He don't look scared to me. He denies bail and we're back in our cells."

The December 21 bail hearing forever changed the relationship between John Gotti and Sammy Gravano.

To demonstrate the high risk the defendants presented to society, prosecutor John Gleeson played excerpts of the Cirelli apartment tapes. It was the first time Sammy learned of their existence.

He was mesmerized by the tapes, especially the critical tape of December 12, 1989, which recorded a meeting between Gotti and Locascio that he had not attended.

On that tape, Sammy heard Gotti acknowledge that he had sanctioned the hit on Robert DiBernardo because Sammy had insisted that DiBernardo was being "subversive," when the fact was that Sammy had done everything he could to spare DiBernardo's life.

He heard Gotti tell Locascio that he had ordered the hit on Louie Milito because Sammy reported Milito's offenses against the family. Ignored was the fact that Sammy had actually saved Milito's life when Milito tried to play both sides against the middle during Castellano's reign as the family boss and finally went along with Gotti's decision that Milito had to go when Milito continued to undermine the family.

He heard Gotti say that Sammy had long wanted Louie DiBono dead, which was true. But in the end it was Gotti who ordered the hit and carried it out without any direct participation by Sammy.

The spin Gotti put on these hits enraged Sammy. The tapes portrayed Gotti as a long-suffering boss saddled with a mad-dog killer who hounded him to obtain authorization for hits until he finally threw up his hands and bowed to Sammy's wishes.

That wasn't all. The December 12 tape, Sammy would learn, contained more of Gotti's nonstop diatribe against him. Every time he turned around, Sammy had some new business he hadn't known anything about. "I tell him a million times," Gotti said to Locascio, 'Sammy, slow it down. Pull it in a fucking notch. You got concrete-pouring. You got Italian floors now. You got construction. You got drywall. You got asbestos. You got rugs. What the fuck next?'" Gotti would compare Sammy to Paul Castellano, who had "sold out the *borgata* [family] for a fuckin' construction company. . . . Three, four guys will wind up with every fuckin' thing. And the rest of the *borgata* looks like a waste. . . . Where, where's my piece of these companies?"

Sammy, said Gotti, had committed the unpardonable. He was "creating a fuckin' army inside an army. . . . I'm not gonna allow that." Locascio suggested that Sammy might be downstairs in the Ravenite. Why didn't he go down and bring him up, so all of this could be thrashed out?

"No, no, no," Gotti exclaimed. "I'm gonna see him tomorrow, and I'm gonna talk to him tomorrow."

Tomorrow, of course, never came.

As some of these excerpts boomed in the courtroom, Sammy glanced at Gotti. "He ain't looking at me," Sammy said. "Only his fingers on his right hand are drumming on the table. They say when I'm really mad, my eyes turn blank, kind of glassy. I guess some of the court officers, the marshals, whatever, caught what I was feeling, because the media reported that afterward I went at John in the hall back of the court, even grabbed him by the throat. I didn't do that at all. This is Cosa Nostra, and he's the boss. I am mad that there's a betrayal, but not to the point that I would raise my hands to him. I never would.

"In the hall, I kind of looked at him, and he finally said, 'You're disturbed?' and I said, 'Fucking A, I'm disturbed. I think we got to talk about these tapes.'

"There's no more conversation, because we're put right back in total sep."

The main defense lawyers, Bruce Cutler and Gerry Shargel, finally obtained a court order from

Judge Glasser to have the defendants moved out of total sep into the general jail population on the grounds that the Bureau of Prisons was breaking its own rules for the treatment of inmates who were not troublemakers.

Now Gotti, Sammy, and Locascio could talk to one another.

Sammy waited in vain for Gotti's explanation of what he had said on the December 12 tape. Instead, Gotti informed Sammy and Locascio that they would not be permitted to listen to the tapes. Nor would either of them be able to meet with their attorneys except in Gotti's presence. Gotti and Cutler would mastermind their mutual defense.

Sammy had retained Shargel, whose legal expertise he admired and who he hoped would strongly represent him in the coming strategy sessions. But then he learned to his dismay that Judge Glasser had disqualified not only Cutler but Shargel as defense attorneys for the trial. Bugs in the hallway adjacent to the Ravenite had shown them to be "house counsels" for the Gambino family in efforts to anticipate and thwart the government in its various investigations. Gleeson successfully argued that they had become "part of the evidence" and thus subject to being called as witnesses. Worse yet, on one of the Cirelli apartment tapes, Gotti, ranting about legal fees, had said, "Gambino crime family? This is the Shargel, Cutler crime family."

Gotti eventually settled on a renowned Brooklyn-born attorney, Albert Krieger, a former president of the National Association of Criminal Defense Lawyers, whose booming courtroom voice was reminiscent of Cutler's. For Sammy, he chose a former Manhattan assistant D.A. named Benjamin Brafman, experienced in representing alleged mob clients.

Clearly, John Gleeson, a deceptively low-key, scholarly graduate of the University of Virginia Law School, was proving to be a formidable adversary. Moreover, Gleeson had a special interest in John Gotti. He'd been an assistant to Diane Giacalone in her ill-fated prosecution of Gotti.

Gotti's behavior grew increasingly bizarre.

He invited Sammy to have a "man-to-man" discussion about what he had said on the December 12 tape. It didn't get very far. His explanation was that he was upset by all of Sammy's business ventures. "It was your fault," he said.

Sammy didn't argue. "What was the point," he said. "It was done. The government had the tape already." But when he asked for permission to seek a severance so that he could attempt a defense without directly contradicting Gotti, Gotti refused. "We're all in this together," he said. "I got to think of the future of the family. I got to think of the future of Cosa Nostra. I got to think of my public."

• • •

The Gulf War was on. "We're watching this bullshit on television every day. John's rooting for Iraq to win the war, for our troops to die and this and that. I told him one day, 'Look, it could be our kids in the army. Some of them could be the kids of people we know. What the fuck. OK, we hate the government. But what do these kids got to do with it? I mean, like it or not, we belong to this country. The country is good, maybe the people running it ain't so good.'

"John don't buy it. I got to root against us in this fucking war. Maybe once or twice a week, they take you to the roof for recreation. Lo and behold, I go to the roof and it's raining and what do they give you to wear? An army jacket! This jacket just brings back every memory I ever had about the army and the military, and now I have to take it off and go back down and root against the army? It really turns me off. It's not me. I'll fight the government, I'll fight anybody who's fucking with me, but this is beyond that, hoping our kids should get bombed and killed and everything."

"One morning Frankie Locascio goes out for his breakfast and robs a half a dozen oranges. Which is a major thing in the can, where you eat shit. 'Hey, Sammy,' he says. 'I got an orange for you. I glommed them out of the refrigerator when I was in the kitchen.'

"About eleven o'clock, the king wakes up. At least, we think he just woke up. He comes out, and he's got a puss on down to the floor. He sat down at the table.

"'Morning, John, How you feeling, bro?' I said.

"Frankie's there and he says, 'Hey, John, I got an orange. You want an orange?'

"John tells him, 'Stick the fucking orange up your motherfucking ass.'

"Other inmates are around. I'm in total shock. 'John, John,' I said, 'what are you doing? He's your *consigliere*.'

"'Shut the fuck up,' he says. He looks at Frankie. 'You fucking bum. You think I was sleeping. I heard you. I'm the fucking boss. You offered him'—meaning me—'a fucking orange first?'

"I said, 'John, he robbed a half a dozen. He gave me one. He's giving you five. You weren't up. I'm up four hours before you.' I saw the other inmates listening to this. 'Fellas,' I told them, 'OK, get back in your cells.'

"John tells me, 'What did you do that for?'

"I said, 'John, he's our acting *consigliere*. You're the boss. You want to abuse him, go ahead. But not in front of all these fucking assholes.'

"'All right,' he says. Then he says, 'Frankie, when we get the fuck out of here, I'll show you who the fuck the boss is.'

"John goes right back in his cell. I put my finger to my lips as if to say to Frankie to be quiet. And Frankie goes back to his cell. He stayed in there all day long. When John came out later, I said, 'John, you're killing this guy. For what? And me, too. For what? You said we're all in this together. We're fighting this case together. What the fuck are we doing wrong here?'

"John don't make any sense. He's talking bullshit. He says, 'Sammy, I'll explain it to you when we get out. But this fucking bum, I got him up to here.'

"'All right, John,' I said. 'But there's other guys around. You know what I mean? We're starting to look bad.'

"The next day, early in the morning, seven, eight o'clock in the morning, I'm standing by the phone and Frankie comes up to me. 'Sammy, can I talk to you?' 'Yeah, sure, what's up?'

"He has tears streaming down his face. A man fifty-nine, sixty years old, a real tough guy, a man's man. He says he's gone crazy, meaning John. He apologizes for not standing up to John when John was bad-mouthing me in the apartment. 'The minute I get out, I'm killing this motherfucker.'

"'Frankie, you know what you're saying?' I said. 'He's your boss.'

"He says, 'Sammy, I never been a punk in my life. Nobody's ever talked to me that way. I don't give a flying fuck if I die trying to do it or afterwards. He made me feel like a punk.'

"I thought about this for a minute. Then I said, 'I agree with you, bro. You know what I'm gonna do? We'll shake hands right now, Frankie. The minute we get out, we'll set up a victory party immediately, and we'll kill him.'

"Frankie said, 'Sammy, two things. I'll bring him to the party myself, and I got to be the shooter.'

"We shake hands. We kiss. He wipes his face. He's a man again. His shoulders are back, his chest is out. He's Frank Locascio again."

"They split myself, John, and Frankie up. I'm in Eleven South. John is in Eleven North. Frankie is in Nine North. One day when we're visiting with the lawyers, John tells me, 'Eleven South and Eleven North has the same library day. Put your name on the list. I'll do the same.' I think this was a Tuesday. He's not so bad when we meet. He seems to have calmed down a little bit, even about Frankie. After we go back up, the prison realizes that me and John were together in the library. So they change Eleven South to a Wednesday for me and a Thursday for John. But when they changed the library days, they put me in with Frankie, Nine North. So me and him are in there together. We talk about the case, how we can't listen to the tapes, how we can't meet with our lawyers without John. Nothing new. No big deal, all bullshit.

"The next day, there's a visit with all the lawyers. John tells them, 'Excuse us a minute,' and they get up, like little puppies, and walk out of the room. And then John says, 'What do you think, I'm a fucking jerk-off? You think I ain't got eyes and ears all over this prison? You two went sneaking down to a meeting in the library.'

"I said, 'Hey, John, we didn't sneak. Like with you and me, the prison put me and Frankie on the same day. What do you mean, sneaking? Everybody knows we were there.'

"'Yeah, well, don't go on another library meeting together again.'

"After I got back upstairs, I thought to myself that Frankie was right. This motherfucker is sick, sick, sick."

"One morning, a guard says to me, 'Gravano, lawyer's visit.' It was about nine o'clock. I'm saying to myself, John's starting to get up early? I'm cuffed up and go down. Who's there but Gerry Shargel. He can't represent me at the trial, but he's allowed to give advice before it begins.

"I said, 'You didn't send for everybody?'

"'No.'

"'What's up?'

"He says that he knows John sleeps in the morning and that I should tell him that Al D'Arco, who's the street boss for the Lucchese family, has flipped.

"In the afternoon, another guard comes over and says, 'Your friend wants to see you.' Now between Eleven South and Eleven North, there's a corridor where the elevators are. The guard says, 'I'm gonna let you in the corridor. Make like you're waiting for an elevator.' So I'm there and John comes in and he starts yelling, 'What did I tell you about meeting lawyers alone?'

"'John,' I said, 'the guard said there's a lawyer waiting. How could I know you and Frankie and everybody ain't down there? That's number one. Number two, Shargel told me Little Al flipped and to give you the message.'

"'Don't ever let it happen again!' John doesn't give a fuck about D'Arco and how it might affect our case. All he cares about is me meeting this lawyer."

"On one visitation day we have, I'm sitting next to my wife. We been married some twenty-some years. Dope that she is, she still loves me, and she's devastated that I'm in this position. As we talk, she's caressing my hand, trying to console me. I don't even realize it. Frankie leans over and whispers, 'Sammy, let your wife stop rubbing your hand.' I look at Frankie. I think he's nuts. He shifts his eyes towards John and gives a little nod. I looked at John. He's smiling, but kind of shaking his head. I turned to Debbie and told her to stop touching my hand. I said, 'It's not supposed to be a contact visit. If the guards see it, they'll stop the visit early.'

"As we're going back in, I said, 'What was that all about with my wife touching my hand?'

"John said, 'Sammy, you're the underboss. We got to carry ourselves a certain way in front of people.'

"'Oh, did she slip and grab my dick at one point that I don't remember?'

"'Don't be fucking cute with me,' he said."

In 1989, in the rigged construction deals Sammy set up with the Teamsters and other unions, he had given Gotti eighty percent of the take—which came to minimally $1.2 million in cash.

For his aboveboard construction contracts, Sammy and his wife, filing separately, paid taxes on nearly $800,000, her recorded income about double Sammy's. After taxes, Sammy then gave Gotti anywhere from 30 to 50 percent, about another $200,000, again in cash. Gotti also received an additional $600,000 or so a year from Sammy's nightclubs, after-hours clubs, various individual scores and street deals. The only income Sammy kept for himself was his loan-sharking profits. By then he had $1.5 million out on the street, which brought in an average $15,000 in interest a week, which, as an aggressive entrepreneur, he continually rolled over.

"No question I was the biggest earner for John," Sammy said. "But he was very cagey about what he got overall, except he was always complaining. You look at Tommy Gambino and the garment center and you know Tommy's bringing in a ton of money. There's also the carting industry, the shipping on the piers, the hijacking scores, the drug money. I mean Patsy Conte had this food market chain, but he was a big heroin dealer. He slips John a hundred thousand every now and then and, believe me, John wouldn't question it. John didn't think, though, that it was coming from Patsy selling tomatoes. It was hard to tell. But if you figured it all out, I would say on the very low side, John was getting five million a year and probably more like ten, twelve million. The only legitimate income he could show was being a plumbing supply salesman and a zipper salesman for this garment center company for, I think, a hundred thousand a year. And he don't even bother paying taxes on that."

"Besides that gang of lies John is telling Frankie Loc on the tape about the hits, he's saying I got this business, I got that business. Those are lies, too. We have them businesses. I shared everything with John that I had in construction and everything else.

"So what is Mr. Machiavelli up to, saying I'm

creating an army within an army? Nobody was more loyal to John in the family than myself. Obviously, in this double-crossing life of ours, John has decided maybe I'm a threat down the road. It's true he don't know everything I'm doing, but that's because he doesn't know nothing about the construction industry.

"Now Frankie ain't standing up to him, but he ain't going along with all this either, so John keeps pushing. He can't just decide to whack me out for nothing. I'm his underboss. I have too much respect in the family and with other families. And I got my old crew, which is the best work crew in the family, who would die for me, no matter what. So John was hoping Frankie would go out and lay the groundwork, dropping little hints to the captains that Sammy's doing this and that. Where is Sammy headed? Maybe it's time for Sammy to go. Only Frankie didn't do that.

"All John had to do was come to me once during that eleven months we were in there together and say, 'Sammy, I'm sorry. My big fucking mouth got you indicted, number one. Number two, let's try to get a severance for you, so you could fight your case. Fuck the public. Let's try to fight this so that one of us, all of us, a couple of us, get out of this fucking mess.

"If he done that, I would have never cooperated with the government, not in a million years would I have cooperated. And if I lost everything and didn't want to play this game anymore, I would have taken myself the fuck out. I don't think I would have a problem in the world doing it. If I could hit somebody else, which I did plenty, I could definitely hit myself for the right reason. Don't get me wrong, I'm not suicidal, but I would do it if I didn't like being in the can forever. I would have taken something. I would have whacked myself out and it'd be, 'OK, God, let's go onto this next life, what do we do now?'

"Instead, it's I still can't listen to the tapes. I can't speak to my own lawyer. He's saying, 'You have no defense. Look what you made me do. Look how mad you got me saying stupid things, things that ain't even true.' It just got worse and worse. He's telling me it's my fault.

"That gets me thinking. No apologies. No severance. I got no defense. He don't say point-blank to me, 'You got to take the weight.' But now I can see that's what he's setting me up for. He sees that December 12 tape could be to his benefit and go against me. If it's played right, the jury could look at John as the boss, the way he dresses and all, and that poor John has lost control of this Sammy the Bull, his underboss. This Sammy has run rampant and John's on tape actually complaining about it. Maybe with his personality, his charisma, with movie stars like Anthony Quinn and Mickey Rourke coming into court and waving at him, the jury would think that he's not such a bad guy and the real monster here is Sammy. So let's convict *him*."

"Comes October, and I'm still not even thinking of cooperating. It's my whining brother-in-law, Eddie Garafola, a whining motherfucker all my life, who puts the idea in my head. He's caused me nothing but trouble with his devious ways, always looking for the angle. A couple of guys in my crew wanted to whack him. You can't trust him, they said. Just the way he wanted me to walk away from that building project in Brooklyn we were going to take a bath on, that was Eddie, pure and simple. But he's got a big edge with me. His wife is my sister and I ain't ever going to hurt her, even though he's treating her like shit.

"So now he comes in for a visit, whining one more time with that crying voice, 'Sammy, you're gonna go down on this case.'

"I said, 'What do you suggest, Eddie?'

"He says, 'I hate to say this, Sammy, but maybe you should cooperate. I'll go with you. Me and you cooperate and we'll go into a whole other life. Take our families and run after it's over.'

"'Cooperate? That's what you think we should do?'

"'Yeah. We have no other choice.'

"'You're willing to pack up your family and go

with me and my family and we'll just duke it out from there on in?'

"He says, 'We'll make another life, Sammy.'

"I said, 'Eddie, think about this when you leave. Next visit, see if your opinion changes. And I'll think about it when I go back to my cell. You're hitting me with something I never thought about in my life.'

"And it's true. Back in '74 when I got pinched in the double murder of the Dunn brothers and the D.A. was offering me total immunity, I didn't even consider cooperating. I'm trying to figure where Eddie's coming from. He knows he ain't too popular with a lot of guys. I've been his protector. With me away, he probably is thinking he's very vulnerable.

"But back in my cell, I say to myself this could be a real possibility. It would be a real rough road. What the fuck would my wife think? My kids? Would I shatter their lives? Would people try to hurt them? That thought went out of my mind because other guys cooperated, and we never ever considered hurting their families. They're innocent. What the fuck did they have to do with this life? What I worried about more was assholes who might think it would help them get to be made.

"While I'm considering all of this, we have a meeting with the lawyers. I make another pitch to try and go for a severance. John says, 'Sammy, a severance? I told you. What would my public think? They would think you don't want to be on trial with me.'

"I said, 'You want me to do the rest of my life in prison without even trying to fight for myself because of what the public may think?'

"John says, 'Sammy, you got to understand this. It's not about me now. Everything has to be to save Cosa Nostra, which is John Gotti. Cosa Nostra needs John Gotti. You got a problem with that?'"

On October 10, through a trusted intermediary, Sammy sent word to the two FBI agents he was sure he could count on to keep his intent confidential: Frank Spero and Matty Tricorico. The message was that he wanted to talk to them. They immediately informed their supervisor, Bruce Mouw, who brought the electrifying news to prosccutor John Gleeson.

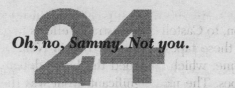

Oh, no, Sammy. Not you.

THROUGHOUT THE SUMMER AND EARLY FALL OF 1991, John Gleeson had been analyzing various defense strategies.

He reached precisely the same conclusion as Sammy.

It would be subtle, Gleeson thought, but its aim would be to allow Gotti to maintain, 'Hey, it wasn't me. It was him.' Its goal would be to persuade the jury that Sammy was the real bad guy, a blank slate upon which could be etched the face of a mad-dog killer. Convict him and cut free John Gotti. Or at least let Gotti off lightly.

Gleeson knew that the weakest part of his case against Gotti was the Castellano killing. Still, he felt that he had strong circumstantial evidence for the large-canvas prosecution he wished to pursue. He intended to trace a line from the Angelo Ruggiero

tapes, which clearly revealed a giant heroin operation, to Castellano's frustrated efforts to gain access
to these tapes and to the bug in Neil Dellacroce's
home, which recorded the bitter debate over the
tapes. The next significant event was the death of
Dellacroce, which cost Gotti his protector. Combined with Gotti's sneering comments about
Castellano in the Cirelli apartment tapes, Gleeson
would argue that Gotti was caught in a kill-or-be-
killed situation. The means of acquiring power and
control in the Gambino family were murder. The
underlying thesis would be: If not Gotti, who could
have ordered the hit on Castellano?

The news Bruce Mouw brought that Sammy
wanted to talk simply bowled Gleeson over. It was
the last thing he expected. He had observed Gotti
and Sammy side by side in court, and Gleeson
had no doubt that the truly tough guy, the true
gangster, was Sammy. If he'd had to bet on who
might turn, it would have been the most marginal
defendant, Frank Locascio. But Locascio had a
serious problem. His son was a made member of
the family. If Frank flipped, he would be signing
his son's death warrant.

Gleeson's immediate question was what did
Sammy want in return? Mouw relayed the answer
from Sammy's intermediary: complete immunity.

That was impossible, Gleeson replied. Unlike a
state prosecutor, a federal prosecutor could not set
the terms for a plea bargain. Only the presiding

federal judge could do that. The best Gleeson could do was to hold out the hope of a twenty-year cap on any prison sentence, and he could not guarantee that. It would depend not only on the judge, but also on the quality of Sammy's testimony and how well he delivered it.

After a couple of anxious days, the word came back that the conditions Gleeson had outlined were acceptable to Sammy.

The next problem was how to meet with him without Gotti's knowledge. Obeying Gotti's demand that a defiant stand be taken on every point, defense counsel gave Gleeson the opening he needed by refusing to stipulate that the voices on the apartment tapes were Gotti's, Sammy's, and Locascio's. Gleeson obtained a court order requiring voice analysis tests. The three defendants were scheduled on three successive days. Sammy was the last, on October 24.

"I was just told that they would reach out to me soon," Sammy said. "Then when this voice bull- shit comes up, I figure this has to be it. I go over to the court in Brooklyn. My lawyer, Brafman, is there. I do the test. Brafman leaves. I'm taken down to go back to jail. There's a couple of guys from the Lucchese family in the bullpen waiting to go back, too. Then a marshal comes by and says, 'Gravano, they want you back upstairs.'

"The Lucchese guys said, 'What do they want you for?'

"I said, 'I probably forgot to sign something. Who knows with these fucking bums?'

Waiting in a room for Sammy were Gleeson and agents Mouw, George Gabriel, Frank Spero, and Matty Tricorico. Spero remembered how great a surge of anticipation they all felt.

The first thing Sammy said was, 'I want to switch governments.' This left Gleeson somewhat nonplussed. He wasn't then aware that Cosa Nostra considered itself a second government.

Gleeson had two concerns. One was that Sammy might try to downplay his criminality. Second, even worse, he might try to tell them what he thought they wanted to hear. Gleeson's fears immediately evaporated. Sammy at once confessed to participating in, one way or another, eighteen or nineteen murders. The government had no idea of his involvement in most of them.

From pretrial discovery, Gleeson knew that Sammy knew there was a citizen witness who was prepared to testify that he had seen Gotti standing on the sidewalk near where Castellano was gunned down. It would have been very easy for Sammy to confirm this if he wanted to curry favor with the prosecution. But he didn't. He told his amazed listeners that he himself had been on the scene, that he had been with Gotti throughout, and that Gotti had never left the car they were both in. After Sammy had named Vinnie Artuso as one of the shooters, Gleeson realized that the witness had made an honest mistake. Artuso bore a close resemblance to Gotti.

Sammy had no legal representation, which could be a problem for Gleeson later on. And Sammy certainly didn't want Brafman present, because he feared that if Brafman was there Gotti would learn what was afoot. Gleeson asked Sammy if he wanted Judge Glasser to appoint counsel for him. Sammy agreed. Glasser was immediately contacted and joined the meeting, where Sammy's request was formally recorded. For Gleeson, Sammy had just crossed the Rubicon.

No one wanted Sammy to return to the detention center. Despite all the precautions, there still could be a leak. Why risk it? But Sammy insisted that he needed at least two weeks to get some of his affairs in order and to inform his wife and children about what he was doing. Although he didn't say this to Gleeson and the agents, he also wanted time to gird himself for what lay ahead.

"I needed some time to think," Sammy said. "This is the most major thing I've ever done in my entire life. It's something against my grain. It's something that I've never even thought of doing, couldn't imagine doing, in any way, shape, or form. And here I was about to do it. It wasn't that

I was going to change my mind. I'm not a half-assed guy in anything I ever did. Once I decide to go forward, that's it. But I knew this was going to be enormous. I needed time to just breathe and relax . . . and just think about everything."

Still, everyone in the room was concerned about what might happen to him if he returned to the detention center. "Well, if it does," said Sammy the Bull, "I guess the deal's off."

"When Eddie is in for another visit, I told him. And he double-crosses me. He backs out. He ain't coming along. You know, it was like when you're kids standing by the edge of the pool, and it's one, two, three, jump! Schmucko jumped, and he didn't. I didn't really care, anyway. It didn't bother me. It's another betrayal on my way out of this life. So it was actually a good reminder. I remembered again when Old Man Paruta and the others would tell me, 'Sammy, there will come a day this guy'll double-cross you, betray you. Go on vacation with your wife and kids and we'll kill him.' And I wouldn't do it.

"Eddie's a schemer, a wheeler-dealer, a conniver. I don't know what was going on in his mind. I think at first, with me away, he was afraid of being shunned, losing clout, losing money, maybe that his number would be up. And then maybe he starts thinking that there's no heat on his ass, really. And he has second thoughts, 'Fuck this. I'm not pinched. Sammy is. Why should I take off ? I could bad-mouth Sammy, grab some of his construction business.' That was Eddie. He's looking at every angle. And he knows I ain't going to do nothing against him because of my sister."

The hardest moments for Sammy were with his wife and children.

"I called them to come to see me, my wife and my daughter, not my son, who was only fourteen. I told them I was going to cooperate.

"Debbie says, 'No!' She's shocked, she's scared, she's everything. My daughter is hysterical. Completely and totally. Her idol, her father, is about to join forces with the enemy. And I'm thinking, Jesus, how did I fuck up my whole life so badly? She's crying. 'No, Dad, *please!*' and she runs right out of the visiting room.

"My wife's eyes are full of tears. She says, 'I have to tell you, Sammy, I'm not going into any witness protection program. I'm not going to be part of this. I was never part of that part of your life, and I'm not going to be part of this. I'm not going to be part of anything.'

"I said, 'Deb, I understand your position and I respect it. You're a mother, not a gangster. You do what you got to do as a mother and I'll understand it one hundred percent.'

"She gives me a hug, and she leaves.

"My heart was breaking. I've never been

through anything like this, never thought it could happen. But I know in my gut that for the first time in my life, I'm finally doing the right thing. I was going the route I chose. I wasn't turning back.

"I was thinking of my son. I was worried about him. I had all kinds of thoughts about him. His father, the underboss, is going to jail. His father is a big hero in the neighborhood. And my son might try to follow in my footsteps, and I can't stop it because I'd be in jail. He's going to be running around, his father is this big underboss, and people are going to cater to him and he's going to wind up in the fucking life. He's a tough kid, but a good kid. He's not for the life. I had always sheltered him from it. And if he winds up in the life, he's sure to end up either being whacked or going to jail himself."

Around midnight on November 8, Sammy was removed from the Metropolitan Correctional Center. The pretext was that he was being transferred to a federal prison in Otisville in upstate New York, a not uncommon occurrence for inmates being held in the MCC.

Sammy had become the leader among the prisoners in Eleven South. When he was moved out, all of them—black, Hispanic, Italian, Irish—were chanting, "Sammy! Sammy! Good luck, Sammy!"

Sammy said, "I knew I wasn't going to no

Otisville. But the worst was yet to come. Frank Spero and Matty are waiting downstairs and they ask, 'How you feeling?' and I say 'OK.' They bring me out to where Bruce Mouw and the other agents are waiting. Just then, this black woman comes by. She's a guard and she patrols the perimeter of the jail. As I'm coming out, she looks at all the agents, and she looks at me, and she says, 'Oh, no, Sammy. Not you.'

"I said, 'Yeah, it's me.' I was literally sick to my stomach. It killed me inside.

"Bruce Mouw walks over and shakes my hand. He opened a car door, and I got in. I told him, 'Are you Mouw?' He says, 'Yes,' and I said, 'I heard you were from Iowa.'

"He said that was right and I said, 'Well, if I got to trust somebody, it might as well be somebody from Iowa.' And off we went."

Sammy was transported under heavy guard to the FBI's training academy at the U.S. Marine base in Quantico, Virginia. There, Gleeson and Sammy hammered out the deal agreement, subject to Judge Glasser's approval. Gleeson found Sammy to be smart, engaging, and a hard bargainer. Sammy tried—and failed—to get the maximum duration of his potential sentence reduced from twenty to ten years. But he did achieve two important points. One was a two-year cap on his availability as a government witness. Clearly, he wanted to avoid, if possible, testifying against any of the loyal members of his old crew. A "good faith" compromise was reached. If, through no fault of the government, a case it wished to prosecute had not been brought to trial before the two years were up, Sammy would cooperate. Otherwise, the decision to testify would be solely Sammy's.

As for the second point, Gleeson had to hand it to Sammy. He wanted Judge Glasser to sign off on the agreement immediately. Normally, a judge's approval was withheld until the time of actual sentencing. Gleeson perceived what was going through Sammy's mind. What if Glasser became incapacitated? Another judge might come in and reject the whole package. Gleeson himself might be out of the picture. To Gleeson's knowledge, no one had ever made a request like this before. But there was no provision against it. Sammy still had to perform, and Judge Glasser granted his approval.

As soon as Benjamin Brafman received a letter from Sammy formally discharging him as his attorney, Brafman dispatched an urgent request to Gleeson asking him to let it be known that Brafman had nothing to do with Sammy's decision to become a government witness. What a wonderful example,

Gleeson would think derisively, of a lawyer looking out for the best interests of his client.

Shortly after Sammy's decision became public, on November 12, 1990, a campaign of vilification was launched.

Gotti's allies and lawyers took frantic steps to influence potential jurors. Stories were leaked that Sammy was an untrustworthy closet homosexual, a womanizer, a drug dealer and addict, a demented serial killer who would do and say anything to save his own skin. Flyers were distributed picturing a loathsome rat with his head on it, a portrait reprinted in the city's tabloids. Tabloid columnists, television commentators, and radio talk-show hosts focused on the "rat" aspect of Sammy's decision.

One columnist pursuing the "Sammy the Rat" scenario would liken him to a "terrorist" bent on "slaughtering innocents," while neglecting to note that the "innocents" were hoodlums themselves operating in a closed society where murder was an everyday part of their lives.

A story inspired by the Gotti camp appeared repeatedly in print. After Sammy had personally killed his wife's brother and had the body chopped up and distributed around the neighborhood, so the story went, the family dog belonging to his in-laws came prancing into their living room holding the victim's hand in its jaws. It made for horrifyingly grisly reading. Except, of course, it hadn't happened.

Seemingly more responsible segments of the local press, including the *New York Times* and *Newsday*, shared a nearly universal perception that Sammy's sole motivation was to spare himself life in prison. Citing anonymous investigative sources, it was reported that he was probably not as tough as advertised, that he was actually "soft" and would "crack" under the pressure of a bleak future behind bars.

No one seemed to recall that at age twenty-nine, newly married and with an infant daughter, Sammy had faced another life sentence and had refused an offer of immunity in the Dunn brothers case.

The FBI's Jim Fox was especially angered by some of the media coverage Sammy was getting. Before heading up the New York office of the FBI, Fox had spent most of his career in foreign counterintelligence during the height of the Cold War. "Whenever we got a Soviet defector," he told me, "he was treated like a hero, a guy who had seen the light and now was helping our side, doing the right thing. Yet Cosa Nostra had done far more to damage the well-being of the United States than the Soviet Union ever did. And here was Gotti being portrayed as some sort of folk hero and Sammy as a Judas. It didn't make any sense. Where were our values?"

•   •   •

In late December, Gleeson brought Sammy secretly to New York for a grand jury appearance. It was a relatively minor case involving the DeCalvacante family in New Jersey and the Genovese family. Gleeson had purposely scheduled it for New Year's Eve. The courthouse was all but vacant. Security would not be much of a factor. The media was not likely to be around.

"We didn't need Sammy to get an indictment," Gleeson said. "But I wanted him to testify. I wanted him to be under oath and speak in front of jurors. To be candid about it, I wanted to get a look at him, to see, when it came to crunch time and he had to raise his right hand and testify, how he comported himself. And he comported himself perfectly, of course."

At Quantico, Sammy was under the control of the FBI's paramilitary Hostage Rescue Team. He remained closely guarded. He was not permitted to leave where he was quartered. He was locked in by himself every night.

Spero and Tricorico observed how stressful his situation was. Finally they prevailed upon the commander of the unit in charge of Sammy to let him go jogging. "Look," we told him, "he needs a little exercise," Tricorico said. "Let him run a little."

The jogging took place in the pitch blackness of cold winter mornings at five-thirty, a three-mile

run along a Marine tank trail. A car was parked
with its lights on to mark the turnaround point
atop a rise. A truck with guards followed to light
the way. "We asked Sammy if he wanted a hat and
gloves," Spero said. "'Yeah, all right.' He wanted
them, but he would never ask. He was a real stoic
type of guy. The first morning, Sammy was huff-
ing and puffing up that hill to where we had to
come back. It didn't look like he was going to
make it. A few days later, he was leaving us all
behind. He wanted to do the run twice, three
times. It just showed you how he did everything a
hundred percent. He was a hood a hundred percent. And when it came time to cooperate and
testify, he was a hundred percent."

After some three weeks of jury selection, the trial of
Gotti and Locascio got under way on February 12,
1991, with an opening statement by U.S. attorney
Andy Maloney.

Prompted by Gotti's Brioni double-breasted
suits, brightly patterned silk ties, and matching
pocket squares, *Newsday* instituted a daily artist-
illustrated fashion watch in its coverage under the
heading "Today's Gotti Garb." Once, as Gotti sat
preening in court for the benefit of jurors, spectators and the press, John Gleeson happened to
pass close by him. "Your wife's a junkie," Gotti
hissed.

Sammy's testimony began on March 2. Emissaries from Gotti sought to have Sammy's wife in court to unnerve him. She refused. She told them what she'd told Sammy. She wasn't part of this.

Spero and Tricorico were on hand to supply moral support. So was Jim Fox. "I was in this back room with them," Sammy said. "There's a recess and Gleeson comes out and said, 'We're calling you out in a couple of minutes.' Of course, I was nervous. I've been reading all this stuff about me, like I'm the devil. I'm a rat. I'm a canary. I'm a stool pigeon. I'm a piece of shit. I'm a traitor. I'm confused. Which side are these reporters on? It's killing me that my wife and kids have to read all this.

"Then I'm called and I walk through that door into court. I thought I was in a funeral parlor. You could literally hear a pin drop. I walked in there, and it's wall-to-wall people. I saw John and Frankie at the defense table. I took the oath, and I sat in the witness chair. My head is spinning a million different thoughts. John is fucking staring at me with this glassy-eyed look. I'm giving it right back to him. He has this little smirk. Believe me, I'm not smirking. Then Gleeson asked me a question, and I had to turn and look at him. That first day John was like he always was. Sitting straight up, not a hair out of place, fancy suit, whatever, the big boss. My last day John ain't so erect anymore. He was slumping down. His hair is a little messy. His tie is crooked. I think he knew he was beat."

For three days, Gleeson led Sammy step-by-step through his life of crime, his life in Cosa Nostra, his life with John Gotti. Sammy was next subjected to five days of withering—and futile—cross-examination by Gotti's attorney, Krieger, and Locascio's lawyer, Anthony Cardinale.

The father of Gleeson's dedicated, savvy lead assistant prosecutor, Laura Ward, was a federal judge. He dropped in periodically. "In all my years on the bench," he told his daughter, "I've never seen a better witness."

On April 2, after only thirteen hours of deliberation, the jury found Gotti guilty of all the racketeering and murder counts against him. Locascio was found guilty of racketeering, racketeering conspiracy, and conspiracy to commit murder.

Both Gotti and Locascio received life sentences without parole. Gotti began his incarceration at the maximum security federal penitentiary in Marion, Illinois. Locascio was shipped to a federal prison in Terre Haute, Indiana.

Epilogue

BY THE TIME SAMMY THE BULL GRAVANO WAS SEN-
tenced, on September 26, 1994, he was responsible for the conviction, guilty pleas, or extended
prison terms of dozens of key Cosa Nostra figures,
the conviction of the corrupt juror in Diane
Giacalone's failed prosecution of Gotti and the
New York criminal intelligence cop who had been
feeding investigative information to Gotti, as well
as for the guilty pleas of eight top trade union
officials for labor racketeering.

In the Gambino family alone, in addition to the
convictions of Gotti and Locascio, seven captains
were in prison on murder and assorted racketeering
counts. Among them was Tommy Gambino, the son
of Carlo Gambino and the czar of the family's
empire in the garment industry, which cost the
American public an average $3.50 in hidden taxes
for every $100 spent on clothing.

The bosses of the Colombo family and New Jersey's DeCalvacante family, the Genovese family underboss, and the Colombo family *consigliere* were also convicted, as well as a Genovese captain and two Lucchese captains.

In addressing Judge Glasser regarding Sammy's law enforcement contributions, John Gleeson noted the unique "ripple" effect of Sammy's testimony. "With respect to all previous cooperators," Gleeson said, ". . . when those people cooperated, there was no ripple effect in the street, in the organized crime community. The take on that was, well, there's something wrong with the guy. . . . What we heard from informants, what we heard from the people who followed Gravano in to become a cooperating witness was that when Salvatore Gravano cooperated, it did not indicate that there was something wrong with Salvatore Gravano, but it indicated that there was something wrong with the mob. It was very much of an attitude adjustment, very much a turning point."

As a result, Gleeson said, a "veritable flood" of cooperating witnesses had stepped forward, including both the acting boss and underboss of the Lucchese family.

Gravano, he told Glasser, "has rendered extraordinary, unprecedented, historic assistance to the government."

•　　•　　•

Before passing sentence, Judge Glasser took pains to note, "I can't recall seeing any reference to Gravano that wasn't preceded by words such as *rat, snitch, turncoat* or some other pejorative word. . . . Would we view it in the same way if, for example, a member of the World Trade Center bombing conspiracy informed on his fellow conspirators, the perpetrators of that disaster? Who, in that context, has Gravano informed against? Is assisting the government to bring major criminals to book a contemptible thing? Is it somehow less commendable because the informant is or was himself a member of that band of criminals? And yet who can provide the information necessary to convict if not one privy to that information?"

Glasser, himself a product of New York's meanest streets, seconded the opinion of a federal agent that Sammy's decision to testify was "the bravest thing I have ever seen."

The judge declared, "There has never been a defendant of his stature in organized crime who has made the leap he has made from one social planet to another. There has never been a defendant whose impact on organized crime, and the suffocating hold of that criminal octopus upon industry and labor that has been so important and so extensive."

He sentenced Sammy to five years, followed by three years of supervised release.

•   •   •

Sammy returned twice more as a witness.

One appearance was at a sanity hearing for Chin Gigante. After six years of differing views from psychiatrists, the government had finally moved for a definitive verdict.

Sammy was the subject of two days of rambling cross-examination which wound up being more of a rehash of the attacks on him by Gotti's defense team than on Gigante's mental competency. But Sammy sealed Gigante's fate with one succinct comment. Asked if he would have met and discussed sensitive Cosa Nostra business with a man whom he believed to be crazy, he replied, "No. Because if I thought he was crazy, how would I know what he was doing? He could walk right into a police station after the meeting."

The presiding judge subsequently ruled that Gigante was fit to stand trial on racketeering and murder charges.

The other case involved Joe Watts, the Gambino family associate who frequently accompanied Gotti during his champagne nights on the town. Along with the *capos* Jimmy Brown Failla and Danny Marino, Watts had been indicted for complicity in the murder of a family soldier that Gotti had ordered. Both Failla and Marino pleaded guilty. Watts, however, reportedly refused to plead. His lawyer at the trial would be F. Lee Bailey, fresh from his triumphant participation in the O. J. Simpson murder case. There was a considerable buildup in the press for the confrontation between Sammy and Bailey, almost as if it were a heavyweight championship fight. Bailey was quoted as saying how much he looked forward to showing what a liar Sammy was.

In fact, in the very beginning, Bailey secretly negotiated a plea bargain for Watts. In return for no jail time, he would become an informer on the post-Gotti Gambino family. Then the Justice Department and the FBI decided that Watts wasn't being as forthcoming as expected and withdrew the proffer.

Watts greatly admired Bailey. As a token of his esteem, he even bought ten Brioni custom-tailored suits for the attorney. Flying in from California during the Simpson trial in the summer and fall of 1995, Bailey would have dinner meetings with Watts at the four-star Lespinasse restaurant in the St. Regis Hotel and at Nello's, a fashionable Madison Avenue restaurant. Watts was assured that he had nothing to worry about, that Sammy had undergone drastic plastic surgery and was sequestered deep in the federal witness protection program. Sammy wouldn't be surfaced again. And without his testimony, the government had no case.

Just after the trial began, Watts learned to his horror that Sammy not only would testify but also was going to take the stand at any moment. Facing a possible life sentence, he instantly pleaded guilty.

• • •

So it was over.

As of this writing, released from prison, Sammy is out there, somewhere.

He is on his own.

He has left the witness protection program.

His wife has divorced him. She sold their home, which was in her name, the Stillwell office building and other property she owned and moved away from New York City with their children.

With his new identity, he is determined to create a new life for himself.

He has found legitimate employment. Now fifty-two, he has the body of a man twenty years his junior. He works out religiously. He continues the early-morning runs, three to five miles daily, that he began at Quantico. He has abandoned cigarettes for cigars. At day's end, he sometimes relaxes with a martini (Beefeater gin, two olives).

He has never testified against members of his old crew. Occasionally, he wonders if they're aware of this. He would be delighted, however, to testify against his brother-in-law, who continues to go around saying what a rat Sammy is, but he never will because of his sister.

"How I could have put Cosa Nostra ahead of loyalty to my wife and my kids is something I will always have to live with," he says. "All my life, growing up, I thought that people who went to school and put their noses to the grindstone were nerds, taking the easy way out. I know now that *I* was the one who took the easy way, that I didn't have the balls to stay in school and try. That was the tough road, which I didn't take.

"They say I broke the oath. But it wasn't the oath I thought I was taking. I thought it was about honor and brotherhood. I mean, when you took the oath, that honor stuff got you as high as a kite when you were being made. You really believed in it, that it was worth living for and dying for and going to jail for. It was none of that. It was all about greed and power. In reality, it was a total joke.

"At least, my own kids know now what the life really is. I hope other kids will realize it, too, from my experience," Sammy said.

"They say Cosa Nostra is on the ropes, which is probably true. But in boxing, when you got a guy like that, that's the time to deliver the knockout punch. Don't kid yourself. Cosa Nostra could come back. I hear the Chinese, the Russians are going to move in. Believe me, they can't put together what took us fifty, sixty, whatever years to do."

I asked Sammy how concerned he was about his physical safety. "A lot of guys in the program," he said, "look over their shoulder every minute. Who was that guy on the corner? What was that car doing parked down the block? A coward dies a thousand deaths. A man only dies once. I'm not saying some kid won't try and make a name for himself taking me out. But if it happens, I'm only going to die once. Not a thousand times. And this kid, whoever he may be, better be good."

In a symbolic effort to wipe away his past, Sammy underwent a painful, nearly yearlong medical process to remove the intricate tattoos he had acquired in his hoodlum youth.

Only one of them has resisted complete elimination, a small head of Christ on his arm. "I guess God still wants me," he joked.

Index

Ace Partitions, 185, 274

Albanese, Sal, 82, 135

Alogna, Iggy, 323

Amusa, Vic, 386

Anastasia, Albert, 51, 105, 129-30, 182

Anastasio, Tough Tony, 130, 272

Apalachin conclave, 51,174-75

Armone, Joe (Joe Piney), 294, 315, 330, 347, 349, 382, 383, 384

Artuso, Vinnie, 327

Atlantic City, 198

Atlas Gem, 373, 376-77

Auletta, Nick, 303

Aurello, Salvatore (Toddo), 115, 143, 146, 153, 168, 195, 248-49, 331, 390

Dunn brothers' murder and, 124, 127

Fiala hit and, 239

Gambino family and, 130-32, 136, 138, 139, 141-43, 178

as Gravano's mentor, 105-14

Ronga's death and Gravano and, 100-104

Simone hit and, 199-200, 201

Bailey, F. Lee, 477-78

Bananas, Tony, 198, 211

Bellino, Frank (Frankie Hearts), 333, 334, 338

Bensonhurst, New York, 1-3, 4, 46, 53, 112, 364

Bergin Hunt and Fish
   Social Club, 256,
   258, 261-64, 278,
   345, 378, 405
Bilotti, Joe, 318, 394
Bilotti, Tommy, 143,
   172, 177, 182-83,
   249, 267, 276, 318
   Castellano and, 294,
      392
   FBI surveillance and,
      263
   Milito's shooting and,
      392-94
   shooting of, 326, 328,
      339, 355, 438
Blakely, G. Robert, 252,
   288, 384
Bonanno, Joseph, 129
Bonanno family, 46,
   93, 270, 306, 345,
   387
Bonavolonta, Jules, 282
Boriello, Bobby, 365,
   380, 406
Boston family, 305
Boxing, 21, 27-28
Brafman, Benjamin,
   444, 460, 467
Brassiere, Jimmy, 97

Brown, Jimmy, see
   Failla, James
Bruno, Angelo, 197-98,
   204, 211
Buffalo family, 174, 306

Cantamesa, Jim, 279-
   80, 282-83
Capone, Al, 3, 113, 344,
   404
Carbonaro, Tommy
   (Huck), 216, 221,
   230, 247, 248, 356,
   359-60, 365, 396,
   400, 429, 431
Cardinale, Anthony, 473
Carneglia, John, 257,
   265, 266, 290, 323,
   350, 384, 396, 415
Casso, Anthony (Gas
   Pipe), 317, 337-38,
   385
Castellano, Joseph, 175,
   263
Castellano, Nina, 285,
   321
Castellano, Paul, 170-
   89, 279-87, 387
   arrest of, 306-7
   background of, 173-74

Castellano, Paul
(*continued*)
construction industry
and, 169, 170, 181-89,
295-300, 373
drug-dealing and,
187-88, 398
FBI surveillance of,
293-97, 300-304
Fiala hit and, 235-41
Gambino family and,
130-31, 132-34,
135-41, 170, 172,
177-78, 259
Gotti and, 132-34,
178, 179, 266-68,
421-23
Gravano and, 145,
156, 158-60, 161,
273-78, 283-87, 304
plot against, 312-27
shooting of, 327, 339,
355, 391, 401, 421-
23, 438
Simone hit and, 197,
199-214
Stymie's death and,
248-50
taste for opulence of,
170-72

Castellano, Paul, Jr.,
175, 263-64
Castellano, Philip, 175
Cement and Concrete
Workers Union, 270
Chicago family, 174,
186, 305, 411
Cirelli, Michael, 420
Cirelli, Nettie, 420, 425,
439, 458
Civella, Nick, 174
Cleveland family, 174,
186, 202, 305
Cody, John, 186, 187
Cohn, Roy, 165
Colletta, Frank, 340
Colombo, Anthony, 54
Colombo, Joseph, 3, 46,
54-55, 64
Colucci hit and, 72, 76
Gallo and, 69-71
Gravano and, 72
Italian-American Civil
Rights League and,
66, 67-69, 113, 408
shooting of, 70, 291
Colombo, Joseph, Jr.,
54
Colombo family, 46-48,
135, 150, 215, 292,

Colombo family,
(continued)
306, 315-17, 345,
386, 400, 409,
475
contract for Grimaldi
from, 194-96
Dunn brothers'
murder and, 120,
124
Gravano and, 49, 51-
59, 61, 64, 70-73,
84, 100, 366
Stymie's death and,
248, 250
Colucci, Camille, 74,
77, 84
Colucci, Joe, 55, 269
killing of, 74-85
Concrete Club, 270,
373
Construction industry,
169, 178-89
Castellano and, 169,
170, 181-89, 295-
300, 373
Gravano's companies
in, 168-69, 185, 217,
268-73, 275, 300,
373-78, 451-56

Gravano's early jobs
in, 116-19
unions and, 168, 185-
89, 268-73, 373
Conte, Pasquale (Pat),
175, 185, 273, 275,
277, 402
Corallo, Anthony (Tony
Ducks), 306, 310,
342, 386, 411
Corrao, Joe (Joe
Butch), 294, 309
Cosa Nostra
Apalachin conclave
and, 51, 173-75
Bensonhurst and, 2-3,
4-5, 46, 53, 112
eligibility for
membership in, 134
Gravano's childhood
experiences with,
4-5, 7-13, 16
Gravano's mentoring
in ways of, 108-14
induction into, 72
Italian-American Civil
Rights League and,
67-69
narcotics trafficking
and, 130-31,

narcotics trafficking and, *(continued)* 257-60, 398-400
organization of, 50-52, 139-43
The Godfather film and myths of, 114-15, 341-43
Costello, Frank, 51, 297, 314
Cuomo, Alley Boy, 96, 101, 103, 119-24, 126, 127
Cutler, Bruce, 352, 379, 411, 442

D'Amico, John (Jackie Nose), 406
D'Angelo, Joe (Stymie), 166-68, 368
death of, 247-50
Fiala hit and, 220-21, 222, 230, 232, 234, 237
Gravano's relationship with, 144-46, 149, 360
Simone hit and, 205, 207-9, 212-14
D'Angelo, Joey, 368

D'Angelo, Karen, 247
D'Arco, Al, 449
DeBatt, Mackie, 153
DeBatt, Mike, 153, 216, 221, 223, 227, 230, 232, 233, 399-400
DeCalvacante family, 47, 55, 139, 470, 475
DeCicco, Boozy, 142, 165
DeCicco, Frank, 142, 143, 149, 165, 168, 179, 180, 182, 183, 236, 237, 239, 249, 265, 267, 275, 284, 294, 300-301, 320-21, 329-33, 334-36, 392
DeCicco, Georgie, 145, 334
Dellacroce, Aniello (Neil), 130, 132, 133, 136-39, 144, 164, 177, 420
death of, 319
FBI surveillance of, 255, 256, 259, 265, 291-92, 307-9

Dellacroce, Aniello
(continued)
Gambino family and,
276, 277, 278
DeMeo, Roy, 168, 180,
267, 287-90, 295,
319, 320
DeSimone, Frank, 174
Dial Meat Purveyors,
Inc., 174-77, 263-
64, 275
DiBernardo, Robert
(DiB), 184, 265,
294-97, 311, 315,
370, 393
FBI surveillance of, 339
shooting of, 348-51,
357, 369, 421, 440
DiBono, Louie, 185,
274-75, 276-77,
401-3, 421, 440-41
DiCicco, Frankie, 392,
394
DiNapoli, Vinnie, 183,
303
Dunn, Arthur, 120-22,
127, 128, 135, 456
Dunn, Joseph, 120-22,
127, 128, 135, 456

Emma, Jimmy, 19,
47-48, 121

Failla, James
(Jimmy Brown),136,
143, 156, 249, 294,
321, 324, 327, 333,
335, 337, 339, 477
Fatico, Carmine
(Charley Wagons),
164, 165, 168, 172,
254, 256
Favara, John, 260-61
FBI, 133, 164
Gotti and, 410
Italian-American Civil
Rights League and
marches on, 67-69,
114, 409
surveillance efforts of,
251, 254-65, 339,
362-73, 420-23
unionization of super-
market chains and,
176-77
Fiala, Frank
party for, 217-24
purchase of the Plaza
Suite by, 224-30
shooting of, 228-42,

shooting of, *(continued)*
390, 391, 392-93
Florida family, 174
Fox, Jim, 436, 469, 472

Gabriel, George, 419-
21, 461
Gaggi, Anthony (Nino),
133, 168, 180, 267,
287, 288
Galione, Ralph
(Ralphie Wigs), 164
Gallo, Joe N., 136, 137,
139, 177, 255, 256,
276, 294, 315, 330-
31
Gallo, Joey (Crazy Joe),
34
Colombo's shooting
and, 69
gang wars and, 19-21
killing of, 70-71
Gallo, Larry, 19-21,
34
Gambino, Carlo, 52,
113, 197, 343
Castellano and, 170,
172
family leadership by,
129-33, 164-65

Gravano and, 60, 62-
63, 64, 130-33
Gambino, Emanuele
(Manny), 164, 259,
343
Gambino, Matty, 60,
62-64, 84
Gambino, Tommy, 131,
183-84, 264, 294,
313, 320-21, 327,
452
Gambino family, 20, 46,
51, 60, 105, 144,
201, 400
businesses of, 143,
186-87, 417
Castellano and, 131,
132-34, 136-42,
170, 172, 177-79,
312-28
FBI surveillance of,
255-56
Gambino's leadership
of, 129-33, 164
Gotti and, 164, 172
Gravano as underboss
in, 419-25
Gravano made in,
127, 134-40,
146

Gravano's growing
stature in, 366, 367
Gravano's switch to,
104-14
Simone hit and, 197,
202, 205-6
unions and, 269, 272
Gangs
Irish, 14, 19, 267, 321,
417
Rampers, 11, 19-21,
22, 24, 32, 35, 36,
38, 46-47, 55
wars between, 19-21
Garafola, Eddie, 116-
19, 161-63, 350,
359-60, 365, 391-
92, 397, 399-400,
429
construction busi-
nesses with Gravano
and, 168-69, 185,
217, 273, 275, 299-
300, 375-76
Fiala hit and, 217,
218, 221, 224-25,
229-34, 238, 241
Gotti and, 335
Gravano's cooperation
and, 455-57, 463

Plaza Suite tax
indictments and,
244, 246
Garafola, Fran, 116
Gem Steel, 269-70, 296,
367, 373, 392
Genovese, Vito, 51, 130,
297, 313
Genovese family, 38,
49, 51, 96, 112, 179,
183, 198, 211, 215,
227, 248, 249, 255,
297, 302, 303, 306,
332, 336, 470
Giacalone, Diane, 345-
46, 352, 378, 404,
444, 474
Giancana, Sam, 174
Giardino, Louie, 300
Gigante, Vincent
(the Chin), 211,
297-98, 302, 306,
317-18, 319, 336-
38, 385, 386-88,
477
Giordano, John (Good-
Looking Jackie),
372, 380, 383
Giuliani, Rudolph, 306,
384

Glasser, I. Leo, 439, 443, 462, 466, 475, 476

Gleeson, John, 423-24, 440, 457, 461, 466-67, 470, 472-73, 475

Godfather, The (film), 114-15, 341-42

Gold, Eugene, 121, 123, 126

Gotti, Frank, 259, 345

Gotti, Gene, 257, 263, 265, 266, 290, 331, 349, 350, 357, 359, 384

  heroin-trafficking case against of, 383-84, 415

  Milito's shooting and, 396

Gotti, John, 28, 134, 249, 404-12

  Castellano and, 133-34, 179, 180, 266-68, 421-22

  conviction of, 473

  Cosa Nostra commission meeting and, 384-88

  death of his son, 259-62

  DiBernardo hit and, 347-52

  Favara disappearance and, 259-62

  FBI surveillance of, 256, 261-63

  first meeting between Gravano and, 163-68

  Gambino family and, 164-65, 172

  Gravano's testimony and, 468-69

  hits ordered by, 400-404, 421-23, 438, 439-42

  indictments of, 345-46, 350-54, 417-18

  media and, 340-45, 404-5

  prison life and, 444-50

  taped conversations about Gravano, 440-45

Gotti, John, Jr., 134, 386-88

Gotti, Pete, 372

Gotti, Victoria, 259

Gravano, Caterina
    (Kay), 4, 9, 14, 17-
    19, 32, 161
  family business of, 4,
    9-12, 107
  son's arrests and, 23,
    124
Gravano, Debra, 99,
    144, 146, 310, 479
  Gravano's arrest
    and decision to
    cooperate, 450-52,
    463-65
  Gravano's Cosa
    Nostra connections
    and, 101-2, 182,
    236, 296
  marriage and family
    life of, 90-96, 116,
    122, 124, 127, 151-
    53, 162-63, 182,
    188-92
Gravano, Gerard, 116,
    192, 465
Gravano, Giorlando
    (Gerry),
    4, 9, 14, 17-19, 32,
    161, 163
  family business of, 4,
    9-12, 19, 107-9

son's arrests and, 23,
    124
son's childhood and,
    9-14, 107-9
Gravano, Karen, 116,
    122, 124, 182, 363-
    64, 464
Gravano, Salvatore
    (Sammy the Bull)
  adolescent arrests and
    trials of, 22-24,
  army years of, 24, 27-
    31
  Bensonhurst
    neighborhood of,
    1-3, 4, 364
  boxing and, 22, 28
  childhood experiences
    with the Cosa Nos-
    tra, 5-6, 8-13, 17
  children of, 166, 122,
    124, 363-64, 464, 465
  clubs and businesses
    run by, 60-68, 86-
    90, 96-100, 126-27,
    153-55, 168, 180-81,
    189, 215-31
  Colombo family and,
    48-49, 51-59, 70-73,
    84, 100, 366

construction

businesses of, 168-69, 186, 216, 268-74, 275, 296-300, 373-78, 451-55

decision to cooperate with prosecutors, 456-65

DiBernardo hit and, 348-51

Dunn murders and, 119-28

early romances of, 33-35, 89

education of, 6-8, 13-19

experiences with the police, 20-24, 40, 47, 64, 86-88

family background of, 2-12

FBI and arrest of, 436-40

FBI surveillance of, 362-73, 426-30

Fiala hit and, 231-41

fighting by, 13-15, 17, 29-30

first hit by, 73, 74-84

Gambino family and, 102-14, 127, 132-40, 366, 368

as Gambino underboss, 419-25

gambling and, 30-33, 151, 199

Gotti's taped conversations about, 440-45

as a government witness, 468-79

haircutting classes and, 41-47

horse farm and, 189-91, 192-94, 235-38, 240-45

IRS case against, 241-43, 244-46, 311

JoJo fight and, 157-62

loan-sharking by, 31, 64-68, 151, 168

marriage and family life of, 90-96, 116, 123, 124, 127, 151-53, 161-63, 182, 189-93, 479

Milito hit and, 389-97

nickname of, 8-10

prison life and, 444-50, 467-69

Rampers gang and, 19-22, 36, 41, 46-48

relationship with Paruta, 355-61

relationship with Stymie, 145-46, 149, 246-48

relationship with Toddo, 105-14

robberies and car-stealing by, 32, 34-42, 47, 55-61, 123-26, 127, 135, 149-52

shootings and, 36-40

Simone hit and, 199-214

Gravanti, Nicholas, 244-46

Grimaldi, Johnny, 34, 194-96

Grimaldi, Little Louie, 33, 194-96

Grimaldi, Louise, 33-34, 89, 92, 194, 196, 432

Gulf War, 445

Halloran, Edward J. (Biff), 271-72, 303

Hardy, Michael, 96, 120-22, 124, 127

Hoover, J. Edgar, 251, 385

Ida, Joseph, 174, 197

Ingrassia, Joe (the Checkcasher), 226, 229, 244, 247

Internal Revenue Service (IRS), Plaza Suite taxes and, 224, 242-43, 244, 310

International Brotherhood of Painters and Allied Trades, 268

Irish gangs, 14, 267, 321, 417

Italian-American Civil Rights League, 66, 67-69, 113

Italians, prejudice against, 6, 13

Jets, Tony, 144

Johnson, Willie Boy, 258-61, 264, 346, 401

Justice Department, 251-53, 424

Kallstrom, Jim, 253-55, 264, 279, 283, 287, 292, 293, 307, 368, 384, 420

Kansas City family, 50, 174, 186, 305

Kennedy, John F., 306

Kennedy, Robert F., 130

Key Food Cooperative, 175, 176, 185

Keys, Johnny, *see* Simone, John

Kravec, John, 279, 282-83

Krieger, Albert, 444, 473

Langella, Gennaro (Gerry Lang), 82, 84, 292-93, 306, 316-17

Lanza, James, 174

LaRossa, James, 318, 324

Las Vegas, 187, 305

LaTorroca, Gerry, 41

LeFrak, Sam, 271

Lino, Eddie, 265, 401

Locascio, Frank (Frankie Loc), 350, 382, 412, 421, 435, 439, 442, 443, 445-49, 452, 459, 473

Los Angeles family, 174, 306

Lucchese family, 46, 131,268, 306, 317, 333, 337, 366, 385, 387, 449, 460, 475

Luciano, Joe, 193

Luciano, Lucky, 51

Madonia, Joe, 185, 273

Magaddino, Stefano, 174

Maloney, Andy, 422-24

Mangano, Benny Eggs, 385, 386

Marathon, 269, 377

Marcello, Carlos, 306

Marino, Danny, 321, 324, 335, 337, 477

Martieri, Larry, 120-22, 127

Mastromarino, Mario, 269, 296, 367, 376

McBratney, James, 164, 259

McIntosh, Hugh (Apples), 82, 150

Media
  Castellano's death and, 327-28
  Gotti and, 341-44, 404-5
  Italian-American Civil Rights League and, 67
  The Godfather myth and, 341-43

Messino, Joe, 317, 387

Milito, Louie, 96, 102, 145-46
  Dunn brothers' murder and, 120, 122, 124, 127
  Fiala hit and, 218, 220-21, 222, 230, 232, 234, 239, 240-41
  Gravano's club and, 61, 62
  shooting of, 389-97, 421, 440
  Simone hit and, 202, 203, 205, 208-9, 210-12

stolen car and, 34-36

Miller, John, 400

Milwaukee family, 186, 305

Montemarano, Dominick (Donnie Shacks), 292-93, 315-17

Morgenthau, Robert, 422

Mormando, Nick (Nicky Cowboy), 230, 232, 398-400

Mosca, Funzi, 183, 296

Mouw, Bruce, 254-56, 261, 264, 280, 292, 293, 295, 296, 318, 328, 339-40, 345, 368, 419, 457, 459, 461, 466

New Jersey family, 47, 55, 139

New Orleans family, 305

New York City, Cosa Nostra families in, 46, 50, 139

New York *Daily News*, 236

New York State
  Organized Crime
  Task Force, 317
New York Times, 328,
  404, 469
North, Oliver, 347

O'Brien, Joe, 176-77
O'Connor, John, 416-
  18, 422-23
Olarte, Gloria, 283-85,
  289, 320
Orena, Vic, 386

Pappa, Gerry, 19, 38-
  39, 48
Paruta, Dottie, 356,
  359, 360
Paruta, Joe (Old Man),
  148-50, 159-61,
  221, 223, 230,
  237, 250, 319, 320-
  21, 350, 355-61,
  399
Patriarca family, 305,
  411
Perdue, Frank, 176-77
Perry, Mike, 118-19,
  124
Persico, Allie Boy, 103

Persico, Carmine, Jr.
  (the Snake), 53, 55,
  58, 69-70, 71-73,
  76, 82, 85, 95, 100,
  105, 147, 150, 194,
  250, 291, 306, 342,
  386
Philadelphia family,
  115, 139, 174, 198,
  305, 411
Piccolo, Frank, 301-2
Piecyk, Romual, 340,
  344, 352
Pileggi, Nicholas, 404
Piney, Joe, *see* Armone,
  Joe
Plaza Suite
  Fiala hit at, 231-41
  Fiala party at, 217-
  24
  Fiala purchase of,
  224-31
  IRS investigation of
  taxes and, 224, 241-
  43, 244-45, 311
Polito, Joseph, 269, 296,
  376, 392
Profaci, Joseph, 3
Profaci family, 19-21,
  46

Racketeer Influenced and Corrupt Organizations Act (RICO), 130, 252, 288, 305, 345, 382, 384, 404, 423, 425

Rampers gang, 11, 19-21, 22, 24, 32, 34, 36, 38, 47, 55

Rampino, Anthony (Tony Roach), 257, 323, 325

Rastelli, Phil (Rusty), 306

Ravenite club, 304, 378-79
FBI surveillance of, 420-23
Gotti at, 379-81, 412-15

Rhode Island family, 305

Rizzo, John, 95, 144, 390-91
Gravano's businesses and, 60, 63-64, 86, 122
Ronga's death and Gravano and, 100, 102-3

Rockefeller, Nelson, 68

Ronga, Ralphie, 55, 99-102, 103

Ruggiero, Angelo,133, 163, 167, 179
arrest and trial of, 290-92, 293, 383-84, 415
DiBernardo hit and, 348-51
FBI surveillance of, 261-63, 265-68, 279, 290, 292-94, 307-8, 339
heroin-trafficking and, 257, 258, 266, 383-84

Ruggiero, Sal, 257, 258, 265

Russo, Nicky, 199, 201, 202-12

Saccente, Louis, 364, 380, 428

Salerno, Anthony (Fat Tony), 179, 297, 306, 342

San Francisco family, 174, 306

Sasso, Bobby, 188, 369, 372

Scalish, John, 174

Scarfo, Nicky, 115, 199, 200, 206, 305

Scarpati, Tony (Scappy), 250

Scialo, Dominick (Mimi), 47, 121

Scibetta, Diane, 90-91, 93

Scibetta, Nick, 144-46

Scopo, Ralph, 270

Scotto, Anthony, 130, 272, 331

Shargel, Gerald, 245, 246, 425, 443

Sicilian, Vinnie, 216

Simone, John (Johnny Keys), 197-214, 389-90

Skaggs, Joe, 217-20, 221-22, 224

Snipes, Renaldo, 432

Spero, Frank, 339, 362, 364, 366, 367, 368-69, 378-80, 426, 436, 457, 461, 466, 470-71, 472

Spero, Ralph, 98-104, 106, 135

Spero, Shorty, 97, 98, 105

Colucci hit and, 74-75, 76, 83

Gravano and Colombo family and, 52-54, 55, 64, 66, 68, 70, 71, 73

Spero, Tommy
Colombo family and, 49, 56, 71

Colucci hit and, 75-76, 77-81, 83-84

fencing operations and, 97-100

Gravano's club and, 154

Ronga's death and Gravano and, 104

robberies and car-stealing by, 35-36, 56-57, 58

Squitieri, Arnold, 396

Stag, Billy, 60, 62

Steele, Frankie, 199, 200-201, 203

Tampa family, 306

Teamsters, 268, 270, 296, 305, 315, 369, 451

Testa, Phil, 198
Time (magazine), 344, 404, 405
Trafficante, Louis, 174
Tricorico, Matty, 339, 362, 364, 366, 367, 368, 378-79, 426, 436-37, 457, 466, 470, 472

Unions
  construction and, 168, 185-89, 268-74
  supermarkets and, 175-77
United Food and Commercial Workers Union, 175, 177

Valachi, Joe, 103, 112
Vallario, Big Louie, 361, 366, 379, 382-83, 395, 411, 429-31, 433
Vietnam War, 32-33

Waldbaum chain, 175, 176
Ward, Laura, 473

Watts, Joe
  (the German), 183, 294, 319, 323, 332, 371-73, 380, 394, 477-79
Webster, William, 253
Westies gang, 267, 321, 417

Yale, Frankie, 3

Zicarelli, Joseph (Bayonne Joe), 93
Zuvito, 11-13, 104